BIBLE DIFFICULTIES
—EXODUS—
CPH Apologetic Commentary

EXAMINE THE
SCRIPTURES DAILY

Reasoning with Them from the
Scriptures, Explaining and Proving

Edward D. Andrews

BIBLE DIFFICULTIES
Exodus

CPH Apologetic Commentary

Edward D. Andrews

Christian Publishing House
Cambridge, Ohio

Christian Publishing House
Professional Conservative Christian Publishing of the Good News!

Unless otherwise indicated, Scripture quotations are from the *Updated American Standard Version of the Holy Scriptures*, 2016 edition (*UASV*).

BIBLE DIFFICULTIES Exodus: CPH Apologetic Commentary

Authored by Edward D. Andrews

ISBN-13: **978-1-945757-20-4**

ISBN-10: **1-945757-20-5**

PREFACE Apologetic Evangelism

Apologetic Evangelism "is tilling the soil of people's hearts of people's minds and hearts to help them be more willing to listen to the truth. - Norman L. Geisler

Evangelism is the work of a Christian evangelist, which seeks to persuade other people to become Christian, especially by sharing the basics of the Gospel, but also the deeper message of biblical truths. Today the Gospel is almost an unknown, so what does the Christian evangelist do? **Preevangelism** is laying a foundation for those who have no knowledge of the Gospel, giving them background information, so that they are able to grasp what they are hearing. The Christian evangelist is preparing their mind and heart so that they will be receptive to the biblical truths. In many ways, this is known as apologetics.

Christian apologetics [Greek: *apologia*, "verbal defense, speech in defense"] is a field of **Christian theology** which endeavors to offer a reasonable and sensible basis for the **Christian faith**, defending the faith against objections. It is reasoning from the Scriptures, explaining and proving, as one instructs in sound doctrine, many times having to overturn false reasoning before he can plant the seeds of truth. It can also be earnestly contending for the faith and saving one from losing their faith, as they have begun to doubt. Moreover, it can involve rebuking those who contradict the truth. It is being prepared to make a defense to anyone who asks the Christian evangelist for a reason for the hope that is in him or her.— Jude 1.3, 21-23; 1 Pet 3.15; Acts 17:2-3; Titus 1:9

What do we mean by **obligated** and what we mean by **evangelism** are at the heart of the matter and are indeed related to each other.

EVANGELISM: An evangelist is a proclaimer of the gospel or good news, as well as all biblical truths. There are levels of evangelism, which is pictured in first-century Christianity. All Christians evangelized in the first century, but a select few fit the role of a full-time evangelist (Ephesians 4:8, 11-12), like Philip and Timothy.

Both Philip and Timothy are specifically mentioned as evangelizers. (Ac 21:8; 2 Tim. 4:5) Philip was a full-time evangelist after Pentecost, who was sent to the city of Samaria, having great success. An angel even directed Philip to an Ethiopian Eunuch, to share the good news about Christ with him. Because of the Eunuch's already having a knowledge of God by way of the Old Testament, Philip was able to help him understand that the Hebrew Scriptures pointed to Christ as the long-awaited Messiah. In the end, Philip baptized the Eunuch. After that, the Spirit again sent Philip on a mission, this time to Azotus and all the cities on the way to Caesarea. (Ac 8:5, 12, 14, 26-40) Paul evangelized in many lands, setting up one congregation after another. (2 Cor. 10:13-16) Timothy was an evangelizer or missionary, and Paul placed distinct importance on evangelizing when he gave his parting encouragement to Timothy. – 2 Timothy 4:5; 1Timothy 1:3.

The office of apostle and evangelist seem to overlap in some areas, but could be distinguished in that apostles traveled and set up congregations, which took evangelizing skills, but also developed the congregations after they were established. The evangelists were more of a missionary, being stationed in certain areas to grow and develop congregations. In addition, if we look at all of the apostles and the evangelists, plus Paul's more than one hundred traveling companions, it seems very unlikely that they could have had Christianity at over one million by the 125 C.E. This was accomplished because all Christians were obligated to carry out some level of evangelism.

OBLIGATED: In the broadest sense of the term for evangelizer, all Christians are obligated to play some role as an evangelist.

- *Basic Evangelism* is planting seeds of truth and watering any seeds that have been planted. [In the basic sense of this word (euaggelistes), this would involve all Christians.] In some cases, it may be that one Christian planted the seed, which was initially rejected, so he was left in a good way because the planter did not try to force the truth down his throat. However, some time later he faces something in life that moves him to reconsider those seeds and another Christian water what had already been planted. This evangelism can be carried out in all of the methods that are available: informal, house-to-house, street, phone, internet, and the like. What amount of time is invested in the evangelism work is up to each Christian to decide for themselves.

- *Making Disciples* is having any role in the process of getting an unbeliever from his unbelief state to the point of accepting Christ as his Savior and being baptized. Once the unbeliever has become a believer, he is still developed until he has become strong. Any Christian could potentially carry this one person through all of the developmental stages. On the other hand, it may be that several have some part. It is like a person that specializes in a certain aspect of a job, but all are aware of the other aspects, in case they are called on to carry out that aspect. Again, each Christian must decide for themselves what role they are to have, and how much of a role, but should be prepared to fill any role needed.

- *Part-Time or* Full-Time Evangelist is one who sees this as their calling and chooses to be very involved as an evangelist in their local church and community. They may work part-time to supplement their work as an evangelist. They may be married with children, but they realize their gift is in the field of evangelism. If it is the wife, the husband would work toward supporting her work as an evangelist and vice-versa. If it were a single person, he or she would supplement their work by being employed part-time, but also the church would help as well. This person is well trained in every aspect of bringing one to Christ.

Congregation Evangelists should be very involved in evangelizing their communities and helping the church members play their role at the basic levels of evangelism. There is nothing to say that one church could not have many within, who have the calling of an evangelist, which would and should be cultivated.

Legal Terms as to How We Should Objectively View Evidence

There are approximately 3,000+ of these supposed errors and contradictions in the Bible. It will take us several volumes to consider such an undertaking. Please do not be disheartened by such a large number, because there are compelling reasons why we have so many Bible difficulties, not errors or contradictions. This will be discussed further in chapter one. These volumes are to serve as an essential source in dealing with Bible difficulties. If we offer reasonable responses and satisfactory answers for these challenging passages, it can be inferred that there would be a reasonable answer for the few that may not have a reply as of yet as well.

One reason for having such publications as this is the new atheist. The unbeliever of decades past was satisfied to believe that everything came about by chance, through evolution, and not concern himself with what others believed. This is no longer the case. Sadly, today's atheist is more involved in leading the Christian down the path of doubt, while the Christian denominations are almost entirely inactive in evangelizing the unbeliever. Hundreds of atheistic books and videos are flooding the market in an attempt to discredit the Bible, the foundation of the Christian belief system. Another enemy of God's Word is found in the agnostic. An agnostic teaches that it is hard to know whether God exists and that we are unable to accept the Bible as a revelation of that existence. Before we begin defining Bible difficulties, it is best that we better define how we should view available evidence.

Burden of Proof: The burden of proof falls on the one making the claims. If the Christian is witnessing to another, he has the burden to prove what he says is so if asked for proof. However, if the critic is challenging the Christian, the burden of disproving lies with the critic. The closer the claim is to socially accepted knowledge, less proof is needed, while the further one moves from conventional knowledge, the more evidence is required. I believe that the legal burden of proof offers the best answers to the witnessing of others. It has been refined over the last 200 years to the point of evaluating a life that is held in its balance, just as everlasting life is held in the balance. Below we will list the levels of legal proof and some percentage and wording to indicate the degree of certainty needed. We have used different Bible objects for each one, but any criticism could be plugged into that particular burden of proof.

Warrants Further Investigation

Reasonable (30%): This is a low-level burden of proof in that it is enough to accept something as *reasonably likely*, being so unless proven otherwise by a deeper look, which may bring in more evidence. For example, at this level, it is *reasonably likely* that Jesus Christ lived, died and was resurrected. This may be achieved in the first conversation with the one which we are sharing the good news.

Probable (40%): This is also a low-level burden of proof in that it is enough to accept something as *likely being so* unless proven otherwise by a deeper look, which may bring in more evidence. At this level, it is *probable* that the Bible is the inspired, inerrant Word of God. This may be achieved in the first 2-3 conversations with the one which we are sharing the good news.

Conviction for Claim

Preponderance of Evidence (51%): This is a higher-level burden of proof that makes Noah surviving a worldwide flood *more likely* to be true than not true.

Clear and Convincing Evidence (85%): This is an even higher level of burden of proof that Adam and Eve were historical persons, created by God is substantially *more likely than not*.

Beyond Reasonable Doubt (99%): This is the highest level of burden of proof that over forty major prophecies about Jesus Christ in the Old Testament came true, being beyond reasonable doubt. It must be understood that feeling as though we have no reason doubt is not the same as 100 percent absolute evidence of certainty. If one has doubts that affect their belief of certainty, it is not beyond reasonable doubt. This too must be qualified, because it is reasonable to have doubts about certain aspects of the whole that does not have all the answers as of yet, but it does not affect the level of certainty as a whole.

Evidentialism only becomes self-defeating the moment one tries to raise the level of certainty to the absolute instead of beyond reasonable doubt (sufficient evidence). The argument against the use of evidentialism that the principle simply does not account for the way we come to have most of our beliefs is no real argument at all. A belief that cold weather makes you sick is not the same as believing there is an Almighty God, Creator. Each of us has hundreds of thousands of core beliefs that are accepted as fact until we come across something that tell us otherwise. Ironically, we are told to investigate before buying a car, or especially a house, as it is a big commitment. Yet, are we to equate the acceptance and commitment to Christ the same way we do that a chair will hold our weight, or our car will get us to work?

The Bible critic generally exaggerates the level of his evidence, presenting it in a sly fashion. At the same time, he will arbitrarily dismiss the Christian evidence, by declaring that all who believes in God and the Bible are foolish and naive. The simple principle to be observed here is to ask, 'which is more likely to be true based on what you know.' Of course, as one grows in knowledge, that is subject to change. A Christian that falls away due to atheism or agnosticism (like Dr. Bart D. Ehrman) will after that require absolute evidence rather that evidence beyond a reasonable doubt. From that time on, God must then show him all that his doubting heart desires. The common expression being, "God if you just _____, I will believe."

The Bible critic runs around like a scavenger looking for an error, not reason. As they come upon a pebble of doubt, they throw it out as though it were a boulder of truth against God. Six months later, an archaeologist digging in Bible lands somewhere finds something that utterly and completely removes this critic's evidence. Does the critic even lean a little closer to God? No, because Christian evidence, no matter how weighty, does not exist on the critic's agenda, which is to sow seeds of doubt regarding the Bible's authenticity. Even if the Ark of the Covenant with the Ten Commandments and Aaron's rod that budded were to be located, the critic would still maintain their stand because the unearthing of these objects does not meet their agenda.

For example, the Bible critic will argue from silence, saying 'Belshazzar of the Bible has not been found in secular history, we have no evidence that he ever existed.' Now, say a year later, a piece of a tablet is found that mentions Belshazzar (this has actually happened), and in connection with the historical account in the Bible. Well, that critic does not draw closer to where the evidence is pointing; he throws it out, dismissing it as though he never raised the argument, and runs to look for another. Sadly this circle of madness just keeps going.

INTRODUCTION A Effectively Reasoning From the Scriptures

Acts 17:2 Updated American Standard Version (UASV)

2 And according to Paul's custom, he went to them, and for three Sabbaths **reasoned with them from the Scriptures,**

The value of God's Word is incomprehensible. With it, we are able to answer some of life's most difficult questions. Why are we here? What is the meaning of life? If there is a God and he is good, why so much suffering? What is the purpose of our existence? What is right and wrong and who should determine it? Will world peace ever be achieved? Will poverty ever end? How can we be happy? What is true freedom and does it exist? What happens after we die? Is there such a thing as **absolute truth**? Moreover, I am certain that each of us could add many more life questions to this list. However, the last question above, is there such a thing as absolute truth, can be answered with an absolute yes and it is found within the Bible alone. In the Bible, we find answers to the above questions and far more. We discover that we have a Creator and why such a loving Creator would allow sickness, old age and death, with much suffering all throughout our limited lives.[1] We also learn the truth about why we are here, what our Creator expects of us, and how his decisions in our behalf have been for our good. – Psalm 19:7-11; Isaiah 48:17.

As true Christians, we accept the Bible as the inspired, fully inerrant Word of God and that it has the power to change lives for the better, so we defend it and share it with others. (Heb. 4:12) When we share these truths with others, we want to help them to realize that it is not our absolute truths, but rather truths that belong to the God of the heavens and the earth, which he has revealed to us within the Scriptures. Thus, we want to use the Bible, as it is the authority, the absolute truth, when we talk with others, literally reading from it. Like Paul, we want to 'reason with them from the Scriptures.' (Ac 17:2) We want to help them accept the Bible for what it is, the inspired Word of God, and accept what it teaches as absolute truth. – 2 Timothy 2:15.

It is highly important that we share what God's Word says rather than what we feel, think, or believe. This can be exemplified in the prophetic book of Jeremiah. The prophets other than Jeremiah were merely saying what the people wanted to hear, pacifying, i.e., seeking to make the people and rulers less angry, upset, or hostile, saying untrue

---

[1] **Suffering & Evil - Why God?**
http://www.christianpublishers.org/suffering-evil-why-god

things to please them. In other words, they were not telling the people the Word of God.

Jeremiah 23:25-28 Updated American Standard Version (UASV)

25 I have heard what the prophets have said who prophesy lies in my name, saying, 'I have dreamed, I have dreamed!' **26** How long will this be in the hearts of the prophets who prophesy lies, even these prophets of the deceit of their own heart, **27** who think to make my people forget my name by their dreams that they tell one another, just as their fathers forgot my name for Baal? **28** The prophet who has a dream may relate his dream, but let him who has My word speak My word in truth. What does straw have in common with grain?" declares Jehovah.

On the other hand, Jeremiah did speak God's Word truthfully, even if it was not well received, or it meant his life was in danger. The apostle Paul tells the Corinthians and us that the historical events of the Old Testament were recorded to serve as "examples for us." Thus, like Jeremiah, we too want to feel obligated to teach only what the authors meant when they penned their particular books and not water down the Word of God or impose modern day thinking into the text, deliberately avoiding offense. For example, today we have an undertaking called the feminist movement, belief in the need to secure rights and opportunities for women equal to those of men, or a commitment to securing these. While the idea of attain the right to vote, equal pay for equal work, among other modern day rights is perfectly fine, it should not retroactively be applied to the Word of God. Paul clearly states at 2 Timothy 2:12, "I do not permit a woman to teach or to exercise authority over a man; rather, she is to remain quiet." The natural reading of 1 Timothy 2:12 is that Paul in his apostolic authority prohibits women from teaching and exercising authority over a man, which means that women cannot serve as pastors or elders in the Christian congregation. We are not to mold to the pressures of the modern day feminist movement because this position goes back to before the fall, has always been applicable, and will always be applicable. For a detail explanation of this text, see the footnote below.[2]

Even Jesus himself said, "My teaching is not mine, but belongs to him that sent me. If anyone wants to do his will, he will know whether the teaching is from God or whether I am speaking on my own authority. The one who speaks on his own authority seeks his own glory, but the one who seeks the glory of him who sent him, this one is true, and there is no unrighteousness in him." (John 7:16-18) Even the Son of God himself

---

[2] **Women in the Pulpit?**
http://www.christianpublishers.org/women-in-the-pulpit

refused to speak of his own authority, but rather the authority of the Father, who had sent him. Therefore, how much more so should we avoid speaking on our own authority? Like, the elders, all Christians want to be "holding fast to the faithful word which is in accordance with the teaching, so that he will be able both to exhort in sound doctrine and to refute those who contradict." (Titus 1:9) Then, there is the counsel from Paul for Timothy to hand off to the congregations, "preach the word; be ready in season and out of season; reprove, rebuke, exhort, with complete patience and teaching." (2 Tim. 4:2) Whether we are answering questions at a Bible study in the congregation, an elder or pastor is giving a lecture, or we are witnessing to someone outside of the congregation, we want to "preach the word."

However, the Bible is a deep, complex book, because it was it was written from 2,000 to 3,500 years ago in many different cultures, the language of biblical Hebrew and Koine (common) Greek, among many other things is it difficult to understand. Therefore, we could never evangelize by just reading the Bible alone, saying no more, especially to this generation that is almost entirely unfamiliar with it. If our listener is to grasp fully what the authors meant and how it applies to us, we are going to have to offer that connection. In the account of the Ethiopian eunuch referred to at Acts 8:26-38, he did not fully understand what was meant in the Book of Isaiah that he was reading in his travels. This Eunuch was familiar with the Hebrew or Greek translation of the Old Testament, as he had come to Jerusalem to worship and was returning to his homeland, and yet he still did not understand Isaiah 53:7-8. How much more help do the unbelievers of today need? Nevertheless, once this eunuch fully understood the importance of the text, seeing how it applied to him personally, he chose to leave the Judaism of the day and become a Christian.

How Jesus Used the Scriptures

Matthew writes, "And when Jesus finished these sayings, the crowds were astonished at his teaching, for he was teaching them as one who had authority, and not as their scribes." (7:28-29) He later writes of Jesus return to his hometown, "He taught them in their synagogue, so that they were astonished." (13:54) After that, when Jesus is speaking on a number of subjects, but especially who shall be saved, Matthew says the disciples "were greatly astonished." (19:25) Later still when Jesus dealt with the resurrection belief of the Sadducees, "when the crowd heard it, they were astonished at his teaching." (22:33)

Why were the crowds astonished at Jesus' way of teaching? What does it mean that he was teaching them as one who had authority? How is it that they say no one had ever spoken as Jesus had? The Greek verb used by Matthew about how Jesus' teaching affected others was *ekplessomai*, which meant that they were "so amazed as to be practically overwhelmed-'to be greatly astounded.'[3] In 7:28, the verb is in the imperfect tense, which suggested an ongoing effect. Jesus taught with the authority of the Scriptures, unlike the scribes, who were busy quoting Rabbis as their authority. Jesus, on the other hand, quoted over 120 Hebrew verses in the dialog that is given to us in the Gospel accounts, accounts that would amount to about a three-hour lecture.

Bible Background on the Scribes

In ancient times, the scribes were merely officers whose duties included writing of various kinds; but, on the return of the Jews from Babylonian captivity, the sopherim, as the scribes were called, were organized by Ezra into a distinct body. Among other duties, they copied the Pentateuch, the Phylacteries, and the Mezuzoth. So great was their care in copying that they counted and compared all the letters to be sure that none were left out that belonged to the text, or none inserted wrongly. On stated occasions they read the law in the synagogues. They also lectured to their disciples. Because of the knowledge they obtained through their work, they became natural interpreters of God's law as well as copyists.

The lawyers (Matthew 22:35; Luke 7:30; 11:45; 14:3) and the doctors of the law (Luke 2:46; 5:17; Acts 5:34) were substantially the same as the scribes. Efforts have been made to show that different classes of duties were assigned to lawyers, doctors, and scribes, but without any measurably different results. It may be, as some believe, that the doctors were a higher grade than the ordinary scribes. The scribes were all carefully educated for their work from early life, and at an appropriate age—some say thirty-years-old—they were admitted to office through a solemn ceremony.

The scribes were not only copyists of the law; they were also keepers of the oral traditional comments and additions to the law. Gradually accumulating with the progress of time, these were numerous, and were regarded by many as of equal value with the law itself. To this Jesus alludes in Mark 7:5–13. Paul represents himself as having been, before his conversion,

---

[3] Johannes P. Louw and Eugene Albert Nida, *Greek-English Lexicon of the New Testament: Based on Semantic Domains* (New York: United Bible Societies, 1996), 311–312.

"exceedingly zealous of the traditions" of his fathers (Galatians 1:14). The scribes also adopted forced interpretations of the law, endeavoring to find a special meaning in every word, syllable, and letter. Thus the Savior charges them: "Woe to you experts in the law, because you have taken away the key to knowledge. You yourselves have not entered, and you have hindered those who were entering" (Luke 11:52).

At the time of Christ, the people were increasingly dependent on the scribes for a knowledge of their Scriptures. The language of the Jews was passing into the Aramaic dialect, and the majority of the people, being unable to understand their own sacred books, were obliged to accept the interpretation that the scribes put upon them. Hence, their astonishment, as indicated in our text-verse, at the peculiar style of teaching adopted by Jesus, and especially illustrated in His Sermon on the Mount. The scribes repeated traditions, but Jesus spoke with authority: "I tell you." The scribes had little sympathy with the masses, but Jesus mingled with the people, explaining to them in a simple, practical way the requirements of religion.[4]

Hendriksen and Kistemaker asked the question that concerned us as well, "What were some of the reasons for this feeling of wonder and astonishment? Matt. 13:54, 55 may supply part of the answer. Nevertheless, on the basis of the sermon itself and of 7:28 ("not as their scribes") the following items are worthy of consideration:"

a. He spoke the truth (John 14:6; 18:37). Corrupt and evasive reasoning marked the sermons of many of the scribes (Matt. 5:21 ff.).

b. He presented matters of great significance, matters of life, death, and eternity (see the entire sermon). They often wasted their time on trivialities (Matt. 23:23; Luke 11:42).

c. There was system in his preaching. As their Talmud proves, they often rambled on and on.

d. He excited curiosity by making generous use of illustrations (5:13–16; 6:26–30; 7:24–27; etc.) and concrete examples (5:21–6:24; etc.), as the sermon shows from beginning to end. Their speeches were often dry as dust.

---

[4] James M. Freeman and Harold J. Chadwick, *Manners & Customs of the Bible* (North Brunswick, NJ: Bridge-Logos Publishers, 1998), 420–421.

e. He spoke as the Lover of men, as One concerned with the everlasting welfare of his listeners, and pointed to the Father and his love (5:44–48). Their lack of love is clear from such passages as 23:4, 13–15; Mark 12:40; etc.

f. Finally, and this is the most important, for it is specifically stated here (verse 28), he spoke "with authority" (Matt. 5:18, 26; etc.), for his message came straight from the very heart and mind of the Father (John 8:26), hence also from his own inner being, and from Scripture (5:17; 7:12; cf. 4:4, 7, 10). They were constantly borrowing from fallible sources, one scribe quoting another scribe. They were trying to draw water from broken cisterns. He drew from himself, being "the Fountain of living waters" (Jer. 2:13).[5]

Clearly, Jesus set the example in how one is to use the Scriptures effectively. Let us examine his use of questions.

Luke 10:25 Updated American Standard Version (UASV)

[25] And behold, a lawyer[6] [an expert in the Mosaic Law] stood up to put him to the test, saying, "Teacher, what shall I do to inherit eternal life?"

A historical note here, "an expert in the law," or "lawyer" as some translations have it, is not a lawyer as we would think of one today. A lawyer was someone that was an expert in the Mosaic Law. However, this person would have the same level of education on the law as a lawyer would today, many years of study and memorization. Thus, this man would certainly know the answer to such an easy question as the one he asked. Now, if a believer is asked a straightforward Bible question, we might be tempted just to offer an answer. Indeed, as the wisest man ever to live, Jesus could have easily answered the question. Instead, Jesus wanted the man to offer his own thoughts, insights or understanding. However, Jesus knew this man was "an expert in the law," and he recognized the man would have had a certain perspective on his question. In other words, the man was not asked because he did not know. Thus, Jesus asked:

Luke 10:26 Updated American Standard Version (UASV)

[26] And he said to him, "What is written in the Law? How do you read it?"

---

[5] William Hendriksen and Simon J. Kistemaker, Exposition of the Gospel According to Matthew, vol. 9, New Testament Commentary (Grand Rapids: Baker Book House, 1953–2001), 382–383.

[6] That is an expert in the Mosaic Law

The man answered correctly,

Luke 10:27 Updated American Standard Version (UASV)

27 And he answered, "You shall love the Lord your God with all your heart and with all your soul and with all your strength and with all your mind, and your neighbor as yourself."

The conversation could have ended there. Again, the man knew the Mosaic Law but seemingly wanted to see if Jesus would agree with what he knew. Jesus gratified him, letting him feel good, by giving the correct answer. Jesus responded:

Luke 10:28-29 Updated American Standard Version (UASV)

28 And he said to him, "You have answered correctly; do this, and you will live."

29 But he, desiring to justify himself, said to Jesus, "And who is my neighbor?"

Here again, the man looks to prove himself righteous, and Jesus could have just stated the truth, even the Samaritan. However, Jesus having insight into the setting, the Jews detested the Samaritans; so, while he would give the correct answer it would be disputed in a long, back-and-forth conversation, and the Jews who listened would have sided with the man. Thus, Jesus boxed the man into giving an answer by having him reason on an illustration.

The Parable of the Good Samaritan

Luke 10:30-37 Updated American Standard Version (UASV)

30 Jesus replied and said, "A man was going down from Jerusalem to Jericho, and he fell among robbers, who stripped him and laid blows upon and departed, leaving him half dead. **31** Now by coincidence a certain priest was going down on that road, and when he saw him, he passed by on the other side. **32** Likewise a Levite also, when he came to the place and saw him, passed by on the other side. **33** But a Samaritan, who was on a journey, came upon him; and when he saw him, he felt compassion, **34** and came to him and bandaged up his wounds, pouring oil and wine on them; and he put him on his own beast, and brought him to an inn and took care of him. **35** And on the next day, he took out two denarii[7] and gave them to the innkeeper, and said, "Take care of him; and whatever more you spend, when I return I will repay you.' **36** Which of these three, do you think, proved to be a neighbor to the man who fell

---

[7] The denarius was equivalent to a day's wages for a laborer

among the robbers?" [37] And he said, "The one who showed mercy toward him." Then Jesus said to him, "Go and do likewise."

This man had to admit the elite in the Jewish religion, the priest, and the Levite, had not been neighborly, but the Samaritan proved to be a good neighbor. Jesus moved him to reason out a new way of viewing exactly what "neighbor" meant. Instead of letting the man walk him into a long debate, Jesus made the man do all of the reasoning in the conversation, and moved him to admit something no Jew would ever utter,[8] as well as grasp a whole new understanding of what it meant to be a neighbor. Jesus took this approach because the circumstances called for it. However, on another occasion, a scribe, another expert in the law, asked him the same question and on that occasion, he chose to give the direct answer. (Mark 12:28-31) Circumstances vary.

What lessons can we take in from the example that Luke provided us? **(1)** Jesus **used Scriptures** initially to answer the man's question. **(2)** Jesus proved **perceptive** enough to **take notice** of the man's agenda. **(3)** Jesus did not just answer the easy Bible question but **shifted the responsibility** to **a question** of his own, by asking the man how he understood the law, giving him a chance to express himself. **(4)** Jesus **complimented** the man for a discerning with the correct answer. **(5)** Jesus made sure the man, and the listeners **made the connection** between the initial question and the Scriptures. **(6)** Jesus **used an illustration** that was able to **reach the heart and mind**, where the answer was kept to the forefront. **(7)** Jesus moved the man **to reason** beyond his basic understanding of a neighbor.

The apostle Paul, as well, was an excellent teacher, one from whom we can learn. His traveling companion, Luke the physician, went with him, and his account of Paul's activity is significant.

Reasoning Adapted to the Listeners

Acts 17:2-3 Updated American Standard Version (UASV)

[2] And according to Paul's custom, he went to them, and for three Sabbaths **reasoned** with them **from the Scriptures**, [3] **explaining and proving** that it was necessary that the Christ had to suffer and rise again from the dead, and saying, "This Jesus whom I am proclaiming to you is the Christ."

---

[8] Notice the hatred ran so deep between Jews and Samaritans that when asked by Jesus, who was the neighbor I the illustration, he did not say, the Samaritan, but rather, "the one who ..."

We have already spoken about the fact that Paul reasoned from the Scriptures. However, he did more, as one can see from the above, that he explained, proved, and made application. Many times, we may read a Scripture to someone, and while it seems straightforward, enough to us, yet the listener fails to see the point. We may highlight a word or phrase or a part of the text and then explain the verse. We are doing that with Acts 17:2-3, as we highlight **explaining and proving**. You could also offer to walk them through the context, as we also did previously with Acts 17:2-3, when we backed up to verse 1, to show that Paul reasoned from the Scriptures because he talked with Jews in the Synagogue, people, who would be familiar with the Hebrew Scriptures. Another option is offering them additional texts that support the one the evangelist used. If the listener does not grasp the text and the explanation, add an illustration like Jesus did over forty times. Then again, asking the right questions might get the listener to reason on things further. We can learn much by looking at Paul's method of teaching. He did not merely quote a Scripture. Thus, we need to do more than just read a Scripture. Not only did he reason from the Scriptures, he adapted his reasoning so that it would fit his audience. He did more than share the gospel with the people; he explained it to them, providing them with proof from the Word of God. Let us consider two examples of how effective Paul's teaching was.

At Acts 13:16-41, we find Paul preaching in the Synagogue at Pisidian Antioch. The first thing Paul did was to attempt to find some common ground with his Jewish audience. (Read 13:16-17) Why take that approach? Well, if he could find some common ground, this would draw his listeners in, making them more willing to reason on a subject that they were not going to agree. Notice too that he did not introduce himself as a Christian, nor did he attempt to bring them the good news of Jesus Christ. He was speaking to Jews, who took issue on both accounts, and he being a former Pharisee, he knew their thinking. Rather he referred to them as 'men of Israel, who fear God, asking them to listen.' He also inferred that he too was like them, a Hebrew from birth. After that, he gave them an important part of Israelite history, which they would have been familiar. Now, here is where the skill comes in, as he held to the common ground he had established when he began to speak about Jesus Christ.

Notice the tie in as Paul moved through the Israelite history, saying God "raised up David to be their king, of whom he testified and said, 'I have found in David the son of Jesse a man after my heart, who will do all my will.' Of this man's offspring God has brought to Israel a Savior, Jesus, as he promised." (13:22-23) Then, he pulled in John the Baptizer as a witness to this fact, a person that these Jews viewed as a prophet of God. (13:24-25; Lu 20:4-6) Knowing that his listeners were well aware that the Jewish leaders in Jerusalem had rejected Jesus, Paul beat them to the punch by mentioning it first; then, establishing that this was fulfilled prophecy. (13:27-29) After that, he drew their attention to the fact that God had not abandoned Jesus, by resurrecting him from the dead, to which there were eyewitnesses among the Jews themselves. (13:30-31) Paul brought this complicated matter home, saying, "We preach to you the good news of the promise made to the fathers." (13:32) From there he went to the Hebrew Old Testament as his evidence of this truth. Paul quoted first from Psalm 2:7 ["'You are my Son, today I have begotten you.'], then Isaiah 55:3 ["'I will give you the holy and sure blessings of David.'], and finally Psalm 16:10 ["'You will not let your Holy One see corruption.']. Paul then went on to reason from those scriptures, "For David, after he had served the purpose of God in his own generation, fell asleep and was laid with his fathers and saw corruption, but he whom God raised up did not see corruption." (13:36-37) Now, Paul closed his argument in a motivating conclusion. Many took serious what he had said. "As they went out, the people begged that these things might be told them the next Sabbath." – Acts 13:38-43.

Now, how did Paul do when he approached a non-Jewish audience? When Paul addressed the Areopagus in Athens, Greece, he used a comparable approach; he essentially adjusted his witness to the new environment and thinking of the Athenians. Here again he sought a common ground. So Paul, standing in the midst of the Areopagus, said: "Men of Athens, I perceive that in every way you are very religious. For as I passed along and observed the objects of your worship, I also found an altar with this inscription, 'To the unknown god.' For as I passed along and observed the objects of your worship, I also found an altar with this inscription, 'To the unknown god.' What therefore you worship as unknown, this I proclaim to you." (Ac 17:22-23) Rather than get explicit with the Scriptures as he did with the Jews, who would have been familiar with such, he paraphrased portions of God's Word, from which he reason from them, proving and explaining what he was saying. Moreover, since Paul had some knowledge of Greek literature, he quoted two different Greek poets.[9] He did not quote these Greek poets as though they were an authority as the Scriptures are, but the portion he quoted was in harmony with Scripture, and he wanted them to realize the points he was making could be found in their own literature. Because of this approach, "some men joined him and believed, among whom also were Dionysius the Areopagite and a woman named Damaris and others with them." – Acts 17:24-31, 34.

---

[9] Verse 28 has a possible quote from Epimenides of Crete, or it could be a traditional Greek formula. The verse also contains a quote from Aratus's poem "Phainomena."

The good news that Paul preached in both Athens and Antioch was the same. The approach he took was very similar, but adapted specifically for a particular audience because he wanted to find a common ground, to reason with them. His love for God and humanity was so deep that Paul took the time to develop his teaching abilities because he cared. Also, such efforts were fruitful because in both cases he found those, who were receptive to the truths he was sharing. It is hoped this book and others by this author will go a long way in helping us to do the same, reasoning from the Scriptures, explaining and proving the points that need to be made, effectively evangelizing our family friends, coworkers, and community.

Exercises

A hypothetical friend loves adventurous sports that are life risking. For example, he likes serious white water rafting, rock climbing up the sides of cliffs and hang-gliding. How would you reason with him that these life-risking sports are unbiblical?

Find someone you know who has strong beliefs that are unbiblical and engage them in a conversation. If you do not know such a person, find them within social media. After the discussion is over, analyze the discussion. What evidence did you present, did you use any illustrations, did you lead him along with questions, and did you evidence concern for his feelings and background.

INTRODUCTION B Effectively Communicating With Others

Whether you are gathering to go out into your community, to share the good news with the locals, or you are just staying at the church to make calls, your frame of mind is important. If you have a negative attitude that day, you must get it right. You need to go to God in prayer before ever leaving the house, asking him for the strength to set aside any mental disposition that may hamper your communication, as well as help endure and overturn any potential negativity from others.

Negative Attitudes

The way you approach others while communicating biblical truths to them will determine if they will be receptive or unreceptive to your message. People love to share their perspective on everything, and so you are bound to hear some whom you will be witnessing to, who will offer incorrect information, irrational thoughts, misconceptions about the Bible, even criticism of the Bible and Christianity as a whole, among other things. We are the ones that must maintain our composure, because "A soft answer turns away wrath, but a harsh word stirs up anger." (Proverbs 15:1)

REVIEW QUESTION: Why is it important that we pray about our mindset before we ever go out to evangelize our community?

Finding Fault

First, you do not want to **find fault** with every incorrect statement that they may make. If you are correct everything they say, you will come across as negative. It is best to choose your battles so to speak. Then, if you **word things thoughtfully**, it will fall on receptive ears. The one you are talking with says, "I have read a few books that claim the Bible has thousands of errors and contradictions, it then listed dozens throughout." First, they are the victim of the Bible critic, so you will need to choose your words carefully.

'Yes, this is a common comment that I hear, and I would add that they are more along the lines of what we call Bible difficulties, not contradictions and errors. A Bible difficulty is something in the Bible that is difficult to understand, because we are thousands of years removed from their culture, because it was written in ancient languages, because the reader has not noticed that two writers are looking at things from two different points of view, among many other things." Then you offer to give an example. "May I give you an example?" He responds with a yes, and you offer an example.

You tell him, "If you were to speak to officers that take accident reports for their police department, you would find that there is cohesion in the accounts, but each person has merely witnessed aspects that have stood out to them. We will see that this is the case as we look at the same account by two different Bible writers." You open your Bible and have him read,

Matthew 8:5: When he entered Capernaum, *a centurion* came forward to him, appealing to him.

Then have him read,

Luke 7:3: When *the centurion* heard about Jesus, he sent to him *elders of the Jews*, asking him to come and heal his servant.

You then say, "Immediately you likely noticed the problem of whether **the centurion** or the **elders of the Jews** spoke with Jesus." He nods his head in agreement. You then say, "The solution is not really hidden from us." You then ask, "Which of the two accounts is the more detailed account?" He responds with, "Luke." "Correct," you respond. Then you explain to him, "The centurion sent the elders of the Jews to represent him to Jesus, so that whatever response Jesus might give, it would be as though he were addressing the centurion; therefore, Matthew gave his readers the basic thought, not seeing the need of mentioning the elders of the Jews aspect. This is how a representative was viewed in the first century, just as some countries see ambassadors today as being the person they represent. Therefore, both Matthew and Luke are correct."

REVIEW QUESTIONS: What balance should someone have if the unbeliever to whom one witnesses to is mistaken on almost everything they believe about the Bible? How might you respond to an unbeliever that has heard that the Bible is full of errors and contradictions?

Respecting the Person

People will have their own view, but you will must come across **respectfully**. You respect the person, not necessarily their view. The person you are talking with may ask, "Why do Christians hate homosexuals?" You would respond with something like, "Christians should not have an irrational hatred for those that struggle with same sex attraction. We are to respect all people. Anyone spewing hatred, he is not truly acting like Jesus. (Matt. 7:12) We are to reject same-sex relationships, the conduct, not the person. For those that are advocates for gay rights, this is their viewpoint, and we **respectfully** disagree, and **respectfully** articulate as to why."

She responds with another question: "Did Jesus not visit sinners and was he not tolerant of others?" You then reply with something like, "Yes, this is partially true, but the inference is mistaken. Jesus spent time with sinners, but he did not ever condone their sin."

"You are right,[10] the Bible does not condone hating those who struggle with same sex attraction, but we are to hate the sin, not the one who may be practicing the sin. However, we are to make a stand against sin that is against the moral code of our Creator, and we are not to cave to public opinion. Our Christian lifestyle is reflective by the moral code within Scripture, and we have a right to our position, by the Creator himself. There is no reason that we should be ashamed of our viewpoint."

REVIEW QUESTIONS: What does it mean to respect the person, but possibly not their view? How might you respond to a person that claims that Christians hate homosexuals? How would you respond to a person who uses Jesus visiting sinners and tolerating others as a means to rationalizing and accepting practicing homosexuals?

Good Communication

Your objective is to share truth, without giving in to popular opinion. However, the truth you want to share will be better received when you afford them the opportunity to share their thoughts and ideas. Then, you express your respectful appreciation for sharing their time with you. You engender trust when they feel that you are listening, and that they are involved in a two-way conversation, as opposed to being on the receiving end of a lecture.

---

[10] You want to say that they are right at every opportunity where that is the case, which helps them to see that you do not just disagree blindly, because not everything is always bland and white.

> **REVIEW QUESTION:** What is one sign of good communication?

Take Notice of Your Surroundings

If you are going to be effective in sharing your Bible beliefs, you will have to be observant to your surroundings. By taking note of what you hear and see, it will help you have far more success. You may be witnessing from house to house, and so you should take note when the person answers the door, or comes from the back yard to greet you. Are there toys, meaning they have children? Is the house immaculately clean? Are there trophies on mantles? Does the house look like it is going through some restoration? Is the newspaper or a magazine laying there with a current affair on the cover? These types of things can be used to generate conversations. However, at the same time, do not come across as being too curious. You should make eye contact, letting them know that you are listening, but not to the point of making them uncomfortable. You may also note body language, as well as the pitch and tone of their words, helping you to know their interest level.

> **REVIEW QUESTION:** What is the benefit of being observant when witnessing to others?

How You Can Be Clear

Do not rush your words, and express them so that the other person can easily understand you. This means that you should be aware of the pace of your speech, and you may want to slow down and pronounce your words more distinctly in private reading. You can practice this in your private Bible reading, where you can read aloud, speaking clearly. However, do not let this become a habit.

In being clear with what you mean to convey, this can be accomplished by not being bogged down in many unnecessary words, but rather being more concise. In other words, if you need to make a point that has multiple parts, it is best that your initial basis of your argument be short and clearly written or stated. Thereafter, you follow it with rational arguments that are mentally clear in their meaning or intention, which your reader or listener is able to easily understand. Jesus was the greatest teacher who ever lived. He on many occasions, took the incredibly complex Mosaic Law, and made it easier to understand for his audience.

In order for you to effectively to teach someone, you must have a solid understanding of the subject yourself, to then help others understand the material. You are ready to teach a subject when you are, in your own words, able to offer reasons as to why it is or is not so. Jesus was able to get his points across by keeping things simple, using indisputable reasoning, stimulating questions, remarkable figures of speech, as well as discernible illustrations that were taken from his listeners everyday life. (Matt. 6:25-30; 7:3-5, 24-27) Jesus was also known for his taking an incident occurring around him and his disciples, which he would then use as an opportunity for teaching a lesson. (John 13:2-16)

Sadly, some Bible scholars have placed their books out of the hands of the common person, as they use language that requires the reader to hold their book in one hand and a Webster's Dictionary in the other. By their nature, these individuals are a polysyllabricator who uses sesquipedalian words. In other words, they use long words with many syllables. Sadly, these individuals spend hundreds, if not thousands of hours researching and writing a book that five people are going to read. In the Sermon on the Mount, Matthew 5:3–7:27, Jesus spoke for a mere half hour, covering such issues as anger toward others, lust, divorce, retaliation, helping the needy, prayer, fasting, anxiety, judging others, materialism. He did not use long words with many syllables here, and could be understood by children, farmers, fishermen and shepherds. (Matt. 7:28)

Jesus expressed word pictures that conveyed the riches of meaning, even today. For example, "No one can serve two masters ... You cannot serve God and money." (Matt. 6:24) "You will recognize them by their fruits." (Matt. 7:20) "Judge not, that you be not judged." (Matt. 7:21) But when he heard it, he said, "Those who are well have no need of a physician, but those who are sick." (Matt. 9:12) Then Jesus said to him, "Put your sword back into its place. For all who take the sword will perish by the sword. (Matt. 26:52) Jesus said to them, "Render to Caesar the things that are Caesar's, and to God the things that are God's." – Mark 12:17.

REVIEW QUESTIONS: Why is clear pronunciation important? What should you do if an unbeliever asks you a Bible question that requires a complex answer? Why have some Bible scholars found themselves out of touch with most people? How did Jesus usually express himself?

Effective Use of Questions

On many occasions, Jesus could have simply told his listeners the point that he wanted to get across, but instead, he chose to ask them questions. For those that were looking to make him look the fool, Jesus asked questions to expose these people. (Matt. 12:24-30; 21:23-27; 22:41-46) However, far more often, he used his questions to convey the point he wanted to make, and he wanted them to remember.

Tax Paid with Coin from mouth of Fish

Matthew 17:24-27 Updated American Standard Version (UASV)

[24] When they arrived in Capernaum, the ones who collected the double drachma tax[11] came up to Peter and said, "Does your teacher not pay the double drachma tax?"[12] [25] He said, "Yes." And when he came into the house, Jesus spoke to him first, saying, "What do you think, Simon? From whom do kings of the earth collect tolls or tax? From their sons or from strangers?" [26] And when he said, "From strangers," Jesus said to him, "Then the sons are free. [27] However, so that we do not cause them to stumble, go to the sea and throw in a hook, and take the first fish that comes up; and when you open its mouth, you will find a shekel.[13] Take that and give it to them for you and me."

REVIEW QUESTION: Who set the example of effective use of questions? Give an example.

Effective Use of Hyperbole

Again, Jesus is by far the most effective teacher of all time, and hyperbole is one method that he used quite often. Hyperbole is a deliberate and obvious exaggeration used for effect, e.g., "I could eat a million of these." The objective is to add emphasis and importance to what is being said. Moreover, like other special literary forms, hyperbole imprints a mental picture in your mind, one that is hard to forget.

There are actually two different types of exaggerations: **(1)** the first being an overstatement, but possible and **(2)** hyperbole, which is a

---

[11] This was two drachmas paid by each male Jew as a yearly temple tax.

[12] This was two drachmas paid by each male Jew as a yearly temple tax.

[13] A stater coin, a silver coin worth two didrachma or approximately one shekel.

statement that is impossible. Our concern is having the ability to recognize either of these when we see them. Let us take a look at a few examples.

Stop Judging

Matthew 7:1-3 Updated American Standard Version (UASV)

7 "Do not judge so that you will not be judged. ² For with the judgment you are judging you will be judged, and by what measure you are measuring, it will be measured to you. ³ Why do you look at the speck that is in your brother's eye, but do not notice **the log** that is in your own eye?

Try to picture what is being emphasized. You have a person who is continuously, and aggressively judging others, who goes up to a brother that is seldom critical, to offer advice on not being critical. A brother that has a log's worth of being judgmental to him is advising the brother that has a mere straw of judgmentalism to him. Is this not a beautiful way to illustrate how a brother, who has immense problems in a particular area, should be slow to offer advice to another brother, who seldom offends in this area? Below Jesus is rebuking some Pharisees, Jewish religious leaders.

Matthew 23:24 Updated American Standard Version (UASV)

²⁴ Blind guides, who strain out a gnat and swallow a camel!

This was a foremost way to use hyperbole. Take note of the fact that he is contrasting a small gnat with a huge camel, which represents the largest animal known to his audience. One religious magazine stated, "It is estimated that it would take up to 70 million gnats to equal the weight of an average camel!" Jesus was also very much aware that the Pharisees strained their wine through a cloth sieve to avoid ceremonial uncleanness by accidently drinking a gnat. However, they were quite eager to gulp down the figurative camel, it also being unclean. (Lev. 11:4, 21-24) How? The Pharisees were very quick to follow the minor points of the Mosaic Law, but set aside the weightier laws, like "justice and mercy and faithfulness." (Matt. 23:23) This one point makes using hyperbole all too clear, and exposed them for the hypocrites they were.

Matthew 17:20 Updated American Standard Version (UASV)

²⁰ And he said to them, "Because of your little faith. For truly I say to you, if you have faith like a mustard seed, you will say to this mountain, 'Move from here to there,' and it will move, and nothing will be impossible for you."

Jesus could have simply said that they need more faith, but that would have not made the impact this figurative comment did. He only stressed the need for a little faith in an effective manner, making the point that a small amount of faith can move mountain-like objects.

Matthew 19:24 Updated American Standard Version (UASV)

²⁴ Again I say to you, it is easier for a camel to go through the eye of a needle than for a rich man to enter the Kingdom of God."

Try if you will to picture a camel fitting through the eye of a sewing needle. It is impossible, not difficult! Of course, this does not mean that rich people are excluded from the kingdom of God. The context is about people, who have a greater love for money than their love of the kingdom. It is their love of money, which makes them ineligible. Jesus' colorful, vivid idioms have an effect so powerful that literally hundreds of millions of people have used them over the last 2,000 years.

Throughout his three and a half years of ministry, Jesus masterfully used hyperbole. Are you not in awe of Jesus' exciting figures of speech and his skill of accomplishing a supreme effect without long words with many syllables?

REVIEW QUESTIONS: What is hyperbole? What two different types of exaggerations are there? How effective was Jesus in his use of hyperbole? Give an example.

Course Project D

Reasoning From The Scriptures: Using several Scriptures, effectively communicate why _____ is not biblical or is biblical. The director or assistant direct will assign a subject.[14]

Overcoming Dismissive Comments

Many today are just not interested in your desire to share the Good News with them. They will attempt to shut you down with one good dismissive comment in the beginning. Your objective is to become effective in your ability to overcome or get around these walls of disinterest. They may hold up their hand, which is a dismissive gesture, and say in a dismissive tone,

- "I am not interested."

---

[14] The Evangelism Program Director or Assistant Director will select the topic.

- "I am not interested in religion."
- "I am busy."
- "Why do Christians feel the need to share?"
- "I am a Buddhist, a Hindu, a Muslim, or a Jew."
- "I don't believe the Bible."
- "Everyone interprets the Bible differently."
- "The Bible is not practical in today's scientific world."
- "The Bible contradicts itself."
- "The Bible is a good book by man, but there is no such thing as absolute truth."

These quick comments are meant to stop us in our tracks. These dismissive comments can be general, "I am not interested," or they could be based on the subject you start the conversation with. People have many reasons as to why they do not want to talk. Most are misconceptions.

- They had a bad experience in a congregation they attended before.
- They have taken many liberal classes throughout their high school and college years.
- They are aware of Christian history, like crusades, inquisitions, or immoral Popes in church history.
- They are aware of major church scandals.
- They have read popular books that tear down the Bible as being full of historical, geographical and scientific errors, and contradictions. To them the book is by imperfect men, not inspired of God.
- Maybe their life has been filled with one tragedy after another, and they cannot grasp how a loving God would allow such suffering.

These are some of the reasons, why they use dismissive comments. They have issues that are not well founded, and need to be reasoned on further. That is why, many times, if you can get beyond the comment, you can get at what really troubles them, and help them reason through it. Below is an example of one trying to be dismissive, using the Bible as a means of shutting down the conversation.

REVIEW QUESTIONS: What are some dismissive comments that the unbeliever might make, and what is his purpose for making such comments? What are some legitimate reasons the Bible critic might not be interested in talking about Christianity or the Bible?

'The Bible contains contradictions, mistakes, and errors'

Whoever makes a claim carries the responsibility, so tactfully inquire, "Yes, this is a common claim, could you take my Bible, and point to an example?" Most will not take the Bible, because they are just repeating a common complaint about the Bible. However, for the sake of those few, who will, he takes your Bible, and turns to Matthew 27:5 and says, "It states that Judas hanged himself," whereas Acts 1:18 says that "falling headlong he burst open in the middle and all his bowels gushed out."

Matthew 27:5 Updated American Standard Version (UASV)

⁵ And he threw the pieces of silver into the temple and departed; and he went away and **hanged himself**.

Acts 1:18 Updated American Standard Version (UASV)

¹⁸ (Now this man acquired a field with the price of his wickedness, and **falling headlong, he burst open in the middle and all his intestines gushed out**.

You Respond: "Neither Matthew, nor Luke made a mistake. What you have is Matthew giving the reader the manner in which Judas committed suicide. On the other hand, Luke is giving the reader of Acts, the result of that suicide. Therefore, instead of a mistake, we have two texts that complement each other, really giving the reader the full picture. Judas came to a tree alongside a cliff that had rocks below. He tied the rope to a branch and the other end around his neck, and jumped over the edge of the cliff in an attempt at hanging himself. One of two things could have happened: (1) the limb broke plunging him to the rocks below, or (2) the rope broke with the same result, and he burst open onto the rocks below."

Then you could add, "Generally, what it comes down to is that many books that criticize the Bible, pointing to Scriptures, showing what they call errors, contradictions, and mistakes. However, what they do not show the reader is that there are reasonable answers for ninety-nine percent of these complaints.'

A longer response might be, "Considering that there are 31,000 plus verses in the Bible, encompassing 66 books written by about 40 writers, ranging from shepherds, to kings, an army general, fishermen, tax collector, a physician and on and on, and being penned over a 1,600 year period, one does find a few hundred *Bible difficulties* (about one percent). However, 99 percent of those are explainable. Yet no one wants to be so arrogant to say that he can explain them all. It has nothing to do with the inadequacy of God's Word, but is based on human understanding. In many cases, science or archaeology and the field of custom and culture of ancient peoples has helped explain difficulties in hundreds of passages. Therefore, there may be less than one percent left to be answered, yet our knowledge of God's Word continues to grow. R. A. Torrey said about 100 years ago, "Some people are surprised and staggered because there are difficulties in the Bible. For my part, I would be more surprised and staggered if there were not."

You explain that these are not contradictions, errors, or mistakes, but are Bible difficulties, which are difficult because the Bible was written in dozens of different cultures and times that range from 2,000 to 3,500 years ago. In addition, the Bible was written in three different ancient languages. Moreover, the Bible was written from the intention of human author back then, and we should not impose our modern world on that author. Today, we say in our news reports that the sun rises and sets at certain times, even though we know this is scientifically inaccurate. However, it is a human observation. Today, we round numbers because it is a way of simplifying things, if we are trying to make a point, like how many people living in America. We would just say 316 million, not, 315,940,341 unless we were doing a census. Jesus spoke of mustard seeds as the smallest of all seeds. This is not accurate. However, was Jesus giving a lesson on botany? No, he was making a point to a people, who knew this seed as being the smallest. Therefore, considering Jesus' audience, the point that he was making, and how the mustard seed was commonly used as a figure of speech, this was the tiniest seed in that setting and circumstance.

Either this person raising issues about the Bible is going to be more receptive to the conversation, or he will ignore your insight as though you never made it, moving on to the next criticism that he has memorized. His response is a way for you to read his heart-attitude. You will not want to throw your pearls before the swine of Bible criticism, so move on, if it is evident that no answer will satisfy this one. However, far more right-hearted ones are going to be receptive to your insightful words. This brings us to our next point, how they listen to you.

REVIEW QUESTION: How might you respond to someone that claims the Bible contains contradictions, mistakes, and errors? How might you explain why there are no contradictions, errors, or mistakes in the Bible, just Bible difficulties?

How the Unbeliever Listens to Us

Getting a sense of how one is listening to us, will enable us to determine if more time should be given to this one. The person we are talking with may very well be what is known as a **judgmental listener**. They are listening to us to ascertain whether we are right or wrong, and are labeling us in their mind ('that was foolish'), as opposed to hearing what we are saying. Then, there is what is known as the **distorted listener**. In other words, this one does not hear us clearly, because he is viewing us in a biased and prejudiced way ('Christians are such fools!'). There is the **stereotype listener**, who also fails to hear our real message, because they are labeling us in their mind, as "just a woman," "Bible thumper," "so naïve," and so on.

Then, there is the **resistive listener**, who will not be receptive to anything that is not a part of his worldview. Moreover, anyone in opposition to their worldview is viewed as the enemy, and they resist anything they say, no matter how reasonable it may be. They think things like, 'Why do these people not see that science has displaced the Bible as a book by man." We also have the **interpretive listener**. These view everything through their preconceptions, ideas based on little or no information, just personal bias. They incorporate their life experience into what they are hearing, making snap interpretations of our every word. They filter everything through their worldview, their knowledge and understanding.

Then, there is the **association listener**, who evaluates our Christian visit with everything bad they have ever heard about Christianity and the Bible, and we are guilty by association. No matter what we say, it is ignored, because they see us as a member of a group that they perceive a certain way. Of course, this could go the other way if they have a favorable view of Christianity. While these are the negative side of listening, it can give us an idea of why and how we could be shut out, before we ever get started. If we feel that we are unfairly dismissed, we could ask some open-ended questions such as 'how do you feel,' 'what do you think,' 'what do you believe,' or 'how do you see these questions.' Open-ended questions enable us to get at their heart condition, enabling us to better formulate our arguments.

Lastly, there are the persons that all Christian evangelizers are looking for, which is the **receptive heart listener**. One who has a receptive heart, will let reasoning from the Scriptures in receptively, which will build confidence in what we are saying is true. We will be able to plant seeds of truth within this person's heart, which God will make grow. In writing to the Corinthians, who were caught up in arguing over who was greater (Paul or Apollos); Paul made the comparison of a Christian evangelist with that of a farmer. The Apostle Paul planted the Corinthian congregation. Apollos came later on the scene, and watered the Bible truths that Paul had already planted. Apollos with his passion and force, as well as his authoritative Scriptural refutations of the arguments that had been raised by the unbelieving Jews was very beneficial to the Corinthian Christians. However, it was God, who made those truths grow.

Corinthians Still Fleshly

1 Corinthians 3:1-9 Updated American Standard Version (UASV)

3 And I, brothers, was not able to speak to you as to spiritual men, but as to fleshly men, as to infants in Christ. **2** I gave you milk to drink, not solid food, for you were not yet ready. But now you are still not able, **3** for you are still fleshly. For since there is jealousy and strife among you, are you not fleshly, and are you not walking like mere men? **4** For when one says, "I am of Paul," and another, "I am of Apollos," are you not mere men?

God Makes It Grow

5 What then is Apollos? And what is Paul? Servants through whom you believed, as the Lord assigned to each. **6** I planted, Apollos watered, but God gave the growth. **7** So then neither the one who plants nor the one who waters is anything, but only God who gives the growth. **8** Now he who plants and he who waters are one; but each will receive his own reward according to his own labor. **9** For we are God's fellow workers; you are God's field, God's building.

Keep in mind, that the receptive heart listener is not just the person, who shakes his head yes, as he agrees with your every word. Peter was sent to the Ethiopian Eunuch (Acts 8:26-38), who had rapid spiritual progress, while the Apostle Paul was sent to the Greek philosophers on Mars Hill.

Mars Hill (Areopagus) was a "prominent rise overlooking the city of Athens where the philosophers of the city gathered to discuss their ideas, some of which revolutionized modern thought. Paul discussed religion with the leading minds of Athens on Mars Hill. He used the altar to an 'unknown god' to present Jesus to them (Acts 17:22)."[15]

The point is that the Apostle Paul was sent to people who were very knowledgeable, intelligent, and wise, people who only lacked the light to see where the real truth lie. This was no easy assignment, but in the end,

---

[15] "Mars Hill", in Holman Illustrated Bible Dictionary, ed. Chad Brand, Charles Draper, Archie England et al., 1084 (Nashville, TN: Holman Bible Publishers, 2003).

"some men joined [Paul] and believed, among whom also were Dionysius the Areopagite and a woman named Damaris and others with them." (Acts 17:34) Yes, Paul reasoned from the Scriptures in the synagogue with the Jews, and he reasoned with Epicurean and Stoic philosophers, who also conversed with him. It says that he was "explaining and proving." This illustrates that a receptive heart listener also includes those who require us to reason from the Scriptures; therefore, we have to have the ability to reason from the Scriptures. – Acts 17: 2-3, 17-18.

REVIEW QUESTIONS: What type of listeners is there, and which one is the evangelist seeking? Are Christians expected to only evangelize those who are easy to convince?

Effective Listening and Responding

In trying to communication with strangers, it can be quite a challenge at times. We may deal with biases, prejudices, a person in the middle of life trauma, someone who has had bad experiences, someone who just lost a loved one, and many more communication challenges. We will be able to overcome some of the anxieties of starting conversation, by taking a moment to consider some of these challenges.

One of the ways to deal with a challenge is empathy. We in our hearts must place ourselves in their shoes, getting their mindset. Just because a person comes across abrasively about talking about the Bible, this does not mean that we let them go. There may very well be a reason as to why they are not open to a Bible conversation. This is where insightful, thought-provoking questions, can get at the significant part that has closed them down.

By employing active listening, allowing them to vent, we will understand whatever issues we need to overcome. We might ask, 'tell me, what has you to where you are unable to talk about the Bible.' This will let them know that we are open to listening. While they are expressing themselves, do not be tempted to resolve their issue, just listen as they fully explain. First, make sure we respond in a calm voice. Then reiterate what they said in a summary point, which will let them know we were listening, and it helps us to know we understand what it is. In the end, we may not agree, but we can empathetically understand in some way.

Now, if we have a solution to what was mention, offer it at this time. If we do not have a biblical answer, be honest, saying something like, "I can understand, and while I do not have a ready answer for you at this time, I will research it at home, and we can talk again." This lets them know that we are going beyond what one would expect and that we are very concerned about them.

> **REVIEW QUESTION:** What are some communication challenges that you may face, and how may you overcome these?

> **Course Project D** **Reasoning From The Scriptures:** Using several Scriptures, effectively communicate why _____ is not biblical or is biblical. The director or assistant direct will assign a subject.[16]

---

[16] The Evangelism Program Director or Assistant Director will select the topic.

32

CHAPTER 1 Bible Difficulties Explained

IT SEEMS THAT the charge that the Bible contradicts itself has been made more and more in the last 20 years. Generally, those making such claims are merely repeating what they have heard, because most have not even read the Bible, let alone done an in-depth study of it. I do not wish, however, to set aside all concerns as though they have no merit. There are many who raise legitimate questions that seem, on the surface anyway, to be about well-founded contradiction. Sadly, these issues have caused many to lose their faith in God's Word, the Bible. The purpose of this books is, to help its readers to be able to defend the Bible against Bible critics (1 Pet. 3:15), to contend for the faith (Jude 1:3), and help those, who have begun to doubt. – Jude 1:22-23.

Before we begin explaining things, let us jump right in, getting our feet wet, and deal with two major Bible difficulties, so we can see that there are reasonable, logical answers. After that, we will delve deeper into explaining Bible difficulties.

Is God permitting Human Sacrifice?

Judges 11:29-34, 37-40? Updated American Standard Version (UASV)

²⁹ Then the Spirit of the Lord was upon Jephthah, and he passed through Gilead and Manasseh; and passed on to Mizpah of Gilead, and from Mizpah of Gilead he passed on to the sons of Ammon. ³⁰ And Jephthah **made a vow** to Jehovah and said, "If You will indeed give the sons of Ammon into my hand, ³¹ then it shall be that **whatever** comes out of the doors of my house to meet me when I return in peace from the sons of Ammon, it shall be Jehovah's, and I will offer it up as a burnt offering." ³² So Jephthah crossed over to the sons of Ammon to fight against them; and Jehovah gave them into his hand. ³³ He struck them with a very great slaughter from Aroer as far as Minnith, twenty cities, and as far as Abel-keramim. So the sons of Ammon were subdued before the sons of Israel.

³⁴ When Jephthah came to his house at Mizpah, behold, **his daughter was coming out to meet him** with tambourines and with dancing. Now she was his one and only child; besides her he had no son or daughter.

³⁷ And she said to her father, "Let this thing be done for me: leave me alone two months, that I may go up and down on the mountains and weep because of my virginity, I and my companions." ³⁸ And he said, "Go." So he sent her away for two months; and **she left with her**

companions, and wept on the mountains because of her virginity. ³⁹ At the end of two months she returned to her father, who **did to her according to the vow that he had made**; and she never known a man.[17] Thus it became a custom in Israel, ⁴⁰ that the daughters of Israel went year by year **to commemorate[18] the daughter** of Jephthah the Gileadite four days in the year.

It is true; to infer that having the idea of an animal sacrifice would really have not been an impressive vow, which the context requires. Human sacrifice will be repugnant if we are talking about taking a life. Jephthah had no sons, so he likely knew it was the daughter, who would come to greet him.

First, the text does not say he killed his daughter. The idea of some that he did kill her is concluded only by inference. While it is not good policy to interpret backward, using Paul on Judges, he does say humans are to be **"as a living sacrifice."** Therefore, Jephthah could have offered his daughter at the temple, "as a living sacrifice" in service, like Samuel.

This is not to be taken dismissively, because, under Jewish backgrounds, it is no small thing to offer a **perpetual virginity** as a sacrifice. This would mean Jephthah's lineage would not be carried on, the family name, was no more.

Second, the context says she went out to weep for two months, not mourn her death. It says, "she left with her companions, and **wept on the mountains because of her virginity**."

If she was facing imminent death, she could have married, and spent that last two months as a married woman. There would be absolutely no reason for her to mourn her virginity if she were not facing perpetual virginity. – Exodus 38:8; 1 Samuel 2:22

Third, it was completely forbidden to offer a human sacrifice. – Leviticus 18:21; 20:2-5; Deuteronomy 12:31; 18:10

Imagine an Israelite believing that he could please God with a human sacrifice that was intended to offer up a human life. To do so would have been a rejection of Jehovah's Sovereignty (the very person you are asking for help), and a rejection of the Law that made them a special people. Worse still, this interpretation would have us believe that Jehovah knew this was coming, allowed the vow, and then aided this type of man to succeed over his enemies.

---

¹⁷ I.e., *never had relations with a man*
¹⁸ Or *lament*

The last point is simple enough. If such a man as one who would make such a vow, in gross violation of the law, and then carry it out; there is no way he would be mentioned by Paul in Hebrews chapter 11 among the most faithful men and women in Israelite history.

In review, there is no way God would have granted and helped in Jephthah's initial success knowing the vow that was coming because both Jehovah and Jephthah would be as bad as the Canaanites. There is no way that God would accept such a vow and then go on to help Jephthah with his enemies yet again. Then, to allow such a vow to be carried out, to then put Jephthah on the wall of star witnesses for God in Hebrews chapter 11.

Does Isaiah 45:7 mean that God Is the Author of Evil?

Isaiah 45:7 King James Version (KJV) 7 I form the light, and create darkness: I make peace, and **create evil**: I the Lord do all these things.	Isaiah 45:7 English Standard Version (ESV) 7 I form light and create darkness, I make well-being and **create calamity**, I am the Lord, who does all these things.[19]

Encarta Dictionary: (Evil) (1) morally bad: profoundly immoral or wrong (2) deliberately causing great harm, pain, or upset

QUESTION: Is this view of evil always the case? No, as you will see below.

Some apologetic authors try to say, 'we do not understand Isaiah 45:7 correctly, because there are other verses that say God is not evil (1 John 1:5), cannot look approvingly on evil (Hab. 1:13), and cannot be tempted by evil. (James 1:13)' Well, while all of these things are Scripturally true, the question at hand is not: Is God evil, can God approvingly look on evil, or can God be tempted with evil? Those questions are not relevant to the one at hand, as God cannot be those things, and at the same time, he can be the yes to our question. The question is, is God the author, the creator of evil?

We would hardly argue that God was **not just** in his bringing "calamity" or "evil" down on Adam and Eve. Thus, we have Isaiah 45:7 saying that God is the creator of "calamity" or "evil."

Let us begin simple, without trying to be philosophical. When God removed Adam and Eve from the Garden of Eden, he sentenced them and humanity to sickness, old age, and death. (Rom. 5:8; i.e., enforce

---

[19] See Jeremiah 18:11, Lamentations 3:18, and Amos 3:6

penalty for sin), which was to bring "calamity" or "evil" upon humankind. Therefore, as we can see "evil" does not always mean wrongdoing. Other examples of God bringing "calamity" or "evil" are Noah and the flood, the Ten Plagues of Egypt, and the destruction of the Canaanites. These acts of evil were not acts of wrongdoing. Rather, they were righteous and just, because God, the Creator of all things, was administering justice to wrongdoers, to sinners. He warned the perfect first couple what the penalty was for sin. He warned the people for a hundred years by Noah's preaching. He warned the Canaanites centuries before.

Nevertheless, there are times, when God extends mercy, refraining from the execution of his righteous judgment to one worthy of calamity. For example, he warned Nineveh, the city of blood, and they repented, so he pardoned them. (Jonah 3:10) God has made it a practice to warn persons of the results of sin, giving them undeservedly many opportunities to change their ways. – Ezekiel 33:11.

God cannot sin; it is impossible for him to do so. So, when did he create evil? Without getting into the eternity of his knowing what he was going to do, and when, let us just say, evil did not exist when he was the only person in existence. We might say the idea of evil existed because he knew what he was going to do. However, the moment he created creatures (spirit and human), the potential for evil came into existence because both have free will to sin (fall short of perfection). Evil became a reality the moment Satan entertained the idea of causing Adam to sin, to get humanity for himself, and then acted on it.

God has the right and is just to bring the *calamity of* or *evil* down on anyone that is an unrepentant sinner. God did not even have to give us the underserved kindness of offering us his Son. God is the author or agent of evil regardless of the source books that claim otherwise. If he had never created free will beings, evil would have never gone from the idea of evil to the potential of evil, to the existence of evil. However, God felt that it was better to get the sinful state out of angel and human existence, recover, and then any who would sin thereafter; he would be justified in handing out evil or calamity to only that person or angel alone.

Who among us would argue that he should have created humans and angels like robots, automatons with no free will? The moment he chose the free will, he moved evil from an idea to a potential, and Satan moved it to reality. God has a moral nature that does not bring about evil and sin when he is the only person in existence. However, the moment he created beings in his image, which had the potential to sin, he brought about evil. The moment we have a moral code of good and evil that is placed upon one's with free will; then, we have evil as a potential.

In English, the very comprehensive Hebrew word ra' is variously translated as "bad," "downcast (sad, NASB)," "ugly," "evil," "grievous (distressing, NASB)," "sore," "selfish (stingy, HCSB)," and "envious," depending upon the context. (Gen 2:9; 40:7; 41:3; Ex 33:4; Deut. 6:22; 28:35; Pro 23:6; 28:22)

Evil as an adjective **describes** the **quality of** a class of people, places, or things, or of a specific person, place, or thing

Evil as a noun, **defines** the **nature** of a class of people, places, or things, or of a specific person, place, or thing (e.g., the evil one, evil eye).

We can agree that "evil" is a thing. Create means to bring something into existence, be it people, places, or things, as well something abstract, for lack of a better word at the moment. We would agree that when God was alone evil was not a reality; it did not exist? We would agree that the moment that God created free will creatures (angels and humans), creating humans in his image, with his moral nature, he also brought the potential for evil into existence, and it was realized by Satan?

Inerrancy: Can the Bible Be trusted?

If the Bible is the Word of God, it should be in complete agreement throughout; there should be no contradictions. Yet, the rational mind must ask, why is it that some passages appear to be contradictions when compared with others? For example, Numbers 25:9 tells us that 24,000 died from the scourge, whereas at 1 Corinthians 10:8, the apostle Paul says it was 23,000. This would seem to be a clear error. Before addressing such matters, let us first look at some background information.

Full inerrancy in this book means that the original writings are fully without error in all that they state, as are the words. The words were not dictated (automaton), but the intended meaning is inspired, as are the words that convey that meaning. The Author allowed the writer to use his style of writing, yet controlled the meaning to the extent of not allowing the writer to choose a wrong word, which would not convey the intended meaning. Other more liberal-minded persons hold with *partial inerrancy*, which claims that as far as faith is concerned, this portion of God's Word is without error, but that there are historical, geographical, and scientific errors.

There are several different levels of inerrancy. *Absolute Inerrancy* is the belief that the Bible is fully true and exact in every way; including not only relationships and doctrine, but also science and history. In other words, all information is completely exact. *Full Inerrancy* is the belief that the Bible was not written as a science or historical textbook, but is phenomenological, in that it is written from the human perspective. In other words, speaking of such things as the sun rising, the four corners of the earth or the rounding off of number approximations are all from a human perspective. *Limited Inerrancy* is the belief that the Bible is meant only as a reflection of God's purposes and will, so the science and history is the understanding of the author's day, and is limited. Thus, the Bible is susceptible to errors in these areas. *Inerrancy of Purpose* is the belief that it is only inerrant in the purpose of bringing its readers to a saving faith. The Bible is not about facts, but about persons and relationships, thus, it is subject to error. *Inspired: Not Inerrant* is the belief that its authors are human and thus subject to human error. It should be noted that this author holds the position of full inerrancy.

For many today, the Bible is nothing more than a book written by men. The Bible critic believes the Bible to be full of myths and legends, contradictions, and geographical, historical, and scientific errors. University professor Gerald A. Larue had this to say, "The views of the writers as expressed in the Bible reflect the ideas, beliefs, and concepts current in their own times and are limited by the extent of knowledge in those times."[20] On the other hand, the Bible's authors claim that their writings were inspired of God, as Holy Spirit moved them along. We will discover shortly that the Bible critics have much to say, but it is inflated or empty.

2 Timothy 3:16-17 Updated American Standard Version (UASV)

[16] All Scripture is inspired by God and profitable for teaching, for reproof, for correction, for training in righteousness; [17] so that the man of God may be fully competent, equipped for every good work.

2 Peter 1:21 Updated American Standard Version (UASV)

[21] for no prophecy was ever produced by the will of man, but men carried along by the Holy Spirit spoke from God.

The question remains as to whether the Bible is a book written by imperfect men and full of errors, or is written by imperfect men, but inspired by God. If the Bible is just another book by imperfect man, there is no hope for humankind. If it is inspired by God and without error, although penned by imperfect men, we have the hope of everything that it offers: a rich, happy life now by applying counsel that lies within and the real life that is to come, everlasting life. This author contends that the Bible is inspired of God and free of human error, although written by imperfect humans.

---

[20] Gerald Larue, "The Bible as a Political Weapon," *Free Inquiry* (Summer 1983): 39.

Before we take on the critics who seem to sift the Scriptures looking for problematic verses, let us take a moment to reflect on how we should approach these alleged problem texts. The critic's argument goes something like this: 'If God does not err and the Bible is the Word of God, then the Bible should not have one single error or contradiction, yet it is full of errors and contradictions.' If the Bible is riddled with nothing but contradictions and errors as the critics would have us believe, why, out of 31,173 verses in the Bible, should there be only 2-3 thousand Bible difficulties that are called into question, this being less than ten percent of the whole?

First, let it be said that it is every Christian's obligation to get a deeper understanding of God's Word, just as the apostle Paul told Timothy:

1 Timothy 4:15-16 Updated American Standard Version (UASV)

[15] Practice these things, be absorbed in them, so that your progress will be evident to all. [16] Pay close attention to yourself and to your teaching; persevere in these things, for as you do this you will ensure salvation both for yourself and for those who hear you.

Paul also told the Corinthians:

2 Corinthians 10:4-5 Updated American Standard Version (UASV)

[4] For the weapons of our warfare are not of the flesh[21] but powerful to God for destroying strongholds.[22] [5] We are destroying speculations and every lofty thing raised up against the knowledge of God, and we are taking every thought captive to the obedience of Christ,

Paul also told the Philippians:

Philippians 1:7 Updated American Standard Version (UASV)

[7] It is right for me to feel thus about you all, because I hold you in my heart, for you are all partakers with me of grace, both in my imprisonment and in the defense and confirmation of the gospel.

In being able to defend against the modern-day critic, one has to be able to reason from the Scriptures and overturn the critic's argument(s) with mildness. If someone were to approach us about an alleged error or contradiction, what should we do? We should be frank and honest. If we do not have an answer, we should admit such. If the text in question gives the appearance of difficulty, we should admit this as well. If we are

---

[21] That is *merely human*
[22] That is *tearing down false arguments*

unsure as to how we should answer, we can simply say that we will look into it and get back to them, returning with a reasonable answer.

However, we do not want to express disbelief and doubt to our critics, because they will be emboldened in their disbelief. It will put them on the offense and us on the defense. With great confidence, we can express that there is an answer. The Bible has withstood the test of 2,000 years of persecution and interrogation and yet it is the most printed book of all time, currently being translated into 2,287 languages. If these critical questions were so threatening, the Bible would not be the book that it is.

When we are pursuing the text in question, be unwavering in purpose, or resolved to find an answer. In some cases, it may take hours of digging to find the solution. Consider this: as we resolve these difficulties, we are also building our faith that God's Word is inerrant. Moreover, we will want to do preventative maintenance in our personal study. As we are doing our Bible reading, take note of these surface discrepancies and resolve them as we work our way through the Bible. We need to make this part of our prayers as well. I recommend the following program. Below are several books that deal with difficult passages. As we daily read and study our Bible from Genesis to Revelation, do not attempt it in one year; make it a four-year program. Use a good exegetical commentary like *The Holman Old/New Testament Commentary* (HOTC/HNTC) or *The New American Commentary* set, and *The Big Book of Bible Difficulties* by Norman L. Geisler, as well as *The Encyclopedia of Bible Difficulties* by Gleason Archer.

We should be aware that men under inspiration penned the originally written books. In fact, we do not have those originals, what textual scholars call autographs, but we do have thousands of copies. The copyists, however, were not inspired; therefore, as one might expect, throughout the first 1,400 years of copying, thousands of errors were transmitted into the texts that were being copied by imperfect hands that were not under inspiration when copying. Yet, the next 450 years saw a restoration of the text by textual scholars from around the world. Therefore, while many of our best literal translations today may not be inspired, they are a mirror-like reflection of the autographs by way of textual criticism.[23] Therefore, the fallacy could be with the copyist error that has simply not been weeded out. In addition, we must keep in mind that God's Word is without error, but our interpretation and understanding of that Word is not.

---

[23] Textual criticism is the study of copies of any written work of which the autograph (original) is unknown, with the purpose of ascertaining the original text. Harold J. Green, *Introduction to New Testament Textual Criticism* (Peabody, MA: Hendrickson, 1995), 1.

It should be noted that the Bible is made up of 66 smaller books that were hand-written over a period of 1,600 years, having some 40 writers of various trades such as shepherd, king, priest, tax collector, governor, physician, copyist, fisherman, and a tentmaker. Therefore, it should not surprise us that some difficulties are encountered as we casually read the Bible. Yet, if one were to take a deeper look, one would find that these difficulties are easily explained. Let us take a few pages to examine some passages that have been under attack.

This chapter's objective is not to be exhaustive, not even close. What we are looking to do is cover a few alleged contradictions and a couple of alleged mistakes. This is to give us a small sampling of the reasonable answers that we will find in the above recommended books. Remember, our Bible is a sword that we must use both offensively and defensively. One must wonder how long a warrior of ancient times would last who was not expertly trained in the use of his weapon. Let us look at a few scriptures that support our need to learn our Bible well so will be able to defend what we believe to be true.

When "false apostles, deceitful workmen, disguising themselves as apostles of Christ" were causing trouble in the congregation in Corinth, the apostle Paul wrote that under such circumstances, we are to *tear down their arguments* and *take every thought captive.* (2 Corinthians 10:4, 5; 11:13–15) All who present critical arguments against God's Word, or contrary to it, can have their arguments overturned by the Christian, who is able and ready to defend that Word in mildness. – 2 Timothy 2:24–26.

1 Peter 3:15 Updated American Standard Version (UASV)

[15] but sanctify Christ as Lord in your hearts, always being prepared to make a defense[24] to anyone who asks you for a reason for the hope that is in you; yet do it with gentleness and respect;

Peter says that we need to be prepared to make a *defense*. The Greek word behind the English 'defense' is *apologia*, which is actually a legal term that refers to the defense of a defendant in court. Our English apologetics is just what Peter spoke of, having the ability to give a reason to any who may challenge us, or to answer those who are not challenging us but who have honest questions that deserve to be answered.

2 Timothy 2:24-25 Updated American Standard Version (UASV)

[24] For a slave of the Lord does not need to fight, but needs to be kind to all, qualified to teach, showing restraint when wronged [25] with

---

[24] Or *argument*; or *explanation*

gentleness correcting those who are in opposition, if perhaps God may grant them repentance leading to accurate knowledge[25] of the truth,

Look at the Greek word (*epignosis*) behind the English "knowledge" in the above. "It is more intensive than *gnosis* (1108), knowledge because it expresses a more thorough participation in the acquiring of knowledge on the part of the learner."[26] The requirement of all of the Lord's servants is that they be able to teach, but not in a quarrelsome way, and in a way to correct his opponents with mildness. Why? Because the purpose of it all is that by God, and through the Christian teacher, one may come to repentance and begin taking in an accurate knowledge of the truth.

Inerrancy: Practical Principles to Overcoming Bible Difficulties

Below are several ways of looking at the Bible that enable the reader to see he is not dealing with an error or contradiction, but rather a Bible difficulty.

Different Points of View

At times, you may have two different writers who are writing from two different points of view.

Numbers 35:14 Updated American Standard Version (UASV)

[14] You shall give three cities across the Jordan and three cities you shall give in the land of Canaan; they will be cities of refuge.

Joshua 22:4 Updated American Standard Version (UASV)

[4] And now Jehovah your God has given rest to your brothers, as he spoke to them; therefore turn now and go to your tents, to the land of your possession, which Moses the servant of Jehovah gave you beyond the Jordan. [on the other side of the Jordan, ESV]

Here we see that Moses is speaking about the east side of the Jordan when he says "on this side of the Jordan." Joshua, on the other hand, is also speaking about the east side of the Jordan when he says "on the other side of the Jordan." So, who is correct? Both are. When Moses was penning Numbers the Israelites had not yet crossed the Jordan River, so the east side was "this side," the side he was on. On the other hand, when

---

[25] *Epignosis* is a strengthened or intensified form of *gnosis* (*epi*, meaning "additional"), meaning, "true," "real," "full," "complete" or "accurate," depending upon the context. Paul and Peter alone use *epignosis*.

[26] Spiros Zodhiates, *The Complete Word Study Dictionary: New Testament*, Electronic ed. (Chattanooga, TN: AMG Publishers, 2000, c1992, c1993), S. G1922.

Joshua penned his book, the Israelites had crossed the Jordan, so the east side was just as he had said, "on the other side of the Jordan." Thus, we should not assume that two different writers are writing from the same perspective.

A Careful Reading

At times, it may simply be a case of needing to slow down and carefully read the account, considering exactly what is being said.

Joshua 18:28 Updated American Standard Version (UASV)

28 and Zelah, Haeleph and the Jebusite (that is, Jerusalem), Gibeah, Kiriath; fourteen cities with their villages. This is the inheritance of the sons of Benjamin according to their families.

Judges 1:21 Updated American Standard Version (UASV)

21 But the sons of Benjamin did not drive out the Jebusites who lived in Jerusalem; so the Jebusites have lived with the sons of Benjamin in Jerusalem to this day.

Joshua 15:63 Updated American Standard Version (UASV)

63 But as for the Jebusites, the inhabitants of Jerusalem, the sons of Judah could not drive them out; so the Jebusites live with the sons of Judah at Jerusalem until this day.

Judges 1:8-9 Updated American Standard Version (UASV)

8 And then the sons of Judah fought against Jerusalem and captured it and struck it with the edge of the sword and set the city on fire. 9 And afterward the sons of Judah went down to fight against the Canaanites living in the hill country and in the Negev[27] and in the Shephelah.[28]

2 Samuel 5:5-9 Updated American Standard Version (UASV)

5 At Hebron he reigned over Judah seven years and six months, and in Jerusalem he reigned thirty-three years over all Israel and Judah.

6 And the king and his men went to Jerusalem against the Jebusites, the inhabitants of the land, and they said to David, "You shall not come in here, but the blind and lame will turn you away"; thinking, "David cannot come in here." 7 Nevertheless, David captured the stronghold of Zion, that is the city of David. 8 And David said on that day, "Whoever would strike the Jebusites, let him get up the water shaft to attack 'the

---

[27] I.e. *South*
[28] I.e., lowland

lame and the blind,' who are hated by David's soul." Therefore it is said, "The blind and the lame shall not come into the house." ⁹ And David lived in the stronghold and called it the city of David. And David built all around from the Millo and inward.

There is no doubt that even the advanced Bible reader of many years can come away confused because the above accounts seem to be contradictory. In Joshua 18:28 and Judges 1:21, we see that Jerusalem was an inheritance of the tribe of Benjamin, yet the Benjamites were unable to conquer Jerusalem. However, in Joshua 15:63 we see that the tribe of Judah could not conquer them either, with the reading giving the impression that it was a part of their inheritance. In Judges 1:8, however, Judah was eventually able to conquer Jerusalem and burn it with fire. Yet, to add even more to the confusion, we find at 2 Samuel 5:5–8 that David is said to have conquered Jerusalem hundreds of years later.

Now that we have the particulars let us look at it more clearly. The boundary between Benjamin's inheritances ran right through the middle of Jerusalem. Joshua 8:28 is correct, in that what would later be called the "city of David" was in the territory of Benjamin, but it also in part crossed over the line into the territory of Judah, causing both tribes to go to war against this Jebusite city. It is also true that the tribe of Benjamin was unable to conquer the city and that the tribe of Judah eventually did. However, if you look at Judges 1:9 again, you will see that Judah did not finish the job entirely and moved on to conquer other areas. This allowed the remaining ones to regroup and form a resistance that neither Benjamin nor Judah could overcome, so these Jebusites remained until the time of David, hundreds of years later.

Intended Meaning of Writer

First, the Bible student needs to understand the level that the Bible intends to be exact in what is written. If Jim told a friend that 650 graduated with him from high school in 1984, it is not challenged, because it is all too clear that he is using rounded numbers and is not meaning to be exactly precise. This is how God's Word operates as well. Sometimes it means to be exact, at other times, it is simply rounding numbers, in other cases, the intention of the writer is a general reference, to give readers of that time and succeeding generations some perspective. Did Samuel, the author of judges, intend to pen a book on the chronology of Judges, or was his focus on the falling away, oppression, and the rescue by a judge, repeatedly. Now, it would seem that Jeremiah, the author of 1 Kings was more interested in giving his readers an exact number of years.

Acts 2:41 Updated American Standard Version (UASV)

⁴¹ So those who received his word were baptized, and there were added that day about three thousand souls.

As you can see here, numbers within the Bible are often used with approximations. This is a frequent practice even today, in both written works and verbal conversation.

Acts 7:2-3 Updated American Standard Version (UASV)

² And Stephen said:

"Brothers and fathers, hear me. The God of glory appeared to our father Abraham when he was in Mesopotamia, before he lived in Haran, ³ and said to him, 'Go out from your land and from your kindred and go into the land that I will show you.'

If you were to check the Hebrew Scriptures at Genesis 12:1, you would find that what is claimed to have been said by God to Abraham is not quoted word-for-word; it is simply a paraphrase. This is a normal practice within Scripture and in writing in general.

Numbers 34:15 Updated American Standard Version (UASV)

¹⁵ The two and a half tribes have received their inheritance beyond the Jordan opposite Jericho, eastward toward the sunrising."

Just as you would read in today's local newspaper, the Bible writer has written from the human standpoint, how it appeared to him. The Bible also speaks of "to the end of the earth" (Psalm 46:9), "from the four corners of the earth" (Isa 11:12), and "the four winds of the earth" (Revelation 7:1). These phrases are still used today.

Unexplained Does Not mean Unexplainable

Considering that there are 31,173 verses in the Bible, encompassing 66 books written by about 40 writers, ranging from shepherds to kings, an army general, fishermen, tax collector, a physician and on and on, and being penned over a 1,600 year period, one does find a few hundred Bible difficulties (about one percent). However, 99 percent of those are explainable. Yet no one wants to be so arrogant to say that he can explain them all. It has nothing to do with the inadequacy of God's Word but is based on human understanding. In many cases, science or archaeology and the field of custom and culture of ancient peoples has helped explain difficulties in hundreds of passages. Therefore, there may be less than one percent left to be answered, yet our knowledge of God's Word continues to grow.

Guilty Until Proven Innocent

This is exactly the perception that the critic has of God's Word. The legal principle of being "innocent until proven guilty" afforded mankind in courts of justice is withheld from the very Word of God. What is ironic here is that this policy has contributed to these Bible critics looking foolish over and over again when something comes to light that vindicates the portion of Scripture they are challenging.

Daniel 5:1 Updated American Standard Version (UASV)

[1] Belshazzar the king made[29] a great feast for a thousand of his nobles, and he was drinking wine in the presence of the thousand.

Bible critics had long claimed that Belshazzar was not known outside of the book Daniel; therefore, they argue that Daniel was mistaken. Yet it hardly seems prudent to argue error from absence of outside evidence. Just because archaeology had not discovered such a person did not mean that Daniel was wrong, or that such a person did not exist. In 1854, some small clay cylinders were discovered in modern-day southern Iraq, which would have been the city of Ur in ancient Babylonia. The cuneiform documents were a prayer of King Nabonidus for "Bel-sar-ussur, my eldest son." These tablets also showed that this "Bel-sar-ussur" had secretaries as well as a household staff. Other tablets were discovered a short time later that showed that the kingship was entrusted to this eldest son as a coregent while his father was away.

He entrusted the 'Camp' to his oldest (son), the firstborn [Belshazzar], the troops everywhere in the country he ordered under his (command). He let (everything) go, entrusted the kingship to him and, himself, he [Nabonidus] started out for a long journey, the (military) forces of Akkad marching with him; he turned towards Tema (deep) in the west."[30]

Ignoring Literary Styles

The Bible is a diverse book when it comes to literary styles: narrative, poetic, prophetic, and apocalyptic; also containing parables, metaphors, similes, hyperbole, and other figures of speech. Too often, these alleged errors are the result of a reader taking a figure of speech as literal, or reading a parable as though it is a narrative.

---

[29] I.e., held

[30] J. Pritchard, ed., *Ancient Near Eastern Texts* (1974), 313.

Matthew 24:35 Updated American Standard Version (UASV)

[35] Heaven and earth will pass away, but my words will not pass away.

If some do not recognize that they are dealing with a figure of speech, they are bound to come away with the wrong meaning. Some have concluded from Matthew 24:35 that Jesus was speaking of an eventual destruction of the earth. This is hardly the case, as his listeners would not have understood it that way based on their understanding of the Old Testament. They would have understood that he was simply being emphatic about the words he spoke, using hyperbole. What he was conveying is that his words are more enduring than heaven and earth, and with heaven and earth being understood as eternal, this merely conveyed even more so that Jesus' words could be trusted.

Two Accounts of the Same Incident

If you were to speak to officers that take accident reports for their police department, you would find that there is cohesion in the accounts, but each person has merely witnessed aspects that have stood out to them. We will see that this is the case as well with the examples below, which is the same account in two different gospels:

Matthew 8:5 Updated American Standard Version (UASV)

[5] When he[31] had entered Capernaum, a centurion came forward to him, imploring him,

Luke 7:2-3 Updated American Standard Version (UASV)

[2] And a centurion's[32] slave, who was highly regarded[33] by him, was sick and about to die. [3] When he heard about Jesus, he sent some older men of the Jews[34] asking him to come and bring his slave safely through.[35]

Immediately we see the problem of whether the centurion or the elders of the Jews spoke with Jesus. The solution is not really hidden from us. Which of the two accounts is the most detailed account? You are correct if you said, Luke. The centurion sent the elders of the Jews to represent him to Jesus, so; that whatever response Jesus might give, it

---

[31] That is *Jesus*

[32] I.e., army officer over a hundred solderiers

[33] Lit *to whom he was honorable*

[34] Or *Jewish elders*

[35] I.e., *save the life of his slave*

would be as though he were addressing the centurion; therefore, Matthew gave his readers the basic thought, not seeing the need of mentioning the elders of the Jews aspect. This is how a representative was viewed in the first century, just as some countries see ambassadors today as being the very person they represent. Therefore, both Matthew and Luke are correct.

Man's Fallible Interpretations

Inspiration by God is infallible, without error. Imperfect man and his interpretations over the centuries, as bad as many of them have been, should not cast a shadow over God's inspired Word. The entire Word of God has one meaning and one meaning only for every penned word, which is what God willed to be conveyed by the human writer he chose to use.

The Autograph Alone Is Inspired and Inerrant

It has been argued by conservative scholars that only the autograph manuscripts were inspired and inerrant, not the copying of those manuscripts over the next 3,000 years for the Old Testament and 1,500 years for the New Testament. While I would agree with this position as well, it should be noted that we do not possess the autographs, so to argue that they are inerrant is to speak of nonexistent documents. However, it should be further understood that through the science of textual criticism, we can establish a mirror reflection of the autograph manuscripts. B. F. Westcott, F. J. A. Hort, F. F. Bruce, and many other textual scholars would agree with Norman L Geisler's assessment: "The New Testament, then, has not only survived in more manuscripts than any other book from antiquity, but it has survived in a purer form than any other great book—*a form that is 99.5 percent pure.*"[36]

An example of a copyist error can be found in Luke's genealogy of Jesus at Luke 3:35–37. In verse 37 you will find a Cainan, and in verse 36 you will find a second Cainan between Arphaxad (Arpachshad) and Shelah. As one can see from most footnotes in different study Bibles, the Cainan in verse 36 is seen as a scribal error, and is not found in the Hebrew Old Testament, the Samaritan Pentateuch, or the Aramaic Targums, but is found in the Greek Septuagint. (Genesis 10:24; 11:12, 13; 1 Chronicles 1:18, but not 1 Chronicles 1:24) It seems quite unlikely that it was in the earlier copies of the Septuagint, because the first-century Jewish historian Josephus lists Shelah next as the son of Arphaxad, and Josephus

---

[36] Norman L. Geisler and William E. Nix: *A General Introduction to the Bible* (Chicago, Moody Press, 1980), 367. (Emphasis is mine.)

normally followed the Septuagint.[37] So one might ask why this second Cainan is found in the translations at all if this is the case? The manuscripts that do contain this second Cainan are some of the best manuscripts that are used in establishing the original text: 01 B L A¹ 33 (Kainam); A 038 044 0102 A¹³ (Kainan).

Look at the Context

Many alleged inconsistencies disappear by simply looking at the context. Taking words out of context can distort their meaning. *Merriam-Webster's Collegiate Dictionary* defines context as "the parts of a discourse that surround a word or passage and can throw light on its meaning."[38] Context can also be "the circumstances or events that form the environment within which something exists or takes place." If we were to look in a thesaurus for a synonym, we would find "background" for this second meaning. At 2 Timothy 2:15, the apostle Paul brings home the point of why context is so important: "Do your best to present yourself to God as one approved, a worker who has no need to be ashamed, rightly handling the word of truth."

Ephesians 2:8-9 Updated American Standard Version (UASV)

8 For by grace you have been saved through faith; and that not of yourselves, it is the gift of God; **9** not from works, so that no man may boast.

James 2:26 Updated American Standard Version (UASV)

26 For as the body apart from the spirit[39] is dead, so also faith apart from works is dead.

So, which is it? Is salvation possible by faith alone as Paul wrote to the Ephesians, or is faith dead without works as James wrote to his readers? As our subtitle brings out, let us look at the context. In the letter to the Ephesians, the apostle Paul is speaking to the Jewish Christians who were looking to the works of the Mosaic Law as a means to salvation, a righteous standing before God. Paul was telling these legalistic Jewish Christians that this is not so. In fact, this would invalidate Christ's ransom because there would have been no need for it if one could achieve salvation by meticulously keeping the Mosaic Law. (Rom. 5:18) But James was writing to those in a congregation who were concerned with their status before other men, who were looking for prominent positions within the congregation, and not taking care of those that were in need.

---

[37] *Jewish Antiquities*, I, 146 [vi, 4].

[38] Merriam-Webster, Inc: *Merriam-Webster's Collegiate Dictionary*. Eleventh ed. (Springfield, Mass.: Merriam-Webster, Inc. 2003).

[39] Or *breath*

(Jam. 2:14–17) So, James is merely addressing those who call themselves Christian, but in name only. No person could truly be a Christian and not possess some good works, such as feeding the poor, helping the elderly. This type of work was an evident demonstration of one's Christian personality. Paul was in perfect harmony with James on this. – Romans 10:10; 1 Corinthians 15:58; Ephesians 5:15, 21–33; 6:15; 1 Timothy 4:16; 2 Timothy 4:5; Hebrews 10:23-25.

Inerrancy: Are There Contradictions?

Below I will follow this pattern. I will list the critic's argument first, followed by the text of difficulty, and conclude with an answer to the critic. What should be kept at the forefront of our mind is this: one is simply looking for the best answer, not absoluteness. If there is a reasonable answer to a Bible difficulty, why are the critics able to set them aside with ease? Because they start with the premise that this is not the Word of God, but only a book by imperfect men and full of contradictions; thus, the bias toward errors has blinded their judgment.

Critic: The critic would argue that there was an Adam and Eve, and an Abel who was now dead, so, where did Cain get his wife? This is one of the most common questions by Bible critics.

Genesis 4:17 Updated American Standard Version (UASV)

[17] Cain had sexual relations[40] with his wife and she conceived, and gave birth to Enoch; and he built a city, and called the name of the city Enoch, after the name of his son, Enoch.

Answer: If one were to read a little further along, they would come to the realization that Adam had a son named Seth; it further adds that Adam "became father to sons *and daughters.*" (Genesis 5:4) Adam lived for a total of 800 years after fathering Seth, giving him ample opportunity to father many more sons and daughters. So it could be that Cain married one of his sisters. If he waited until one of his brothers and sisters had a daughter, he could have married one of his nieces once she was old enough. In the beginning, humans were closer to perfection; this explains why they lived longer and why at that time there was little health risk of genetic defects in the case of children born to closely related parents, in contrast to how it is today. As time passed, genetic defects increased and life spans decreased. Adam lived to see 930 years. Yet Shem, who lived after the Flood, died at 600 years, while Shem's son Arpachshad only lived 438 years, dying before his father died. Abraham saw an even

---

[40] Lit *knew*

greater decrease in that he only lived 175 years while his grandson Jacob was 147 years when he died. Thus, due to increasing imperfection, God prohibited the marriage of closely related people under the Mosaic Law because of the likelihood of genetic defects.—Leviticus 18:9.

Critic: If God is here hardening Pharaoh's heart, what exactly makes Pharaoh responsible for the decisions he makes?

Exodus 4:21 Updated American Standard Version (UASV)

21 Jehovah said to Moses, "When you go and return to Egypt see that you perform before Pharaoh all the wonders which I have put in your hand; but I will harden his heart so that he will not let the people go.

Answer: This is actually a prophecy. God knew that what he was about to do would contribute to a stubborn and obstinate Pharaoh, who was going to be unwilling to change or give up the Israelites so they could go off to worship their God. Therefore, this is not stating what God is going to do; it is prophesying that Pharaoh's heart will harden because of the actions of God. The fact is, Pharaoh allowed his own heart to harden because he was determined not to agree with Moses' wishes or accept Jehovah's request to let the people go. Moses tells us at Exodus 7:13 (ESV) that "Pharaoh's heart was hardened, and he would not listen to them, as the Lord had said." Again, at 8:15 we read, "When Pharaoh saw that there was a respite, he hardened his heart and would not listen to them, as the Lord had said."

Critic: The Israelites had just received the Ten Commandments, with one commandment being: "You shall not make for yourself a carved image or any likeness of anything that is in heaven above, or that is in the earth beneath, or that is in the water under the earth." Therefore, how is the bronze serpent not a violation of this commandment?

Numbers 21:9 Updated American Standard Version (UASV)

9 And Moses made a bronze serpent and set it on the standard;41 and it came about, that if a serpent bit any man, when he looked to the bronze serpent, he lived.

Answer: First, an idol is "a representation or symbol of an object of worship; *broadly*: a false god."42 Second, it should be noted that not all images are idols. The bronze serpent was not made for the purpose of worship, or for some passionate devotion or veneration. There were times, however, when images were created with absolutely no intention

---

41 I.e., *pole*

42 Merriam-Webster, Inc: *Merriam-Webster's Collegiate Dictionary*. Eleventh ed. (Springfield, Mass.: Merriam-Webster, Inc., 2003).

of it receiving devotion, veneration, or worship, yet were later made into objects of veneration. That is exactly what happened with the copper serpent that Moses had formed in the wilderness. Many centuries later, "in the third year of Hoshea son of Elah, king of Israel, Hezekiah the son of Ahaz, king of Judah, began to reign. He removed the high places and broke the pillars and cut down the Asherah. And he broke in pieces the bronze serpent that Moses had made; for until those days the people of Israel had made offerings to it (it was called Nehushtan)."—2 Kings 18:1, 4.

Critic: Deuteronomy 15:11 (NET) says: "*There will never cease to be some poor people in the land;* therefore, I am commanding you to make sure you open your hand to your fellow Israelites who are needy and poor in your land." Is this not a contradiction of Deuteronomy 15:4? Will there be no poor among the Israelites, or will there be poor among them? Which is it?

Deuteronomy 15:4 Updated American Standard Version (UASV)

⁴ However, there will be no poor among you, since Jehovah will surely bless you in the land which Jehovah your God is giving you as an inheritance to possess,

Answer: If you look at the context, Deuteronomy 15:4 is stating that if the Israelites obey Jehovah's command to take care of the poor, "there should not be any poor among" them. Thus, for every poor person, there will be one to take care of that need. If an Israelite fell on hard times, there was to be a fellow Israelite ready to step in to help him through those hard times. Verse 11 stresses the truth of the imperfect world since the rebellion of Adam and inherited sin: there will always be poor among mankind, the Israelites being no different. However, the difference with God's people is that those who were well off financially were to offset conditions for those who fell on difficult times. This is not to be confused with the socialistic welfare systems in the world today. Those Jews were hard-working men, who labored from sunup to sundown to take care of their families. But if disease overtook their herd or unseasonal weather brought about failed crops, an Israelite could sell himself into the service of a fellow Israelite for a period of time; thereafter, he would be back on his feet. And many years down the road, he may very well do the same for another Israelite, who fell on difficult times.

Critic: Joshua 11:23 says that Joshua took the land according to what God had spoken to Moses and handed it on to the nation of Israel as planned. However, in Joshua 13:1, God is telling Joshua that he has grown old and much of the Promised Land has yet to be taken possession of. How can both be true? Is this not a contradiction?

Joshua 11:23 Updated American Standard Version (UASV)

23 So Joshua took the whole land, according to all that Jehovah had spoken to Moses, and Joshua gave it for an inheritance to Israel according to their divisions by their tribes, and the land had rest from war.

Joshua 13:1 Updated American Standard Version (UASV)

13 Now Joshua was old and advanced in years, and Jehovah said to him, "You are old and advanced in years, and there remains yet very much land to possess.

Answer: No, it is not a contradiction. When the Israelites were to take the land, it was to take place in two different stages: the nation as a whole was to go to war and defeat the 31 kings of this land; thereafter, each Israelite tribe was to take their part of the land based on their individual actions. (Joshua 17:14–18; 18:3) Joshua fulfilled his role, which is expressed in 11:23 while the individual tribes did not complete their campaigns, which is expressed in 13:1. Even though the individual tribes failed to live up to taking their portion, the remaining Canaanites posed no real threat. Joshua 21:44, *ASV*, reads: "Jehovah gave them rest round about."

Critic: The critic would point out that John 1:18 clearly says that "*no one has ever seen God*," while Exodus 24:10 explicitly states that Moses and Aaron, Nadab and Abihu, and seventy of the elders of Israel "*saw the God of Israel*." Worse still, God informs them in Exodus 33:20: "You cannot see my face, for man shall not see me and live." The critic with his knowing smile says, 'This is a blatant contradiction.'

John 1:18 Updated American Standard Version (UASV)

18 No one has seen God at any time; the only begotten god[43] who is in the bosom of the Father,[44] that one has made him fully known.

Exodus 24:10 Updated American Standard Version (UASV)

10 and they saw the God of Israel; and under his feet was what seemed like a sapphire pavement, as clear as the sky itself.

Exodus 33:20 Updated American Standard Version (UASV)

20 But he [God] said, "You cannot see my face, for no man can see me and live!"

---

[43] Jn 1:18: "only-begotten god", P66א*BC*Lsyrhmg,p; **[V1]** "the only-begotten god," P75א¹33copbo; **[V2]** "the only-begotten Son." AC³(W¹)ΘΨf1.13 MajVgSyrc

[44] Or *at the Father's side*

Answer: Exodus 33:20 is one-hundred percent correct: No human could see Jehovah God and live. The apostle Paul at Colossians 1:15 tell us that Christ is the image of the invisible God, and the writer informs us at Hebrews 1:3 that Jesus is the "exact representation of His nature." Yet if you were to read the account of Saul of Tarsus (the apostle Paul), you would see that a mere partial manifestation of Christ's glory blinded Saul – Acts 9:1–18.

When the Bible says that Moses and others have seen God, it is not speaking of *literally* seeing him, because first of all He is an invisible spirit person. It is a *manifestation* of his glory, which is an act of showing or demonstrating his presence, making himself perceptible to the human mind. In fact, it is generally an angelic representative that stands in his place and not him personally. Exodus 24:16 informs us that "the glory of the Lord dwelt on Mount Sinai," not the Lord himself personally. When texts such as Exodus 24:10 explicitly state that Moses and Aaron, Nadab and Abihu, and seventy of the elders of Israel *"saw the God of Israel,"* it is this "glory of the Lord," an angelic representative. This is shown to be the case at Luke 2:9, which reads: "And *an angel of the Lord* appeared to them, and *the glory of the Lord shone around them* [the shepherds], and they were filled with fear."

Many Bible difficulties are cleared up elsewhere in Scripture; for example, in the New Testament, you will find a text clarifying a difficulty from the Old Testament, such as Acts 7:53, which refers to those "who received the law *as delivered by angels* and did not keep it." Support comes from Paul at Galatians 3:19: "Why then the law? It was added because of transgressions until the offspring should come to whom the promise had been made, and it was put in place through angels by an intermediary." The writer of Hebrews chimes in at 2:2 with "For since the message *declared by angels* proved to be reliable, and every transgression or disobedience received a just retribution. . . ." As we travel back to Exodus again, to 19:19 specifically, we find support that it was not God's own voice, which Moses heard; no, it was an angelic representative, for it reads: "Moses was speaking, and God was answering him with a voice." Exodus 33:22–23 also helps us to appreciate that it was the back of these angelic representatives of Jehovah that Moses saw: "While my glory passes by . . . Then I will take away my hand, and you shall see my back, but my face shall not be seen."

Exodus 3:4 states: "God called to him out of the bush, 'Moses, Moses!' And he said, 'Here I am.'" Verse 6 informs us: "I am the God of your father, the God of Abraham, the God of Isaac, and the God of Jacob." Yet, in verse 2 we read: "And the angel of the Lord appeared to him in a flame of fire out of the midst of a bush." Here is another example of using God's Word to clear up what seems to be unclear or difficult to understand at first glance. Thus, while it speaks of the Lord making a direct appearance, it is really an angelic representative. Even today, we hear such comments, as 'the president of the United States is to visit the Middle East later this week.' However, later in the article it is made clear that he is not going personally, but it is one of his high-ranking representatives. Let us close with two examples, starting with,

Genesis 32:24-30 Updated American Standard Version (UASV)

24 And Jacob was left alone, and a man wrestled with him until daybreak. **25** When he saw that he had not prevailed against him, he touched the socket of his thigh; so the socket of Jacob's thigh was dislocated as he wrestled with him. **26** Then he said, "Let me go, for the dawn is breaking." But he said, "I will not let you go unless you bless me." **27** And he said to him, "What is your name?" And he said, "Jacob." **28** And he said, "Your name shall no longer be called Jacob, but Israel,[45] for you have struggled with God and with men and have prevailed." **29** Then Jacob asked him and said, "Please tell me your name." But he said, "Why is it that you ask my name?" And he blessed him there. **30** So Jacob named the place Peniel,[46] for he said, "I have seen God face to face, yet my soul has been preserved."

It is all too obvious here that this man is simply a materialized angel in the form of a man, another angelic representative of Jehovah God. Moreover, the reader of this book should have taken in that the Israelites as a whole saw these angelic representatives, and spoke of them as though they were dealing directly with Jehovah God himself.

This proved to be the case in the second example found in the book of Judges where an angelic representative visited Manoah and his wife. Like the above mentioned account, Manoah and his wife treated this angelic representative as if he were Jehovah God himself: "And Manoah said to the angel of the Lord, 'What is your name, so that, when your words come true, we may honor you?' And the angel of the Lord said to him, 'Why do you ask my name, seeing it is wonderful?' Then Manoah knew that he was the angel of the Lord. And Manoah said to his wife, "We shall surely die, *for we have seen God*." – Judges 13:3–22.

---

[45] Meaning *he contends with God*
[46] Meaning *face of God*

Inerrancy: Are There Mistakes?

I have addressed the alleged contradictions, so it would seem that our job is done here, right? Not hardly. Yes, there are just as many who claim that the Bible is full of mistakes.

Critic: Matthew 27:5 states that Judas hanged himself, whereas Acts 1:18 says, "Falling headlong, he burst open in the middle and all his intestines gushed out."

Matthew 27:5 Updated American Standard Version (UASV)

⁵ And he threw the pieces of silver into the temple and departed; and he went away and hanged himself.

Acts 1:18

¹⁸ (Now this man acquired a field with the price of his wickedness, and falling headlong, he burst open in the middle and all his intestines gushed out.

Answer: Neither Matthew nor Luke made a mistake. What you have is Matthew giving the reader the manner in which Judas committed suicide. On the other hand, Luke is giving the reader of Acts, the result of that suicide. Therefore, instead of a mistake, we have two texts that complement each other, really giving the reader the full picture. Judas came to a tree alongside a cliff that had rocks below. He tied the rope to a branch and the other end around his neck and jumped over the edge of the cliff in an attempt at hanging himself. One of two things could have happened: (1) the limb broke plunging him to the rocks below, or (2) the rope broke with the same result, and he burst open onto the rocks below.

Critic: The apostle Paul made a mistake when he quotes how many people died.

Numbers 25:9 Updated American Standard Version (UASV)

⁹ The ones who died in the plague were twenty-four thousand.

1 Corinthians 10:8 Updated American Standard Version (UASV)

⁸ Neither let us commit sexual immorality, as some of them committed sexual immorality, only to fall, twenty-three thousand of them in one day.

Answer: We must keep in mind the above principle that we spoke of, the *Intended Meaning of the Writer*. We live in a far more precise age today, where specificity is highly important. However, we round large numbers off (even estimate) all the time: "there were 237,000 people in Time Square last night." The simplest answer is that the number of people slain was in between 23,000 and 24,000, and both writers rounded the number off. However, there is even another possibility, because the book of Numbers specifically speaks of "all the chiefs of the people" (25:4-5), which could account for the extra 1,000, which is mentioned in Numbers 24,000. Thus, you have the people killing the chiefs of the people and the plague killing the people. Therefore, both books are correct.

Critic: After 215 years in Egypt, the descendants of Jacob arrived at the Promised Land. As you recall they sinned against God and were sentenced to forty years in the wilderness. But once they entered the Promised Land, they buried Joseph's bones "at Shechem, in the piece of land that *Jacob bought* from the sons of Hamor the father of Shechem," as stated at Joshua 24:32. Yet, when Stephen had to defend himself before the Jewish religious leaders, he said that Joseph was buried "in the tomb that *Abraham had bought* for a sum of silver from the sons of Hamor." Therefore, at once it appears that we have a mistake on the part of Stephen.

Acts 7:15-16 Updated American Standard Version (UASV)

[15] And Jacob went down to Egypt and died, he and our fathers. [16] And they were brought back to Shechem and buried in the tomb that Abraham had bought for a sum of silver from the sons of Hamor in Shechem.

Genesis 23:17-18 Updated American Standard Version (UASV)

[17] So Ephron's field, which was in Machpelah, which faced Mamre, the field and cave which was in it, and all the trees which were in the field, that were in all its border around, were made over [18] to Abraham for a possession in the presence of the sons of Heth, before all who went in at the gate of his city.

Genesis 33:19 Updated American Standard Version (UASV)

[19] And he bought the piece of land where he had pitched his tent from the hand of the sons of Hamor, Shechem's father, for one hundred qesitahs.[47]

Joshua 24:32 Updated American Standard Version (UASV)

[32] As for the bones of Joseph, which the sons of Israel brought up from Egypt, they buried them at Shechem, in the piece of land that Jacob bought from the sons of Hamor the father of Shechem for one hundred qesitahs.[48] It became an inheritance of the sons of Joseph.

---

[47] Or *pieces of money*; money of unknown value
[48] Or *pieces of money*; money of unknown value

Answer: If we look back to Genesis 12:6-7, we will find that Abraham's first stop after entering Canaan from Haran was Shechem. It is here that Jehovah told Abraham: "To your offspring I will give this land." At this point Abraham built an altar to Jehovah. It seems reasonable that Abraham would need to purchase this land that had not yet been given to his offspring. While it is true that the Old Testament does not mention this purchase, it is likely that Stephen would be aware of such by way of oral tradition. As Acts chapter seven demonstrates, Stephen had a wide-ranging knowledge of Old Testament history.

Later, Jacob would have had difficulty laying claim to the tract of land that his grandfather Abraham had purchased, because there would have been a new generation of inhabitants of Shechem. This would have been many years after Abraham moved further south and Isaac moved to Beersheba, and including Jacob's twenty years in Paddan-aram (Gen 28:6, 7). The simplest answer is that this land was not in use for about 120 years because of Abraham's extensive travels and Isaac's having moved away, leaving it unused; likely it was put to use by others. So, Jacob simply repurchased what Abraham had bought over a hundred years earlier. This is very similar to the time Isaac had to repurchase the well at Beersheba that Abraham had already purchased earlier. – Genesis 21:27–30; 26:26–32.

Genesis 33:18–20 tells us that 'Jacob bought this land for a hundred pieces of money, from the sons of Hamor.' This same transaction is also mentioned at Joshua 24:32, in reference to transporting Joseph's bones from Egypt, to be buried in Shechem.

We should also address the cave of Machpelah that Abraham had purchased in Hebron from Ephron the Hittite. The word "tomb" is not mentioned until Joshua 24:32, and is in reference to the tract of land in Shechem. Nowhere in the Old Testament does it say that Abraham bought a "tomb." The cave of Machpelah obtained by Abraham would eventually become a family tomb, receiving Sarah's body and, eventually, his own, and those of Isaac, Rebekah, Jacob, and Leah. (Genesis 23:14–19; 25:9; 49:30, 31; 50:13) Gleason L. Archer, Jr., concludes this Bible difficulty, saying:

> The reference to a *mnema* ("tomb") in connection with Shechem must either have been proleptic [to anticipate] for the later use of that shechemite tract for Joseph's tomb (i.e., 'the tomb that Abraham bought' was intended to imply 'the tomb location that Abraham bought"); or else conceivably the dative relative pronoun *ho* was intended elliptically [omission] for *en to topo ho onesato Abraam* ("in the place that Abraham bought") as describing the location of the *mnema* near the Oak

of Moreh right outside Shechem. Normally Greek would have used the relative-locative adverb *hou* to express 'in which' or 'where'; but this would have left *onesato* ("bought") without an object in its own clause, and so *ho* was much more suitable in this context. (Archer 1982, 379–81)

Another solution could be that Jacob is being viewed as a representative of Abraham, for he is the grandson of Abraham. This was quite appropriate in Biblical times, to attribute the purchase to Abraham as the Patriarchal family head.

Critic: 2 Samuel 24:1 says that God moved David to count the Israelites, while 1 Chronicles 21:1 Satan, or a resister did. This would seem to be a clear mistake on the part of one of these authors.

2 Samuel 24:1 Updated American Standard Version (UASV)

[1] Now again the anger of Jehovah burned against Israel, and it incited David against them to say, "Go, number Israel and Judah."

1 Chronicles 21:1 Updated American Standard Version (UASV)

[1] Then Satan stood up against Israel and moved David to number Israel.

Answer: In this period of David's reign, Jehovah was very displeased with Israel, and therefore he did not prevent Satan from bringing this sin on them. Often in Scripture, it is spoken of as though God did something when he allowed an event to take place. For example, it is said that God 'hardened Pharaoh's heart' (Exodus 4:21), when he actually allowed the Pharaoh's heart to harden.

Inerrancy: Are There Scientific Errors?

Many truths about God are beyond the scope of science. Science and the Bible are not at odds. In fact, we can thank modern day science as it has helped us to better under the creation of God, from our solar system to the universes, to the human body and mind. What we find is a level of order, precision, design, and sophistication, which points to a Designer, the eyes of many Christians, to an Almighty God, with infinite intelligence and power. The apostle Paul makes this all too clear, when he writes, "For his invisible attributes, namely, his eternal power and divine nature, have been clearly perceived, ever since the creation of the world, in the things that have been made. So they are without excuse." – Romans 1:20.

Back in the seventeenth century, the world-renowned scientist Galileo proved beyond any doubt that the earth was not the center of the universe, nor did the sun orbit the earth. In fact, he proved it to be the other way around (no pun intended), with the earth revolving around the sun. However, he was brought up on charges of heresy by the Catholic Church and ordered to recant his position. Why? From the viewpoint of the Catholic Church, Galileo was contradicting God's Word, the Bible. As it turned out, Galileo and science were correct, and the Church was wrong, for which it issued a formal apology in 1992. However, the point we wish to make here is that in all the controversy, the Bible was never in the wrong. It was a misinterpretation on the part of the Catholic Church and not a fault with the Bible. One will find no place in the Bible that claims the sun orbits the earth. So where would the Church get such an idea? The Church got such an idea from Ptolemy (b. about 85 C.E.), an ancient astronomer, who argued for such an idea.

As it usually turns out, the so-called contradiction between science and God's Word lies at the feet of those who are interpreting Scripture incorrectly. To repeat the sentiments of Galileo when writing to a pupil– Galileo expressed the same sentiments: "Even though Scripture cannot err, its interpreters and expositors can, in various ways. One of these, very serious and very frequent, would be when they always want to stop at the purely literal sense."[49] I believe that today's scholars, in hindsight, would have no problem agreeing.

While the Bible is not a science textbook, it is scientifically accurate when it touches on matters of science.

The Circle of the Earth Hangs on Nothing

Isaiah 40:22 Updated American Standard Version (UASV)

[22] It is he who sits above **the circle of the earth**,
    and its inhabitants are like grasshoppers;
who stretches out the heavens like a curtain,
    and spreads them like a tent to dwell in.

More than 2,500 years ago, the prophet Isaiah wrote that the earth is a circle or sphere. First, how would it be possible for Isaiah to know the earth is a circle or sphere, if not from inspiration? Scientific America writes, "As countless photos from space can attest, Earth is round–the "Blue Marble," as astronauts have affectionately dubbed it. Appearances, however, can be deceiving. Planet Earth is not, in fact, perfectly round."[50] Scientifically speaking, the sun is not perfectly, absolutely 100 percent round but in everyday speech, this verse is both acceptable and accurate,

---

[49] Letter from Galileo to Benedetto Castelli, December 21, 1613.

[50] Charles Q. Choi (April 12, 2007). Scientific America. Strange but True: Earth Is Not Round. Retrieved Monday, August 03, 2015.
http://www.scientificamerican.com/article/earth-is-not-round/

when we keep in mind it is written from a human perspective, not from a scientific perspective. Moreover, Isaiah was not discussing astronomy; he was simply making an inspired observation that man came to realize once he was in space, looking back at the earth, it is round. See the section about title, "Intended Meaning of Writer."

Job 26:7 Updated American Standard Version (UASV)

7 "He stretches out the north over empty space
and hangs the earth on nothing.

Here the author describes the earth as hanging upon nothing. Many have never heard of the Greek mathematician and astronomer Eratosthenes. He was born in about 276 B.C.E. and received some of his education in Athens, Greece. In 240 B.C., the "Greek astronomer, geographer, mathematician and librarian Eratosthenes calculates the Earth's circumference. His data was rough, but he wasn't far off."[51] While man very early on used their God given intelligence to arrive at some outstanding conclusion that were actually very accurate, we learn two points here. Eratosthenes was a very astute scientist, while Isaiah, who wrote some 500 years earlier, was no scientist at all. Moreover, Moses, who wrote the book of Job over 1,230 years before Eratosthenes, knew that the earth hung upon nothing.

How Is the Sun Standing Still Possible?

Joshua 10:13 Updated American Standard Version (UASV)

13 And the sun stood still, and the moon stopped,
until the nation avenged themselves of their enemies.
Is this not written in the Book of Jashar? The sun stopped in the midst of heaven and did not hurry to set for about a whole day.

The Canaanites had besieged the Gibeonites, a group of people that gained Jehovah God's backing because they had faith in Him. In this battle, Jehovah helped the Israelites continue their attack by causing "the sun [to stand] still, and the moon stopped, until the nation took vengeance on their enemies." (Jos 10:1-14) Those who accept God as the creator of the universe and life can accept that he would know a way of stopping the earth from rotating. However, there are other ways of understanding this account. We must keep in mind that the Bible speaks from an earthly observer point of view, so it need not be that he stopped the rotation. It could have been a refraction of solar and lunar light rays, which would have produced the same effect.

---

[51] Alfred, Randy (June 19, 2008). "June 19, 240 B.C.E: The Earth Is Round, and It's This Big". Wired. Retrieved Monday, August 03, 2015.

Psalm 136:6 Updated American Standard Version (UASV)

⁶ to him who spread out the earth above the waters,
   for his lovingkindness is everlasting;

Hebrews 3:4 Updated American Standard Version (UASV)

⁴ For every house is built by someone, but the builder of all things is God.

2 Kings 20:8-11 Updated American Standard Version (UASV)

⁸ And Hezekiah said to Isaiah, "What shall be the sign that Jehovah will heal me, and that I shall go up to the house of Jehovah on the third day?" ⁹ And Isaiah said, "This shall be the sign to you from Jehovah, that Jehovah will do the thing that he has spoken: shall the shadow go forward ten steps or go back ten steps?" ¹⁰ And Hezekiah answered, "It is an easy thing for the shadow to decline ten steps; no, but let the shadow turn backward ten steps." ¹¹ And Isaiah the prophet cried to Jehovah, and he brought the shadow on the steps back ten steps, by which it had gone down on the steps of Ahaz.

How is it that the stars fought on behalf of Barak?

Judges 5:20 Updated American Standard Version (UASV)

²⁰ From heaven the stars fought, from their courses they fought against Sisera.

Judges 4:15 Updated American Standard Version (UASV)

¹⁵ And Jehovah routed Sisera and all his chariots and all his army with the edge of the sword before Barak; and Sisera alighted from his chariot and fled away on foot.

In the Bible, you have Biblical prose, and Biblical poetry.

Prose: language that is not poetry: (1) writing or speech in its normal continuous form, without the rhythmic or visual line structure of poetry **(2)** ordinary style of expression: writing or speech that is ordinary or matter-of-fact, without embellishment.

Poetry: literature in verse: (1) literary works written in verse, in particular verse writing of high quality, great beauty, emotional sincerity or intensity, or profound insight **(2) beauty or grace:** something that resembles poetry in its beauty, rhythmic grace, or imaginative, elevated, or decorative style.

We have a beautiful example of both of these forms of writing communication in chapters four and five of the book of Judges. Judges,

Chapter 4 is a prose account of Deborah and Barak, while Judges Chapter 5 is a poetic account. As we have learned from the above, poetry is less concerned with accuracy than evoking emotions. Poetry has a license to say things like what we find in of 5:20, which is in the poetry chapter: "from heaven the stars fought." This can be said, and the reader is expected not to take the language literally. What we can surmise from it though, is that God was acting against Sisera in some way, there was divine intervention.

Procedures for Handling Biblical Difficulties

1. You need to be completely convinced a reason or understanding exists.

2. You need to have total trust and conviction in the inerrancy of the Scripture as originally written down.

3. You need to study the context and framework of the verse carefully, to establish what the author meant by the words he used. In other words, find the beginning and the end of the context that your passage falls within.

4. You need to understand exegesis: find the historical setting, determine author intent, study key words, and note parallel passages. You need to slow down and carefully read the account, considering exactly what is being said

5. You need to find a reasonable harmonization of parallel passages.

6. You need to consider a variety of trusted Bible commentaries, dictionaries, lexical sources, encyclopedias, as well as books on Bible difficulties.

7. You should investigate as to whether the difficulty is a transmission error in the original text.

8. You must always keep in mind that the historical accuracy of the biblical text is unmatched; that thousands of extant manuscripts some of which date back to the second century B.C. support the transmitted text of Scripture.

9. We must keep in mind that the Bible is a diverse book when it comes to literary styles: narrative, poetic, prophetic, and apocalyptic; also containing parables, metaphors, similes, hyperbole, and other figures of speech. Too often, these alleged errors are the result of a reader taking a figure of speech as literal, or reading a parable as though it is a narrative.

10. The Bible student needs to understand what level that the Bible intends to be exact in what is written. If Jim told a friend that 650 graduated with him from high school in 1984, it is not challenged, because it is all too clear that he is using rounded numbers and is not meaning to be precise.

CHAPTER 2 View of Bible Difficulties

By R. A. Torrey

Updated By Edward D. Andrews

Every careful student and every thoughtful reader of the Bible finds that the words of the Apostle Peter concerning the Scriptures, that there are some things in them hard to be understood is true. The apostle Peter says of Paul's letters, "as *he does* also in all his [Paul's] letters, speaking in them about these *things*, in which there are some *things* **hard to understand**, which the ignorant and unstable distort to their own destruction, as *they* also *do* the rest of the scriptures." (2 Peter 3:16, LEB) If this were true of Peter, how much more so of us 2,000 years removed, of a different language and culture? This is abundantly true for us! Who of us has not found things in the Bible that have puzzled us, yes, that in our early Christian experience have led us to question whether the Bible was, after all, the Word of God? We find some things in the Bible, which it seems impossible to reconcile with other things in the Bible. We find some things, which seem incompatible with the thought that the whole Bible is of divine origin and absolutely inerrant.

It is not wise to attempt to conceal the fact that these difficulties exist. It is the part of wisdom, as well as of honesty, to frankly face them and consider them.

What shall we say concerning these difficulties that every thoughtful student will eventually encounter?

The first thing we have to say about these difficulties in the Bible is that from the very nature of the case *difficulties are to be expected*.

Some people are surprised and staggered because there are difficulties in the Bible. For my part, I would be more surprised and staggered if there were not. What is the Bible? It is a revelation of the mind and will and character and being of an infinitely great, perfectly wise and absolutely holy God. God Himself is the Author of this revelation. However, one would ask, to who specifically is the revelation made? To men, to finite beings who are imperfect in intellectual development and consequently in knowledge, and who are imperfect in character and consequently in spiritual discernment. The wisest man measured on the scale of eternity is only a babe, and the holiest man compared with God is only an infant in moral development.

Therefore, there must from the very necessities of the case, be difficulties in such a revelation from such a source made to such persons. In addition, when the finite is attempting to understand the infinite, there is bound to be difficulty. When the ignorant contemplate the utterances of one perfect in knowledge, there must be many things hard to be understood, and some things, which to their immature and inaccurate minds appear absurd. When beings whose moral judgments as to the hatefulness of sin and as to the awfulness of the penalty that it demands, listen to the demands of an absolutely holy Being, they are bound to be staggered at some of His demands, and when they consider His dealings, they are bound to be staggered at some of His dealings. These dealings will appear too severe, too stern, and too harsh.

It is plain that there must be difficulties for us in such a revelation as the Bible has proved to be. If someone should hand me a book that was as simple to me as the multiplication table, and say, "This is the Word of God; in it He has revealed His whole will and wisdom," I should shake my head and say, "I cannot believe it; that is too easy to be a perfect revelation of infinite wisdom." There must be in any complete revelation of God's mind and will and character and being, things hard for the beginner to understand; and the wisest and best of us are but beginners.

The second thing to be said about these difficulties is that a difficulty in a doctrine, or a grave objection to a doctrine, does not in any way prove the doctrine untrue.

Many people think that it does. If they come across some difficulty in the way of believing in the divine origin and absolute inerrancy and infallibility of the Bible, they at once conclude that the doctrine is exploded. That is very illogical. They should stop a moment and think, and learn to be reasonable and fair.

There is scarcely a doctrine in science generally believed today, that has not had some great difficulty in the way of its acceptance.

When the Copernican theory (the earth revolves around the sun and not vice versa), now so universally accepted, was first proclaimed, it encountered a very grave difficulty. If this theory were true, the planet Venus should have phases as the moon has, but the best glass could discover no phases then in existence. However, the positive argument for the theory was so strong that it was accepted in spite of this apparently unanswerable objection. When a more powerful glass was made, it was found that Venus had phases after all. The whole difficulty arose, as most; all of those in the Bible arise, from man's ignorance of some of the facts in the case.

The nebular hypothesis (the formation of the solar system) is commonly accepted in the scientific world today. Nevertheless, when this theory was first announced, and for a long time afterward, the movements of the planet Uranus could not be reconciled with the theory.

Uranus seemed to move in just the opposite direction from that in which it was thought it ought to move in accordance with the demands of the theory. However, the positive arguments for the theory were so strong that it was accepted in spite of the inexplicable movements of Uranus.

If we apply to Bible study the commonsense logic recognized in every department of science (with the exception of Biblical criticism, if that be a science), then we must demand that if the positive proof of a theory is conclusive, it must be believed by rational men in spite of any number of difficulties in minor details. He is a shallow thinker who gives up a well-attested truth because there are some apparent facts, which he cannot reconcile with that truth. In addition, he is a very shallow Bible scholar who gives up his belief in the divine origin and inerrancy of the Bible because there are some supposed facts that he cannot reconcile with that doctrine. There are in the theological world today many shallow thinkers of that kind.

The third thing to be said about the difficulties in the Bible is: there are many more, and much greater, difficulties in the way of the doctrine that holds the Bible to be of human origin, and hence fallible, than there are in the way of the doctrine that holds the Bible to be of divine origin, and hence infallible.

Turning the Tables

Oftentimes a man will put forth some difficulty and say, "How do you explain that, if the Bible is the Word of God?" You may not be able to answer him satisfactorily. Then he thinks he has you cornered. Not at all, turn on him, and ask him, "How do you account for the fulfilled prophecies of the Bible if it is of human origin? How do you account for the marvelous unity of the Book? How do you account for its inexhaustible depth? How do you account for its unique power in lifting men up to God?" For every insignificant objection he can bring to your view of the Bible, you can bring very many more deeply significant objections to his view of the Bible. Moreover, any candid man who desires to know and obey the truth will have no difficulty in deciding between the two views.

Some time ago a young man, who was of a bright mind and unusually well read in skeptical, critical, and agnostic literature, told me he had given the matter a great deal of candid and careful thought, and as a result he could not believe the Bible was of divine origin.

I asked him, "Why not?"

He pointed to a certain teaching of the Bible that he could not and would not believe to be true.

I replied, "Suppose for a moment that I could not answer that specific difficulty; that would not prove that the Bible is not of divine origin. I can bring you many things far more difficult to account for on the hypothesis that the Bible is not of divine origin than on the hypothesis that the Bible is of divine origin. You cannot deny the fact of fulfilled prophecy. How do you account for it if the Bible is not God's Word? You cannot shut eyes to the marvelous unity of the sixty-six books of the Bible, written under such divergent circumstances and at periods of time so remote from one another. How do you account for it if God is not the real Author of the Book back of the forty or more human authors? You cannot deny that the Bible has a power—to save men from sin, to bring men peace and hope and joy, to lift men up to God—that all other books taken together do not possess. How do you account for it if the Bible is not the Word of God in a sense that no other book is the Word of God?"

The objector did not answer. The difficulties that confront one who denies that the Bible is of divine origin and authority are far more numerous and vastly more weighty than those which confront the one who believes it to be of divine origin and authority.

The fourth thing to be said about the difficulties in the Bible is: *the fact that you cannot solve a difficulty does not prove it cannot be solved, and the fact that you cannot answer an objection does not prove at all that it cannot be answered.*

It is remarkable how often we overlook this very evident fact. There are many, who meet a difficulty in the Bible and give it a little thought and can see no possible solution, at once jump at the conclusion that a solution is impossible, and so they give up their faith in the inerrancy of the Bible and in its divine origin. Any man should have a sufficient amount of modesty, being so limited in knowledge, to say, "Though I see no possible solution to this difficulty, someone a little wiser than I might easily find one."

If we would only bear in mind that we do not know everything, and there are a great many things that we cannot solve now which we could very easily solve if we only knew a little more, it would save us from all this foolishness. We ought never to forget that there may be a very easy solution to infinite wisdom even for that which to our finite wisdom—or ignorance—appears unsolvable. What would we think of a beginner in algebra who, having tried in vain for half an hour to solve a difficult problem, declared that there was no possible solution to the problem because he could find none!

A man of unusual experience and ability one day left his work and drove a long distance to see me, as he was in great uneasiness of mind because he had discovered what he believed to be a flat contradiction in the Bible. He had lain awake all night thinking about it. It had defied all his attempts at reconciliation, but when he had fully stated the case to me, in a very few moments I showed him a very simple and satisfactory solution of the difficulty. He went away with a happy heart. Nevertheless, why had it not occurred to him at the outset that, though it appeared impossible to him to find a solution, after all, someone else might easily discover a solution? He supposed that the difficulty was an entirely new one, but it was one that had been faced and answered long before either he or I were born.

The fifth thing to be said about the difficulties in the Bible is that *the seeming defects of the Book are exceedingly insignificant when put in comparison with its many and marvelous areas of excellence.*

It certainly reveals great perversity of both mind and heart that men spend so much time focusing on and exaggerating such insignificant points, which they consider defects in the Bible, and pass absolutely unnoticed the incomparable beauties and wonders that adorn and glorify almost every page. This is even taking place in some prominent institutions of learning, where men are supposed to be taught to appreciate and understand the Bible and where they are sent to be trained to preach its truth to others. These institutions are spending much more time on minute and insignificant points that seem to point toward an entirely human origin of the Bible than is spent upon studying and understanding and admiring the unparalleled glories that make this Book stand apart from all other books in the world. What would we think of any man who in studying some great masterpiece of art concentrated his whole attention upon what looked like a flyspeck in the corner? A large proportion of the much boasted about "critical study of the Bible" is a laborious and scholarly investigation of supposed flyspecks. The man who is **not** willing to squander the major portion of his time in this intellectualized investigation of flyspecks but prefers to devote it to the study of the unrivaled beauties and majestic splendors of the Book is counted in some quarters as not being "scholarly and up to date."

The sixth thing to be said about the difficulties in the Bible is that *they have far more weight with superficial readers than with profound students.*

Take a man like Colonel Ingersoll, who was very ignorant of the real contents and meaning of the Bible, or that class of modern preachers who read the Bible for the most part for the sole purpose of finding texts to serve as pegs to hang their own ideas. To such superficial readers of the

Bible these difficulties seem of immense importance, but to one who has learned to meditate upon the Word of God day and night they have scarcely any weight at all. That rare man of God, George Müller, who had carefully studied the Bible from beginning to end more than one hundred times, was not disturbed by any difficulties he encountered; but to the man who is reading it through for the first or second time there are many things that perplex and stagger.

The seventh thing to be said about the difficulties in the Bible is that *they rapidly disappear upon careful and prayerful study.*

How many things there are in the Bible that once puzzled and staggered us, but which have since been perfectly cleared up and no longer present any difficulty whatever! Every year of study finds these difficulties disappear more and more rapidly. At first they go by ones, and then by twos, and then by dozens, and then by scores. Is it not reasonable then to suppose that the difficulties that remain will all disappear upon further study?

CHAPTER 3 Some Types of Bible Difficulties

By R. A. Torrey

Updated by Edward D. Andrews

All the difficulties found in the Bible can be included under ten general headings:

The Text from which our English Bible was Translated

No one, as far as I know, holds that the English translation of the Bible is absolutely infallible and inerrant. The doctrine held by many is that the Scriptures as originally given were absolutely infallible and inerrant, and that our English translation is a *substantially accurate* rendering of the Scriptures as originally given.

We do not possess the original manuscripts of the Bible. These original manuscripts were copied many times with great care and exactness, but naturally, some errors crept into the copies that were made. We now possess so many good copies that by comparing one with another, we can tell with great precision just what the original text was. Indeed, for all practical purposes the original text is now settled.

Update: After Torrey's death in 1928, we have made the extremely important discovery over 100 papyrus manuscripts that date before 300 C.E. Quite a few date to the second century, with one small fragment being dated to about 125 C.E. The modern textual scholar can now say with certainty that we have establish the Greek New Testament to a ninety-nine percent reflect of the originally publish book(s). Moreover, we have more than 100 English translations today, with many of them being a very good representation of the Hebrew and Greek in English: NASB, ESB, HCSB, LEB, and others. **Edward D. Andrews**

There is not one important doctrine, which hangs upon any doubtful reading of the text. However, when our Authorized Version (KJV) was published in 1611, some of the best manuscripts were not within reach of the translators, and the science of textual criticism was not so well understood as it is today, and so the translation was made from an imperfect text. Not a few of the apparent difficulties in the Bible arise from this source.

For example, we are told in John 5:4 that "an angel went down at a certain season into the pool, and troubled the water: whosoever then first after the troubling of the water stepped in was made whole of whatsoever disease he had." This statement for many reasons seems improbable and difficult to believe, but upon investigation, we find that it is all a mistake of the copyist. Some early copyist, reading John's account, added in the margin his explanation of the healing properties of this intermittent medicinal spring. A late copyist embodied this marginal note in the body of the text, and so it came to be handed down and got into the Authorized Version (KJV). Very properly, it has been omitted from the Revised Version.

Note: It is omitted from almost all of our modern-day translations as well, with the exception of the NASB and the HCSB, which retained it out of esteem to the KJV. **Edward D. Andrews**

The discrepancies in figures in different accounts of the same events as, for example, the differences in the ages of some of the kings as given in the text of Kings and Chronicles, doubtless arise from the same cause, errors of copyists. Such an error in the matter of figures would be very easy to make, as in the Hebrew; letters, and letters that appear very much alike have a very different value as figures denote numbers. For example, the first letter in the Hebrew alphabet denotes one, and with two little points above it, no larger than flyspecks, it denotes a thousand. The twenty-third or last letter of the Hebrew alphabet denotes four hundred, but the eighth letter of the Hebrew alphabet that looks very much like it and could be easily mistaken for it, denotes eight. A very slight error of the copyist would therefore make an utter change in figures. The remarkable thing when one contemplates the facts in the case is that so few errors of this kind have been made.

Inaccurate Translations

For example, in Matthew 12:40 Jonah is spoken of as being in "the whale's belly." Many a skeptic has made a mockery over the thought of a whale with the peculiar construction of its mouth and throat swallowing a man. However, if the skeptic had only taken the trouble to look the matter up, he would have found the word translated "whale" really means "sea monster" [or great fish] without any definition as to the character of the sea monster. We will take this up more in detail in considering the story of Jonah. Therefore, the whole difficulty arose from the translator's mistake and the skeptic's ignorance. Many skeptics today are so densely ignorant of matters clearly understood by many Sunday school children that they are still harping in the name of scholarship on this supposed error in the Bible.

False Interpretations of the Bible

What the Bible teaches is one thing, and what men interpret it to mean is oftentimes something widely different. Many difficulties that we have with the Bible arise not from what the Bible actually says, but from what men interpret it to mean.

A striking illustration of this is found in Genesis 1. If we were to take the interpretation put upon this chapter by many, it would indeed be difficult to reconcile it with much that modern science regards as established. However, the difficulty is not with what Genesis 1 says, but with the interpretation put upon it. There is no contradiction whatever between what is really proven by science and what is really said in Genesis 1.

Another difficulty of the same character is with Jesus' statement that He would be three days and three nights in the heart of the earth. Many interpreters would have us believe that He died Friday and rose early Sunday morning, and the time between these two is far from being three days and three nights. However, it is a matter of biblical interpretation, and the trouble is not with what the Bible actually says, but with the interpretation that men put upon the Bible. We will take this matter up at length below by Edward D. Andrews.

Matthew 12:40 How many days was Jesus in the tomb?

Some argue for three days, based on Jesus' words,

Matthew 12:40 English Standard Version (ESV)

⁴⁰ For just as Jonah was three days and three nights in the belly of the great fish, so will the Son of Man be three days and three nights in the heart of the earth.

This would seem to suggest a full 72 hours. However, we should not set aside similar expressions that may allow us to get at the intent of the words. Many times in Scripture, three days does not always mean a full 72 hours of three days. For example, look at the words of Rehoboam,

1 Kings 12:5, 12 English Standard Version (ESV)

⁵ He said to them, "Go away for three days, then come again to me." So the people went away. ¹² So Jeroboam and all the people came to Rehoboam the third day, as the king said, "Come to me again the third day."

You see that the king told the people to go away for three days, and then return to him. But you also will notice that they returned on the third day, which was not a full 72 hours of three days. Now, consider what Jesus said of himself, something that Scripture repeatedly says,

Luke 24:46 English Standard Version (ESV)

⁴⁶ and said to them, "Thus it is written, that the Christ should suffer and **on the third day** rise from the dead

Now, if he had remained in the grave for a full 72 hours of three days, it mean that he would have been raised on the fourth day. Jewish days ran from sundown to sundown. Jesus died on Friday afternoon about 3:00 p.m., Nisan 14, 33 C.E.

- Jesus' death Friday Nisan 14, about 3:00 p.m. (Matt 27:31-56; Mk 15:20-41; Lu 23:26-49; Jn 19:16-30)

- Jesus was in Tomb before sundown Friday evening (Matt 27:57-61; Mk 15:42-47; Lu 23:50-56; Jn 19:31-42)

- Jesus in tomb all of Nisan 15th from sundown Friday to sundown Saturday, which began Nisan 16 (Matt 27:62-66)

- Jesus resurrected early Sunday morning of Nisan 16th (Matt 28:1; Mk 16:1; Lu 24:1; Jn 20:1)

Therefore, Jesus was dead and in the tomb for at least a period of time on Friday Nisan 14, was still in the tomb during the course of the whole day of Nisan 15, and spent the nighttime hours of Nisan 16 in the tomb.

- Now after the Sabbath, toward the dawn of the first day of the week, Mary Magdalene and the other Mary went to see the tomb. (Matt 28:1)

- When the Sabbath was past, Mary Magdalene, Mary the mother of James, and Salome bought spices, so that they might go and anoint him. (Mk 16:1)

- But on the first day of the week, at early dawn, they went to the tomb, taking the spices they had prepared. (Lu 24:1)

- Now on the first day of the week Mary Magdalene came to the tomb early, while it was still dark, and saw that the stone had been taken away from the tomb. (Jn 20:1)

Certain women came to the tomb on Sunday morning, it was still dark, he had already been resurrected. Thus, Jesus had been in the tomb for parts of three days.

A Wrong Conception of the Bible

Many think that when we say the Bible is the Word of God, of divine origin and authority, we mean that God is the speaker in every utterance it contains; but this is not what is meant at all. Oftentimes, it simply records what others say, i.e., what good men say, what bad men say, what inspired men say, what uninspired men say, what angels and demons say, and even what the devil says. The record of what they said is from God and absolutely true, but what those other persons are recorded as saying may be true or may not be true. It is true that they said it, but what they said may not be true.

For example, the devil is recorded in Genesis 3:4 as saying, "You will not surely die." It is true that the devil said it, but what the devil said is not true, but an infamous lie that shipwrecked our race. That the devil said it is God's Word, but what the devil said is not God's word but the devil's word. It is God's Word that this was the devil's word.

Very many careless readers of the Bible do not notice who is talking, God, good men, bad men, inspired men, uninspired men, angels or devil. They will tear a verse right out of its context regardless of the speaker and say, "There, God said that." However, God said nothing of the kind. God's Word says that the devil said it or a bad man said it or a good man said it or an inspired man said it, or an uninspired man said it, or an angel said it. What God says is true, namely, that the devil said it, or a bad man, or a good man, or an inspired man, or an uninspired man, or an angel. However, what they said may or may not be true.

It is very common to hear men quote what Eliphaz, Bildad or Zophar said to Job as if it were necessarily God's own words because it is recorded in the Bible, in spite of the fact that God disavowed their teaching and said to them, "you have not spoken of me what is right" (Job 42:7). It is true that these men said the thing that God records them as saying, but often they gave the truth a twist and said what is not right. A very large share of our difficulties thus arises from not noticing who is speaking. The Bible always tells us, and we should always note it. Below, under the subheadings of "the Case of Job" and "The Comforters" Andrews demonstrates how the erroneous interpretations come about.

The Case of Job

What we have covered thus far will help us understand one of the more complex books of the Bible, the book of Job.

Job was a "blameless and upright man, who fears God and turns away from evil." Job was living the happy life; he had seven sons and the daughters. He was a wealthy landowner. "He possessed 7,000 sheep, 3,000 camels, 500 yoke of oxen, and 500 female donkeys, and very many servants, so that this man was the greatest of all the people of the east." (1:3) Even so, he is not a materialistic person; he was simply following a proverb like the above, 'if you work hard, your efforts will be blessed.'

Job 1:13-19; 2:7-8 English Standard Version (ESV)

[13]Now there was a day when his sons and daughters were eating and drinking wine in their oldest brother's house, [14]and there came a messenger to Job and said, "The oxen were plowing and the donkeys feeding beside them, [15]and the Sabeans fell upon them and took them and struck down the servants with the edge of the sword, and I alone have escaped to tell you." [16]While he was yet speaking, there came another and said, "The fire of God fell from heaven and burned up the sheep and the servants and consumed them, and I alone have escaped to tell you." [17]While he was yet speaking, there came another and said, "The Chaldeans formed three groups and made a raid on the camels and took them and struck down the servants with the edge of the sword, and I alone have escaped to tell you." [18]While he was yet speaking, there came another and said, "Your sons and daughters were eating and drinking wine in their oldest brother's house, [19]and behold, a great wind came across the wilderness and struck the four corners of the house, and it fell upon the young people, and they are dead, and I alone have escaped to tell you." [2:7]So Satan went out from the presence of the LORD and struck Job with loathsome sores from the sole of his foot to the crown of his head. [8]And he took a piece of broken pottery with which to scrape himself while he sat in the ashes.

The Comforters

Job 4:7-8 English Standard Version (ESV)

[7]"Remember: who that was innocent ever perished? Or where were the upright cut off? [8]As I have seen, those who plow iniquity and sow trouble reap the same.

Eliphaz in an attempt at dealing with Job's atrocities assumes Job's tragedies are a result of his own actions. Eliphaz has reasoned wrong by taking a proverb and making it an absolute. In essence, he asks Job, 'do those that are innocent die? When have those that live a righteous life been destroyed?' Eliphaz goes on by saying, 'my experience suggests that it is those who are doing wrong and entertain bad that will get back what they gave out.' In other words, Eliphaz is assuming that only the wicked reap bad times.

76

Job 5:15 English Standard Version (ESV)

¹⁵But he saves the needy from the sword of their mouth and from the hand of the mighty.

Eliphaz again assumes that Job is at fault. Eliphaz is assuming that it was Job's great riches, which were ill gotten, and this is why he is suffering. Is Eliphaz's statement wrong in and of itself? No, God does rescue the poor from the oppressive, by their following his counsel on the right way to live. However, this is no absolute; saying all who live by God's will and purposes will never be mistreated. Moreover, the whole idea is misplaced, in that maybe Job is the rich oppressor and this is his punishment from God.

Job 8:3-6 English Standard Version (ESV)

³Does God pervert justice? Or does the Almighty pervert the right? ⁴If your children have sinned against him, he has delivered them into the hand of their transgression.⁵If you will seek God and plead with the Almighty for mercy, ⁶if you are pure and upright, surely then he will rouse himself for you and restore your rightful habitation.

Bildad too is stating true statements, but in absolute terms that are misplaced when it comes to Job, or anyone. Certainly, God does not pervert justice. Therefore, Bildad is right on that, but his application and understanding is what is twisted, as he assumes that children died because they had sinned, and justice was being meted out to them. Again, in verse 5-6, we have a true thought, in that if one is in an impure state, and turns to God with pleadings, he will restore them. However, in verses 5-6, Bildad is assuming that Job is unrighteous, because he sees that proverb as an absolute.

As can be seen from the above, one must be aware that proverbs are not absolutes, but are general truths. True enough, there are likely a couple of exceptions to this rule, but that would not negate this rule, and approach of correct interpretation of proverbs.

In the Psalms, we have sometimes, what God said to man and that is always true; but on the other hand, we often have what man said to God, and that may or may not be true. Sometimes, and far oftener than most of us see, it is the voice of the speaker's personal vengeance or despair. This vengeance may be and often is prophetic, but it may be the wronged man committing his cause to Him to whom vengeance belongs (Romans 12:19), and we are not obliged to defend all that he said. In the Psalms, we have even a record of what the fool said, "There is no God" (Psalm 14:1). Now it is true that the fool said it, but the fool lied when he said it. It is God's Word that the fool said it, but what God reports the fool as saying is not God's own word at all but the fool's own word.

Therefore, in studying our Bible, if God is the speaker we must believe what He says. If an inspired man is the speaker, we must believe what he says. If an uninspired man is the speaker, we must judge for ourselves, it is perhaps true, perhaps false. If it is the devil who is speaking, we do well to remember that he was a liar from the beginning; but even the devil may tell the truth sometimes.

The Language in Which the Bible was Written

The Bible is a book of all ages and for all kinds of people, and therefore it was written in the language that continues the same and is understood by all, the language of the common people and of appearances. It was not written in the terminology of science.

Thus, for example, what occurred at the Battle of Gibeon (Joshua 10:12–14) was described in the way it appeared to those who saw it, and the way in which it would be understood by those who read about it. There is no talk about the refraction of the sun's rays, and so forth, but the sun is said to have "*stood still*" (or tarried) in the midst of heaven. It is one of the perfections of the Bible that it was not written in the terminology of modern science. If it had been, it would never have been understood until the present day, and even now it would be understood only by a few. Furthermore, as science and its terminology are constantly changing, the Bible if written in the terminology of the science of today would be out of date in a few years; but being written in just the language chosen, it has proved the Book for all ages, all lands and all conditions of men.

Other difficulties from the language in which the Bible was written arise from the fact that large portions of the Bible are poetical and are written in the language of poetry, the language of feeling, passion, imagination and figure. Now if a man is hopelessly matter-of-fact, he will inevitably find difficulties with these poetical portions of the inspired Word.

For example, in Psalm 18 we have a marvelous description of a thunderstorm, but let the dull, matter-of-fact fellow get hold of that, for example, verse 8: "Smoke went up from his nostrils, and devouring fire from his mouth; glowing coals flamed forth from him," and he will be head over heels in difficulty at once. However, the trouble is not with the Bible, but with his own stupid, thickheaded plainness.

Our Defective Knowledge of the History, Geography and Usages of Bible Times

For example, in Acts 13:7 Luke speaks of "the deputy" (more accurately "the proconsul," see English Standard Version) of Cyprus. Roman provinces were of two classes, imperial and senatorial. The ruler of the imperial provinces was called a propraetor, of a senatorial province a proconsul. Up to a comparatively recent date, according to the best information we had, Cyprus was an imperial province and therefore its ruler would be a propraetor, but Luke calls him a proconsul. This certainly seemed like a clear case of error on Luke's part, and even the conservative commentators felt forced to admit that Luke was in slight error, and the destructive critics were delighted to find this "mistake." Further and more thorough investigation has brought to light the fact that just at the time of which Luke wrote the senate had made an exchange with the emperor whereby Cyprus had become a senatorial province, and therefore its ruler was a proconsul. Luke was right after all, and the literary critics were themselves in error.

Repeatedly further researches and discoveries, geographical, historical and archaeological, have vindicated the Bible and put to shame its critics. For example, the book of Daniel has naturally been one of the books that unbelievers and destructive critics have most hated. One of their strongest arguments against its authenticity and truthfulness was that such a person as Belshazzar was unknown to history, that all historians agreed that Nabonidus was the last king of Babylon, and that he was absent from the city when it was captured. Therefore, Belshazzar must be a purely mythical character, and the whole story legendary and not historical. Their argument seemed very strong. In fact, it seemed unanswerable. However, Sir H. Rawlinson discovered at Mugheir and other Chaldean sites clay cylinders on which Belshazzar (Belsaruzar) is named by Nabonidus as his eldest son. Doubtless he reigned as regent in the city during his father's absence, an indication of which we have in his proposal to make Daniel third ruler in the kingdom (Daniel 5:16). He himself being second ruler in the kingdom, Daniel would be next to him. So the Bible was vindicated again.

The critics asserted most positively that Moses could not have written the Pentateuch because writing was unknown in his day. However, recent discoveries have proved beyond a question that writing far antedates the time of Moses. So the critics have been compelled to give up their argument, though they have had the bad grace to hold on stubbornly to their conclusion.

The Ignorance of Conditions under Which Books Were Written and Commands Given

For example, to one ignorant of the conditions, God's commands to Israel as to the extermination of the Canaanites seem cruel and horrible. However, when one understands the moral condition to which these nations had sunk, the utter hopelessness of reclaiming them and the weakness of the Israelites themselves, their extermination seems to have been an act of mercy to all succeeding generations and to themselves.

The Many-Sidedness of the Bible

The broadest-minded man is one-sided, but the truth is many-sided, and the Bible is all-sided. Therefore, to our narrow thought one part of the Bible seems to contradict another.

For example, religious men as a rule are either Calvinistic or Arminian in their mental makeup. In addition, some portions of the Bible are decidedly Calvinistic and present great difficulties to the Arminian type of mind, while other portions are decidedly Arminian and present difficulties to the Calvinistic type of mind. However, both sides are true. Many men in our day are broad-minded enough to be able to grasp at the same time the Calvinistic side of the truth and the Arminian side of the truth; but some are not, so the Bible perplexes, puzzles and bewilders them. The trouble is not with the Bible, but with their own lack of capacity for comprehensive thought.

Expansion: These schools of doctrinal positions are initially established religious leaders and their followers, such as John Calvin and Jacob Arminius. There are even more, such as the Lutheran, from Martin Luther, The Wesleyan, from John Wesley, and the Mennonites, from Menno Simons, and Society of Friends (Quakers) under George Fox. Actually, I would disagree with Torrey here, I believe that he should have used his earlier point of argument, it boils down to the truth of the Bible as being absolute, but man may misinterpret that truth. Therefore, it will lay concealed until discovered. This misinterpretation does not refute the infallibility or inerrancy of Scripture. Actually, doctrine plays no part in inerrancy of Scripture. Whether one believes the earth was created in six literal 24-hour days, or six creative periods called days, has no impact on the doctrine of inerrancy. The Bible is inerrant and one of those interpretations is wrong and the other is correct. This has to do with the person interpreting the Bible, not the inerrancy of the Bible. **Edward D. Andrews**

Therefore, Paul seems to contradict James, and James seems sometimes to contradict Paul; and what Paul says in one place seems to contradict what he says in another place. However, the whole trouble is that our narrow minds cannot take in God's large truth.

The Bible has to do with the Infinite, and our Minds are Finite

It is necessarily difficult to put the facts of infinite being into the limited capacity of our finite intelligence, just as it is difficult to put the ocean into a pint cup. To this class of difficulties belong those connected with the Bible doctrines of the Trinity and of the divine-human nature of Christ. To those who forget that God is infinite, the doctrine of the Trinity seems like the mathematical monstrosity of making one equal three. However, when one bears in mind that the doctrine of the Trinity is an attempt to put into forms of finite thought the facts of infinite being, and into material forms of expression the facts of the spirit, the difficulties vanish. The simplicity of the Unitarian conception of God arises from its shallowness.

The Dullness of our Spiritual Perception

The man who is farthest advanced spiritually is still so immature that he cannot expect to see everything yet as an absolutely holy God sees it, unless he takes it upon simple faith in Him. To this class of difficulties belong those connected with the Bible doctrine of eternal punishment. It often seems to us as if this doctrine cannot be true, must not be true, but the whole difficulty arises from the fact that we are still so blind spiritually that we have no adequate conception of the awfulness of sin, and especially of the awfulness of the sin of rejecting the infinitely glorious Son of God. However, when we become so holy, so like God, that we see the enormity of sin as He sees it, we shall have no difficulty with the doctrine of eternal punishment.

Expansion: Torrey is like many other Calvinist or Lutheran minded individuals, he wishes to follow the evidence, but instead, desires to call those, who do not find this doctrine Biblical, spiritually blind. I hope that even the most conservative reader can see that as dismissive. Without arguing the evidence, I will say that once again, the truth is biblical, and we must follow it objectively, and not allow theological bias to cloud our judgment. I am recommending that you read, *WHAT IS HELL? Basic Bible Doctrines of the Christian Faith* by Edward D. Andrews[52]

As we look back over the ten classes of difficulties, we see they all arise from our imperfection, and not from the imperfection of the Bible. The Bible is perfect, but we, being imperfect, have difficulty with it. As we grow more and more into the perfection of God, our difficulties grow ever less and less, and so we are forced to conclude that when we become as perfect as God is, we shall have no more difficulties whatever with the Bible.

---

[52] http://www.christianpublishers.org/apps/webstore/products/show/5346167

CHAPTER 4 Dealing With Bible Difficulties

By R. A. Torrey

Updated By Edward D. Andrews

Honestly

Whenever you find a difficulty in the Bible frankly, acknowledge it. Do not try to obscure it. Do not try to dodge it. Look it square in the face. Admit it frankly to whoever mentions it. If you cannot give a good, square, honest explanation, do not attempt any at all. Those, who in their zeal for the infallibility of the Bible have attempted explanations of difficulties that do not commend themselves to the honest, fair-minded man, have done untold harm. People have concluded that if these are the best explanations, then there are really no explanations at all, and the Bible instead of being helped has been injured by the unintelligent zeal of foolish friends. If you are not really convinced that the Bible is the Word of God, you can far better afford to wait for an honest solution of a difficulty than you can afford to attempt a solution that is evasive and unsatisfactory.

Humbly

Recognize the limitations of your own mind and knowledge, and do not for a moment imagine that there is no solution just because you have found none. There is, in all probability, a very simple solution, even when you can find no solution at all.

Determinedly

Make up your mind that you will find the solution if you can by any amount of study and hard thinking. The difficulties of the Bible are our heavenly Father's challenge to us to set our brains to work. Do not give up searching for a solution because you cannot find it in five minutes or ten minutes. Ponder over it and work over it for days if necessary. The work will be more beneficial than the solution does. There is a solution somewhere, and you will find it if you will only search for it long enough and hard enough.

Fearlessly

Do not be frightened when you find a difficulty, no matter how unanswerable or how insurmountable it appears at first sight. Thousands of men have encountered just such difficulties, and still the old Book has withstood the test of time, being the bestseller that will never be touched, in the untold billions of copies. The Bible that has stood eighteen centuries of rigid examination, and of incessant and awful assault, is not likely to go down before your discoveries or before the discharges of any modern critical guns. To one who is at all familiar with the history of critical attacks on the Bible, the confidence of those modern critics who think they are going to annihilate the Bible at last is simply amusing.

Patiently

Do not be discouraged because you do not solve every problem in a day. If some difficulty persistently defies your very best efforts at a solution, lay it aside for a while. Later it will likely be resolved, and you will wonder how you were ever perplexed by it.

Scripturally

If you find a difficulty in one part of the Bible, look for another scripture to throw light upon it and dissolve it. Nothing explains scripture like scripture. Repeatedly people have come to me with some difficulty in the Bible that had greatly staggered them, and asked for a solution. I have been able to give a solution by simply asking them to read some other chapter and verse, and the simple reading of that scripture has thrown such light upon the passage in question that all the mists have disappeared and the truth has shone as clear as day.

Prayerfully

It is simply wonderful how difficulties dissolve when one looks at them on his knees. Not only does God open our eyes in answer to prayer to behold wonderful things out of His law, but He also opens our eyes to look straight through a difficulty that seemed impenetrable before we prayed. One great reason why many modern Bible scholars have learned to be destructive critics is that they have forgotten how to pray. Please see,

HOW TO PRAY: The Importance of Prayer [Updated and Expanded] by R. A. Torrey and Edward D. Andrews

CHAPTER 5 Bible Difficulties in the Book of Exodus

Exodus 1:15 How could two Hebrew midwives deliver the children of so many women?

When we look at Exodus 12:37 and Numbers chapters 1-4, there were about 600,000 men besides women and children, which would mean about three million. This would mean that there must have been hundreds of thousands of women of childbearing age. Pharaoh is said to have spoken to the midwives Shiphrah and Puah. How is it possible for these two midwives to deliver children for so many women?

It is like any profession, in which a leader would deal with those that he had placed in charge of the midwives. The Egyptian society was one of the more organized. The Pharaohs had someone serving in the position of oversight in almost every conceivable profession. Of course, the Pharaoh would not personally assign people to oversight positions, he would have an administer of affairs, the position that Joseph served at while he was in Egypt. (Gen. 41:37-44, 46) The administer of affairs would likely have had a person over the nation of Israel, who was responsible to assign the Hebrews professions and report to him.

Exodus 1:15 How could God bless Hebrew midwives for defying the Pharaoh's decree?

The Hebrew women Shiphrah and Puah, who likely were the heads of the midwife profession, over the other midwives, did not carry out king of Egypt's order. They apparently did not instruct the midwives under them as ordered. The result was: "The people multiplied and grew very strong." Romans 13:1 says that we are commanded to "be subject to the governing authorities. For there is no authority except from God, and those that exist have been instituted by God."

While the above is true, this is a rule that was applicable for Christians, and was not in existence at the time of the midwives dealing with Pharaoh. Even so, no Scripture is an island. They must be understood in conjunction with the Bible as a whole. Are we to just blindly follow anything that a government requires, based on Roman 13:1. No. Acts 5:29 gives us a balanced principle, "But Peter and the apostles answered, 'We must obey God rather than men.'" If the government is asking a servant of God to do anything that would cause him or her to violate God's laws, the servant should not obey. Notice the response of the midwives, "But **the midwives feared God** and did not do as the king of Egypt commanded them, but let the male children live." – Exodus 1:17.

We might understand that they wanted to obey God rather than the Egyptian King. How are we to understand their deception?

Exodus 1:18-19 Updated American Standard Version (UASV)

[18] So the king of Egypt called for the midwives and said to them, "Why have you done this thing, and let the boys live?" [19] The midwives said to Pharaoh, "Because the Hebrew women are not as the Egyptian women; for they are vigorous and give birth before the midwife comes to them."

In short, while malevolent lying is certainly condemned in the Bible, this does not mean that a person is under compulsion to disclose truthful information to people who are not entitled to it. We can see that the midwives were favored by Jehovah God for all of their actions, "And because the midwives feared God, he gave them families." –Exodus 1:21.

The standard of God is that there is no lying, which Exodus 20:16 makes all too clear, "You shall not bear false witness against your neighbor." However, When Abram was forced to go down to Egypt, because of a famine, he "said to Sarai his wife, 'I know that you are a woman beautiful in appearance, and when the Egyptians see you, they will say, 'This is his wife.' Then they will kill me, but they will let you live. Say you are my sister, that it may go well with me because of you, and that my life may be spared for your sake.'" (12:12-13) In Genesis chapter 20, we find Abraham repeating this behavior, even though it did not bode well for him the first time. Did Abraham lie these two times, and if so, why does the entire account of Abraham present him as righteously walking with God, the epitome of faith?

First, it should be mentioned that Sarah was the half-sister and wife of Abraham. Therefore, in essence, he did not lie about their relationship; he simply withheld information that would have been used by the enemy, resulting in Abraham being possibly killed. It is true malicious lying is prohibited in the Bible, which is to say something that is not true in a conscious effort to deceive or hurt somebody that is deserving of the truth. However, the Bible has examples or cases where a person has withheld information from an enemy, who would have used that information to hurt or cause harm to the person or another. The Bible seems to suggest that we are not under obligation to divulge information to the enemy, or that would cause oneself harm. The American legal system allows something like this as well. It is called The Fifth Amendment (Amendment V), which guarantees you do not have to testify against yourself.

Jesus Christ counseled, "Do not give dogs what is holy, and do not throw your pearls before pigs, lest they trample them underfoot and turn to attack you." (Matt 7:6) Even Jesus himself, who is incapable of malicious lying, on occasion, withheld information from those who were not worthy of it, and would have only used it to hurt him. (Matt 15:1-6; 21:23-27; John 7:3-10) We see this same principle under way with Abraham, Isaac, Rehab, and Elisha, as all pointed in the wrong direction or withheld all the facts from the enemies or nonworshipers.—Gen 12:10-19; 20:1-18; 26:1-10; Josh 2:1-6; Jas 2:25; 2Ki 6:11-23.

- A crazed gunman breaks into your house, and asks you, "Is anyone else here?" Are you obligated to tell him that your two little girls are upstairs hiding under the bed?

- What if you see a woman run into an alley to escape someone who's trying to kill her, and they ask you, "Where is she?" What do you do? Do you send them on a wild goose chase to protect the woman's life? Or do you lead them to their victim?—William Lane Craig

- During World War II, you are bringing a food box into a concentration camp. The guard asks if there is any contraband inside. Are you obligated to tell him that you have a small Bible smuggled into one of the packages?

- Do you endanger a human life, or do you withhold information that they do not deserve, nor have the right to, even giving them misinformation?

Exodus 3:1 What kind of priest was Jethro?

In the days of Abraham, Isaac, Jacob, the patriarchal times [a culture in which men were the ones who lead the family, especially the oldest living male]. Jethro, Moses' father-in-law, a Kenite, was the patriarchal head of the Midianite tribe. The Midianites were actually related to the Israelites, as they were descendants of Keturah. Therefore, it is quite possible that they might have been familiar with the worship of Jehovah, the Israelite God. Genesis 25:1-2

Exodus 3:22 How could a God that is the epitome of love command the Israelites to plunder the Egyptians for their riches?

Exodus 3:22 Updated American Standard Version (UASV)

²² But every woman shall ask of her neighbor and the woman who lives in her house, articles of silver and articles of gold, and clothing; and you will put them on your sons and on your daughters; **and you will plunder the Egyptians.**"

We must look at the whole text, because the reality is that Jehovah had commanded the Israelites to "ask" their neighbor. To plunder is to gain or acquire something by superior strength, generally by force. By their asking them, they would not be plundering in the sense that we understand the English equivalent, but the result is the same as if they had. Also, it should be mentioned that the Hebrew here is used in a figurative sense, as this was a request, not a forceful taking, and they received what they had asked for. Of course, it is true that the Egyptians were motivated by the ten plagues that they had just experienced at the hands of the Israelite God.

However, to address the idea of whether a loving God, who was simply using force, to free his people from slavery, was now exploiting that fear for the riches of the land, this is not the case at all. What the Israelites received was long overdue. For centuries the Israelites had been abused as slaves, working in a physically, mentally, emotionally and spiritually abusive environment, for nothing more than barely enough food to exist, while the Pharaoh's treasure house grew. In a modern day perspective, we can just view it as the Israelites received their back pay.

Exodus 4:11 How is it that Jehovah "makes mute or deaf or sighted or blind?"

There have been times in Scripture, where Jehovah had the right to cause blindness and muteness. (Genesis 19:11; Luke 1:20-22, 62-64) Those are the only cases where he is directly responsible, and thus this text should not be understood as a saying that he is responsible for all such cases through human history. Of course, he is indirectly responsible for all cases, because he all imperfection to enter into humankind. Blindness and muteness are a result of inherited sin. (Job 14:4; Romans 5:12) However, the direct responsibility falls on the angel known as Satan the Devil, as well as Adam and Eve, when they rebelled in the Garden of Eden. (Gen 3:1-6) Thus, since God has permitted sin to enter into the world, he can speak of himself as making ones 'mute or deaf or sighted or blind.' The follow-up question would then be, why has God permitted or allowed wickedness and suffering?

"God has morally sufficient reasons for permitting the evil and suffering in the world." – William Lane Craig

That *morally sufficient reason* lies below.

"The significant issue that drove me to Agnosticism [Bible Scholar Dr. Bart D. Ehrman is now an Agnostic] has to do not with the Bible, but with the pain and suffering in the world." He writes, "I eventually found it impossible to explain the evil so rampant among us—whether in terms of genocides (which continue), unspeakable human cruelty, war, disease, hurricanes, tsunamis, mudslides, the starvation of millions of innocent children, you name it—if there was a good and loving God who was actively involved in this world." *Misquoting Jesus* (p. 248)

As you will see below, Ehrman's issue is simply a matter of starting with the wrong assumption. **Point One**: He starts with 'if God is a God of love, who has the power to fix anything, how can there have been such horrific pain and suffering in imperfection over the last 6,000 years?' **Point Two**: He also likely begins with the premise that 'God is responsible for everything that happens.' If one starts with the wrong assumption, there is no doubt that he will reach the wrong conclusion(s). **Point One** is dealt with below, but let it be said that Ehrman is looking through the binoculars from the opposite end, the big side through the small. When we do that, we get a narrow, focused outlook. God looks through the binoculars the correct way, and can see the big picture. Ehrman can only see but a fraction and a moment of time, 70 – 80 years, while God has seen everything that has happened over these past 6,000 plus years in the greatest of detail, and can see what the outcome would be if he had handled things in a variety of ways.

Point Two is certainly one reason suffering and evil is often misunderstood. God is responsible for everything, but not always directly. If he started the human race, and we end up with what we now have, in essence, he is responsible. Just as parents, who have a child are similarly responsible for the child committing murder 21 years into his life, because they procreated and gave birth to the child. The mother and father are indirectly responsible. King David commits adultery with Bathsheba and has her husband Uriah killed to cover things up, and impregnates Bathsheba, but the adulterine child, who remains nameless, died. Is God responsible for the death of that child? We can answer yes and no to that question. He is responsible in two ways: **(1)** He created humankind, so there would have been no affair, murder, adulterine child if he had not. **(2)** He did not step in and save the child when he had the power to do so. However, he is not directly responsible, because he did not make King David and Bathsheba commit the acts that led to the child being born, nor did he bring an illness on the adulterine child, he just did not move in to protect the child, in a time that had a high rate of infant deaths.

The reason people think that God does not care about us is the words of some religious leaders, which have made them, feel this way. When tragedy strikes, what do some pastors and Bible scholars often say? When 9/11 took place, with thousands dying in the twin towers of New York, many ministers said: "It was God's will. God must have had some good reason for doing this." When religious leaders make such comments or similar ones, they are actually blaming God for the bad things that happened. Yet, the disciple James wrote, "Let no one say when he is tempted, 'I am being tempted by God,' for God cannot be tempted with evil, and he himself tempts no one." (James 1:13) God never directly causes what is bad. Indeed, "far be it from God that he should do wickedness, and from the Almighty that he should do wrong." Job 34:10.

The history of humans has been inundated with pain and suffering on an unprecedented scale, much of which they have brought on themselves. The problem/question that has plagued many persons is, 'why if there is a loving God, would he allow it to start with, and worse still, why allow it to go on for over 6,000 years?' Some apologist scholars have struggled to answer this question, because they are over analyzing, as opposed to just looking for the answer in God's Word. Therefore, if we are to answer this question, we must go back to Adam and Eve at the time of the first sin. Many have read this account, but I will list the texts as a refresher.

Genesis 2:17 Updated American Standard Version (UASV)

[17] but from the tree of the knowledge of good and evil you shall not eat,[53] for in the day that you eat from it you shall surely die."[54]

Genesis 3:1-5 Updated American Standard Version (UASV)

[1] Now the serpent was more crafty than any beast of the field which Jehovah God had made. And he said to the woman, "Did God actually say, 'You[55] shall not eat of any tree in the garden'?" [2] And the woman said to the serpent, "From the fruit of the trees of the garden we may eat,

---

[53] Lit *eat from it*

[54] Lit *dying you* [singular] *shall die*. Heb *moth tamuth*; the first reference to death in the Scriptures

[55] In Hebrew *you* is plural in verses 1–5

³ but from the tree that is in the midst of the garden, God said, 'You shall not eat from it, nor shall you touch it, lest you die.'" ⁴ And the serpent said to the woman, "You shall not surely die. ⁵ For God knows that when you eat of it your eyes will be opened, and you will be like God, knowing good and evil." knowing good and evil.

Later Bible texts establish Satan the Devil as the one using a serpent as his mouthpiece like a ventriloquist would a dummy. Anyway, take note that Satan contradicts the clear statement that God made to Adam at Genesis 2:17, "you will not surely die." Backing up a little, we see Satan asking an inferential question, "Did God actually say, 'You shall not eat of any tree in the garden'?" First, he is overstating what he knows to be true, not "any tree," just one tree. Second, Satan is inferring, 'I can't believe that God would say . . . how dare he say such.' Notice too that Eve has been told so thoroughly about the tree that she even goes beyond what Adam told her, not just that you 'do not eat from it,' no, 'you do not even touch it!' Then, Satan out and out lied and slandered God as a liar, saying that 'they would not die.' To make matters much worse, he infers that God is withholding good from them, and by rebelling they would be better off, being like God, 'knowing good and bad.' This latter point is not knowledge of; it is the self-sovereignty of choosing good and bad for oneself and act of rebellion for created creatures. What was symbolized by the tree is well expressed in a footnote on Genesis 2:17, in The Jerusalem Bible (1966):

> This knowledge is a privilege which God reserves to himself and which man, by sinning, is to lay hands on, 3:5, 22. Hence it does not mean omniscience, which fallen man does not possess; nor is it moral discrimination, for unfallen man already had it and God could not refuse it to a rational being. It is the power of deciding for himself what is good and what is evil and of acting accordingly, a claim to complete moral independence by which man refuses to recognize his status as a created being. The first sin was an attack on God's sovereignty, a sin of pride.

The Issues at Hand

(1) Satan called God a liar and said he was not to be trusted, as to the life or death issue.

(2) Satan's challenge, therefore, took into question the right and legitimacy of God's rightful place as the Universal Sovereign.

(3) Satan also suggested that people would remain obedient to God only as long as their submitting to God was to their benefit.

(4) Satan all but said that humankind was able to walk on his own, there being no need for dependence on God.

(5) Satan argued that man could be like God, choosing for himself what is right and wrong.

(6) Satan claimed that God's way of ruling was not in the best interests of humans, and they could do better without God.

Job 1:6-11 Updated American Standard Version (UASV)

6 Now there was a day when the sons of God came to present themselves before Jehovah, and Satan also came among them. **7** Jehovah said to Satan, "From where do you come?" Then Satan answered Jehovah and said, "From roaming about on the earth and walking around on it." **8** Jehovah said to Satan, "Have you considered my servant Job? For there is no one like him on the earth, a blameless and upright man, fearing God and turning away from evil." **9** Then Satan answered Jehovah, "Does Job fear God for nothing? **10** Have you not made a hedge about him and his house and all that he has, on every side? You have blessed the work of his hands, and his possessions have increased in the land. **11** But put forth your hand now and touch all that he has; he will surely curse you to your face."

Job 2:4-5 Updated American Standard Version (UASV)

4 Satan answered Jehovah and said, "Skin for skin! Yes, all that a man has he will give for his life. **5** However, put forth your hand now, and touch his bone and his flesh; he will curse you to your face."

This general reference to "a man," as opposed to explicitly naming Job, is suggesting that all men [and women] will only obey God when things are good, but when the slightest difficulty arises, he will not obey. If you were put to the test, would you prove your love for your heavenly Father and show that you preferred His rule to that of any other?

God Settles the Issues

There is one thing that Satan did not challenge, namely, the power of God. Satan did not suggest that God was unable to destroy him as an opposer. However, he did challenge God's way of ruling, not His right to rule. Therefore, a moral issue must be settled.

An illustration of how God chose to deal with the issue can be demonstrated in human terms. A neighbor down the street slandered a man, who had a son and daughter. The slanderer said that he was not a good father, i.e., he withheld good from his children and was so overbearing, to the point of being abusive. The slanderer stated that the children would be better off without their father. He further argued that the children had no real love for their father and only obeyed him because of the food and shelter. How should the father deal with these false, i.e., slanderous accusations? If he were to go down the road and pummel the slanderer, it would only validate the lies, making the neighbors believe the accuser is telling the truth.

The answer lies within his family as they can serve as his witnesses. (Pro 27:11; Isa 43:10) If the children stay obedient and grow to be successful adults, turning out to be loving, caring, honest people with spotless character, it proves the accusations false. If the children accept the lies and rebel and grow up to be despicable people, it just further validates that they would have been better off by staying with the father. This is how God chose to deal with the issues. The issues that were raised must be settled beyond all reasonable doubt.

If God had destroyed the rebellious three: Satan, Adam, and Eve; he would not have resolved the issues of

(1) Whether man could walk on his own,

(2) if he would be better off without his Creator,

(3) if God's rulership were not best, and

(4) if God were hiding good from man.

(5) In addition, there was an audience of untold billions of angelic spirit creatures looking on.

If God destroyed without settling things, these spirit persons would be following God out of dreadful fear, not love, fear of displeasing God. Moreover, say He did kill them, and start over, and ten thousand years down the road (with billions of humans now on earth), the issues were raised again, He would have to destroy billions of people again, and again, and again all throughout time, until these issues were laid to rest.

What God has done is, allow time to pass, and the issues to be resolved. Man thought he was better off without God, and could walk on his own. In addition, man has attempted every kind of rulership imaginable, and one must ask, 'have they proven themselves better than rulership under the sovereignty of their Creator?' (Proverbs 1:30-33; Isaiah 59:4, 8) Sadly, the issues must be taken up to the brink of destroying man. (Rev 11:18) Otherwise, the argument would be that if given enough time, they could have turned things around. If man goes up to the point of destroying himself and Armageddon comes at the last minute, it will have set a case law, solved the issue, and the Bible can serve as the example forever. If the issues of God's sovereignty or the loyalty of His created creatures, angelic or human, is ever questioned again, we would have the Holy Bible that will serve as a law established based on previous verdicts of not guilty, please see below.

What Have the Results Been?

(1) God does not cause evil and suffering. Romans 9:14.

(2) The fact that God has allowed evil, pain and suffering has shown that independence from God has not brought about a better world. Jeremiah 8:5, 6, 9.

(3) God's permission of evil, pain, and suffering has also proved that Satan has not been able to turn all humans away from God. Exodus 9:16; 1 Samuel 12:22; Hebrews 12:1.

(4) The fact that God has permitted evil, pain, and suffering to continue has provided proof that only God, the Creator, has the capability and the right to rule over humankind for their eternal blessing and happiness. Ecclesiastes 8:9.

(5) Satan has been the god of this world since the sin in Eden (over 6,000 years), and how has that worked out for man, and what has been the result of man's course of independence from God and his rule? Matthew 4:8-9; John 16:11; 2 Corinthians 4:3-4; 1 John 5:19; Psalm 127:1.

Satan's impact on the earth's activities has carried with it conflict, evil and death, and his rulership has been by means of deception, power and his own self-interest. He has demonstrated himself an unfit ruler of everything. Therefore, God is now completely vindicated in putting an end to this corrupted rebel along with all who have shared in his evil deeds.—Romans 16:20.

God has tolerated evil, sickness, pain, suffering and death until our day in order to resolve all the issues raised by Satan. We are self-centered in thinking that this has only pained us. Imagine that you are holding a rope on a sinking ship that 20 other men, women, and children are clinging to, when your child loses her grip and falls into the ocean. You can hold the rope, saving 20 people, or you can let go and attempt to rescue your daughter. God has been watching the suffering of billions from the day of Adam and Eve's sin. Moreover, it has been His great love for us, which causes Him to cling to the rope of issues, saving us from a future of repeated issues. Nevertheless, he will not allow this evil to remain forever. He has set a fixed time when He will end this wicked system of Satan's rule.

Daniel 11:27 Updated American Standard Version (UASV)

²⁷ As for both kings, their heart will be inclined to do what is evil, and they will speak lies to each other at the same table; but it will not succeed, for the end is still to come <u>at the appointed time</u>.

Unlike what many people of the world may think (the world that lies in the hands of Satan), being obedient to God is not difficult. We simply must set our pride aside and accept that the wisdom of God is so far greater than our own, and accept that He has worked for the good of obedient humankind, as He loves each one of us.

Matthew 7:21 Updated American Standard Version (UASV)

²¹ "Not everyone who says to me, 'Lord, Lord,' will enter the kingdom of heaven, but <u>the one who does the will of my Father</u> who is in heaven.

1 John 2:15-17 Updated American Standard Version (UASV)

¹⁵ Do not love the world or the things in the world. If anyone loves the world, the love of the Father is not in him. ¹⁶ For all that is in the world, the lust of the flesh and the lust of the eyes and the boastful pride of life, is not from the Father, but is from the world. ¹⁷ The world is passing away, and its lusts; but the one who does the will of God remains forever.

As Christians, there is a love we must not have. We must 'not love the world or anything in it.' Instead, we need to keep from becoming infected by the corruption of unrighteous human society that is alienated from God and must not breathe in its mental disposition or be moved by its sinful dominant attitude. (Ephesians 2:1, 2; James 1:27) If we were to have the views of those in the world that are in opposition to God, "the love of the Father" would not be in us. (James 4:4)

Was Satan Punished?

Yes.

COMMON QUESTION: Why did God not destroy the Satan, Adam, and Eve right away?

I would follow up with what would have happened if God had chosen that path. Hundreds of billions of angels with free will were watching, and they knew of the issues raised. What would their love of God have been like if God did not address the issues raised? Was Satan right? Was God lying? Would free will creatures, spirit and humans, be better off? Will God just destroy us over anything? First, the spirit creatures would have followed God out of dreadful fear, rather than fear of displeasing the one they loved so much up to that point, like a child to a parent. Second, what happens if the issue is raised a hundred thousand years after a restart and there are 30 billion perfect humans on the planet? Would God simply destroy everyone again and start over. Do we think it wise that he does this reboot every time or was it not better that he settled the issue once and for all?

POINT: Satan raised Issues of sovereignty in the Garden of Eden.

POINT: Can humans walk on their own; do they really need their Creator? Are they better off without God?

POINT: Was God lying and withholding?

When a teenager becomes a rebel in our house, we have a choice: (1) severe punishment or (2) teach them an object lesson.

HUMANS AND ANGELS are a created product no different than a car coming off of an assembly line, i.e., (1) they owe their existence to their creator and (2) they were created to function based on the design of the creator. If we take a ford escort and treat it like a heavy duty four-wheel drive truck and go off roading (not what the car was designed to do), what will happen?

God wisely chose to teach both angels and humans an object lesson. Neither was designed to walk on their own. Both angel and human were given relative freedom (under the sovereignty of God), not absolute freedom. They were not designed to choose what is right and what is wrong on their own. They were given God's moral standards by way of an internal conscience. How can we tell a rebel that we do not have absolute freedom, we are better off under the umbrella of our creator's sovereignty, we cannot walk on our own? They will just reject it as a rebel teenager would.

OBJECT LESSON: We let them learn from their choice, no matter how painful it is, and hard love means that we do not step in until the lesson is fully learned. Humankind was essentially told, "Oh, you think you can walk on your own, well go ahead, we will see how that works out." After six-thousand-years, God could actually use a common saying among young people today: "How is that absolute freedom working out for you?"

When will the lesson fully be learned? Humankind will walk right up to the very edge of the cliff of killing themselves, actually falling over, when God will step in and stop the object lesson. To stop it anytime before, will cause doubts. If it had been stopped a century ago, the argument would have been; God simply stepped in before we got to the scientific age because he knew we were going to find true peace and security, along with something to give us eternal life. However, if humanity has actually fallen over the edge of the cliff and the destruction of us is definite, and God steps in, no argument can be raised, the object lesson is learned.

Why Was Satan Not Kicked Out of Heaven Right Away?

Satan stayed in his realm, just as humans stayed in theirs. God changed nothing right away because he would have been accused of adjusting the pieces on the chessboard to get the desired outcome, i.e., cheating. When will Satan be kicked out of heaven? Satan and the Demons lost access to the person of God long age, and they lost some of their powers, such as being able to materialize in human form, like they did when they took human women for themselves at the flood, producing the Nephilim.

Satan would be thrown to the earth very shortly before the end of his age of rulership, when "he knows that his time is short." (Rev 12:9-12) This, then, means that Satan will be thrown from heaven likely sometime before the Great Tribulation and Christ's return. Revelation 12:12 says, "'Therefore, rejoice, O heavens and you who dwell in them! But woe to you, O earth and sea, for the devil has come down to you in great wrath because he knows that his time is short!'"

Notice that it is at a time, when "Satan knows that his time is short!" What comes next for Satan? He will be abyssed, thrown into a super-maximum-security prison for a thousand years (for lack of a better way to explain it) while Jesus fixes all that Satan done. After the thousand years, he will be let loose for a little while, and he will tempt perfect humans, and sadly some will fall away. In the end, Satan and those humans will be destroyed, and Jesus will hand the kingdom back over to the father.

Exodus 4:16 How was Moses to Be God to Aaron?

Moses represented Jehovah God to the Israelites, as well as any other people they came into contact with. Jehovah God gave Moses miraculous powers and authority. Therefore, Aaron served as a representative of Moses; Like Moses had done for Jehovah. Elohim, the Hebrew word for God, means 'mighty one' or 'powerful one.' Moses was mighty and powerful as a result of the miraculous powers he was given. When Moses received his instruction to go before the older men of Israel or Pharaoh, he would give those same instructions to Aaron, who would then serve as his spokesman. (Ex 2:23; 4:10-17) Jehovah even spoke of Aaron as Moses' prophet at Exodus 7:1. Just as Jehovah God directed Moses, Moses directed Aaron. Finally, also at Exodus 7:1, we read, "Jehovah said to Moses, 'See, I have made thee as God to Pharaoh.'" In other words, Moses had far greater power than Pharaoh because his support came from Jehovah, while Pharaoh had his power and support from Satan.

Exodus 4:21 Why did God hardened Pharaoh's heart?

Exodus 4:21 Updated American Standard Version (UASV)

²¹ Jehovah said to Moses, "When you go and return to Egypt see that you perform before Pharaoh all the wonders which I have put in your hand; but **I will harden his heart** so that he will not let the people go.

The Hardening of Pharaoh's Heart

Exodus mentions that a heart is hardened or unbending 19 times. In the list below, each of the situations is listed, along with the Hebrew verb used and the subject of that verb. At times the text states that the heart itself grows hard, while in other instances there is an agent— Jehovah or Pharaoh—who does the hardening.

Reference	Verb	Subject
4:21	*ḥzq*	Jehovah
7:3	*qšh*	Jehovah
7:13	*ḥzq*	heart
7:14	*kbd*	heart
7:22	*ḥzq*	heart
8:15	*kbd*	Pharaoh
8:19	*ḥzq*	heart
8:32	*kbd*	Pharaoh
9:7	*kbd*	heart
9:12	*ḥzq*	Jehovah
9:34	*kbd*	heart
9:35	*ḥzq*	heart
10:1	*kbd*	Jehovah
10:20	*ḥzq*	Jehovah
10:27	*ḥzq*	Jehovah
11:10	*ḥzq*	Jehovah
14:4	*ḥzq*	Jehovah
14:8	*ḥzq*	Jehovah
14:17	*ḥzq*	Jehovah

It should be noted, Jehovah is the subject of *kbd* only once (10:1); all of the other times it is the heart of Pharaoh or Pharaoh himself

Jehovah God had to bring ten plagues on the land of Egypt. With each plague, the Pharaoh hardened his heart, and this allowed the people to see the great power of the real God. (Ex 7:3-5, 14–11:10) Throughout the process, many Egyptians had seen, who the true God of heaven and earth is, and that he deserves obedience. For instance, the seventh plague of hail was announced, and many Egyptians made sure their livestock was under shelter, thus they exercised faith in the Israelite God. (Ex 9:20, 21) Even in the end, when Pharaoh finally released the Israelites, he hardened his heart yet again, coming after the Israelites with his army. (Ex 14:8, 9; 15:9) However, he met destruction along with his army in the Red Sea, drawing even more attention to the great power of Jehovah God. (Ex 14:27, 28; Ps 136:15) This event promoted God's name and reputation for decades throughout the land, as to what Jehovah did when the pharaoh hardened his heart against Him.—Ex 18:10, 11; Jos 2:10, 11; 9:9; 1Sa 6:6.

Since God gives the people advance warnings, it could never be His fault, if they choose to become stubborn. Having said that, now let us look at what the Scriptures really say:

Exodus 7:13 Updated American Standard Version (UASV)

¹³ And Pharaoh's **heart was hardened**,⁵⁶ and he **would not listen** to them, as Jehovah had said.

We see that Pharaoh's heart grew hard, because he would not listen.

Exodus 8:15 Updated American Standard Version (UASV)

¹⁵ But when Pharaoh saw that there was a relief, **he hardened**⁵⁷ **his heart** and **would not listen** to them, as Jehovah had said.

Exodus 4:21 Updated American Standard Version (UASV)

²¹ Jehovah said to Moses, "When you go and return to Egypt see that you perform before Pharaoh all the wonders which I have put in your hand; but **I will harden his heart** so that he will not let the people go.

This is really prophetic, in that God is saying what will happen as the result of His actions. In other words, it is spoken of as though God did something, because his actions are what brought about the outcome that He knew would come.

God does not harden hearts against people's freewill, but He does tell us what to expect, and if we stubbornly ignore that loving insight, he did harden our heart by his actions, but it came about because of our stubbornness. In support of the above, the appendix to Rotherham's

---

⁵⁶ Lit *strong*

⁵⁷ Lit *made heavy*

translation shows that in Hebrew the occasion or permission of an event is often presented as if it were the cause of the event, and that "even positive commands are occasionally to be accepted as meaning no more than permission." After quoting Hebrew scholars M. M. Kalisch, H. F. W. Gesenius, and B. Davies in support, Rotherham states that the Hebrew sense of the texts involving Pharaoh is that "God permitted Pharaoh to harden his own heart, spared him, gave him the opportunity, the occasion, of working out the wickedness that was in him. That is all."— The Emphasised Bible, appendix, p. 919; compare Isa 10:5-7.

Exodus 5:2 Who was the Exodus Pharaoh?

Genesis 15:13-16 Updated American Standard Version (UASV)

[13] Then He said to Abram: "Know for certain that your seed[58] will be foreigners[59] in a land not theirs and they shall serve them[60] and they[61] shall oppress them for **four hundred years**. [14] But also on the nation that they[62] serve I will bring judgment, and afterward they will come out with great possessions. [15] As for you, you shall go to your fathers in peace; you shall be buried in a good old age. [16] And in the fourth generation shall return here, for the error of the Amorites is not yet complete."[63]

The 400-year oppression had to await the promised seed. Shortly after God's statement about the 400 years of oppression, when Abraham was 86 years old (1932 B.C.E.), his Egyptian concubine gave birth to his son, Ishmael. However, it was 14 years later (1918 B.C.E.) that Sarah bore him a son, Isaac, and God chose this son as the one who would produce the coming promised seed. However, God's time had not yet come for giving Abraham or his seed the land of Canaan, and so they were, as foretold, 'strangers and exiles on the earth.' – Genesis 16:15, 16; 21:2-5; Hebrews 11:13.

When did the 400 years of oppression begin, and when did it end? While Jewish tradition begins the 400 years at the birth of Isaac, the more accurate biblical evidence come when Isaac is 5 years old and Ishmael is 19, as the start of the oppression. It was "at that time he who was born according to the flesh [Ishmael] persecuted him who was born according to the Spirit [Isaac]." (Gal. 4:29) Ishmael, who was part Egyptian, in

---

[58] I.e. *offspring* or *descendants*

[59] Or *aliens, strangers, sojourners*

[60] Israel would become enslaved to the Egyptians.

[61] The Eqyptians would appress the Israelites, who would become their slaves some four hundred years later.

[62] I.e. the *Israelites*

[63] I.e. *has not yet reached its full measure*

distrust and detestation, began "mocking." (YLT; RSV, ftn) at Isaac, the young child, this amounting to much more than a mere children's quarrel. (Gen. 21:9) This incident occurred in 1846 B.C.E. Therefore, the 400-year period of oppression began in 1846 B.C.E. and ended at the exodus of 1446 B.C.E. The years of Solomon's reign were 970 to 930 B.C.E.; and David's, 1010 to 970 B.C.E. The date of the exodus, then, based on 1 Kings 6:1 and Judges 11:26, is 1446 B.C.E.

Support for the early date comes from the biblical record and archeological evidence. First, in 1 Kings 6:1 the time between the Exodus and the beginning of Solomon's temple construction (in the fourth year of his reign) was 480 years. Since the fourth year of Solomon's reign was 966 B.C., the Exodus was in 1446. Also in the time of Jephthah (ca. 1100 B.C.) Israel had been in the land for 300 years (Jud. 11:26). Therefore 300 years plus the 40 years of the wilderness sojourn and some time to conquer Heshbon places the Exodus in the middle of the 15th century.

Second, archeological evidence from Egypt during this period corresponds with the biblical account of the Exodus (see Merrill F. Unger, *Archaeology and the Old Testament*. Grand Rapids: Zondervan Publishing House, 1954, pp. 140–5; and Gleason L. Archer, Jr., *A Survey of Old Testament Introduction*. Chicago: Moody Press, 1964, pp. 215–6). For example, though Thutmose IV succeeded his father, Amenhotep II, Thutmose was not the eldest son. (The eldest son was killed by the Lord on the night of the first Passover, Ex. 12:29.) Amenhotep II (1450–1425 B.C.) repressed insurgents in the early part of his reign. Semites were forced to make bricks (cf. 5:7–18). Several of the Pharaohs of Egypt's 18th dynasty (ca. 1567–1379 B.C.) were involved in building projects in northern Egypt. "Since Eighteenth Dynasty Pharaohs were very active in Palestinian campaigns, it would seem reasonable that they would have established garrisons and store cities (cf. 1:11) somewhere in the Delta regions to facilitate movement between Syro-Palestinian sites and Egypt itself" (John J. Davis, *Moses and the Gods of Egypt*, p. 27).

Third, events in Palestine about 1400 B.C. correspond with the Conquest under Joshua. Archeological evidence suggests that Jericho, Ai, and Hazor were destroyed about 1400. One scholar has concluded, "All the accredited Palestinian artifactual evidence supports the literary account that the Conquest occurred at the time specifically dated by the biblical historians" (Bruce K. Waltke, "Palestinian Artifactual Evidence

Supporting the Early Date of the Exodus," *Bibliotheca Sacra* 129. January–March, 1972:47).[64]

The pharaohs, who are named in the Bible, are Shishak, So, Tirhakah, Nechoh, and Hophra. Some have considered Zerah the Cushite as a ruler of Egypt. Other pharaohs are left nameless. Because of the confused state of Egyptian chronology, it is not probable to connect these pharaohs to those of secular history with confidence. These nameless pharaohs include: The one who tried to take Sarah (Gen. 12:15-20); the pharaoh who placed Joseph in authority (Gen. 41:39-46); the pharaoh (or pharaohs) of the period of oppression of the Israelites prior to Moses' return from Midian (Ex. chaps 1-2); the pharaoh ruling during the Ten Plagues and at the time of the Exodus (Ex. 5-14); the pharaoh who gave refuge to Hadad of Edom in David's time (1 Ki 11:18-22); the father of the Egyptian wife of Solomon (1 Ki 3:1); and the pharaoh who struck down Gaza during the time of the prophet Jeremiah. – Jeremiah 47:1.

Exodus 6:3 In what way had God's name not been made known to Abraham, Isaac, and Jacob?

Exodus 3:13 Updated American Standard Version (UASV)

[13] Then Moses said to God, "Behold, I am going to the sons of Israel, and I will say to them, 'The God of your fathers has sent me to you.' Now they may say to me, 'What is his name?' What shall I say to them?"

Exodus 6:3 Updated American Standard Version (UASV)

[3] And I appeared to Abraham, to Isaac, and to Jacob, as God Almighty,[65] but by my name Jehovah I did not make myself known to them.

How can Exodus 3:13 and 6:13 be accurate, because the patriarchs knew used the divine name Jehovah? . . .

Genesis 2:4 Updated American Standard Version (UASV)

[4] These are the generations of the heavens and of the earth when they were created, in the day that Jehovah[66] God made earth and heaven. (see also 5, 7, 8-9, and 15)

---

[64] John D. Hannah, "Exodus," in *The Bible Knowledge Commentary: An Exposition of the Scriptures*, ed. J. F. Walvoord and R. B. Zuck, vol. 1 (Wheaton, IL: Victor Books, 1985), 104.

[65] Heb *El Shaddai*

[66] The first occurrence of God's personal name, יהוה (JHVH/YHWH), which is found in the Hebrew Old Testament 6,828 times.

As well as . . .

Genesis 4:1 Updated American Standard Version (UASV)

4 Now the man knew[67] Eve his wife, and she conceived and bore Cain,[68] and said, "I have gotten a man <u>with the help of Jehovah</u>."

Jehovah chose his own name, one rich in meaning. "Jehovah" literally means "He Causes to Become." The divine name certainly was not new. The divine name was known and used clear back in the beginning with Adam and Eve. The Patriarchs also knew and used the divine name, as well as received promises from Jehovah. However, keeping in mind the meaning of God's name, "He Causes to Become," the patriarchs did not know Jehovah in an experiential way, as the one that would cause the promises to be fulfilled. (Genesis 12:1, 2; 15:7, 13-16; 26:24; 28:10-15.) They knew the promises, but Moses was about to experience the results. No matter what was to get in the way of Moses and the Israelites, no matter the difficulties they faced, Jehovah was going to become whatever they needed, to deliver them from slavery and into the Promised Land.

Exodus 6:9 Did the Israelites listen to Moses, or did they ignore his words?

Exodus 4:31 Updated American Standard Version (UASV)

31 And <u>the people believed</u>; and <u>when they heard</u> that Jehovah had visited the sons of Israel and that he had seen their affliction, they bowed their heads and worshiped.

Exodus 6:9 Updated American Standard Version (UASV)

9 And Moses spoke thus to the sons of Israel, but <u>they did not listen to Moses</u>, because of their lack of spirit[69] and harsh slavery.

How can both of the above texts be true? Did the children of Israel listen to Moses or not? Obviously, they were in an emotional state, having served as slaves their entire lives, and to hear that their God, Jehovah was going to bring about their release was very overwhelming. Therefore, they were initially excited by such news, and listened to Moses every word. However, when this release was not immediate, they became disheartened, and annoyed with Moses, choosing to no longer listen to him.

---

[67] Meaning Adam had *sexual relations* with Eve

[68] That is, gotten one

[69] I.e *their discouragement* or *their despondency*

Exodus 6:10-13 Did Moses receive his call in Egypt or Midian?

Exodus 3:10 Updated American Standard Version (UASV)

¹⁰ Come now, and I will send you to Pharaoh, so that you may bring my people, the sons of Israel, out of Egypt."

Exodus 4:19 Updated American Standard Version (UASV)

¹⁹ And Jehovah said to Moses in Midian, "return to Egypt, for all the men who were seeking your life are dead."

Exodus 6:10-11 Updated American Standard Version (UASV)

¹⁰ And Jehovah spoke to Moses, saying, ¹¹ "Go, speak to Pharaoh, the king of Egypt, to let the sons of Israel go out from his land."

Initially, Moses was commissioned in Egypt (Ch. 3-4). However, Pharaoh rejected Moses (Ch. 5), and Moses himself was reluctant to take on the task (4:1, 10). Therefore, it became necessary for God to reassure Moses and restate his call in Exodus 6.

Exodus 6:16-20 How is it possible that the Israelites were in Egypt for 430 years, when there were only three generations between Levi and Moses?

The period from Abraham's move to Canaan until Jacob's going down into Egypt was 215 years. This figure is arrived at from the following facts: 25 years between Abraham's departure from Haran to the birth of Isaac (Gen 12:4; 21:5); from then to the birth of Jacob was 60 years (Gen 25:26); and Jacob was 130 at the time of his entry into Egypt (Gen 47:9); thus giving a total of 215 years (from 1943 to 1728 B.C.E.). This means that an equal period of 215 years was thereafter spent by the Israelites in Egypt (from 1728 to 1513 B.C.E.).

Again, we must keep in mind that Jehovah told Abraham that in the fourth generation his descendants would return to Canaan. (Gen 15:16) In the entire 430 years from the time when the Abrahamic covenant took effect to the Exodus there were more than four generations, even bearing in mind the long life spans that they enjoyed during that time, according to the record. However, it was only 215 years that the Israelites were in fact, in Egypt. The 'four generations' following their entering Egypt can be calculated in this way, using as an example just one tribe of Israel, the tribe of Levi: (1) Levi, (2) Kohath, (3) Amram, and (4) Moses.—Ex 6:16, 18, 20.

Exodus 6:26-27 How is it possible that Moses wrote this when it speaks of him in third person?

Exodus 6:26-27 Updated American Standard Version (UASV)

²⁶ **These are** the Aaron and Moses to whom Jehovah said, "Bring out the sons of Israel from the land of Egypt by their hosts." ²⁷ It was **they** who spoke to Pharaoh king of Egypt about bringing out the people of Israel from Egypt, this Moses and this Aaron.

We must consider the context of the account, and that means going back to verse 14, which is a historical account of the genealogies of Moses and Aaron's ancestors. The customary way of writing, would then require that the writer refer to himself in third person, if he is referenced. This is the common practice throughout history. The record needed to be clear as to the genealogy of the one whom God had chosen to bring Israel out of slavery of Egypt, for future generations of Hebrews. This would have not been quite the case with "It was Aaron and I to whom Jehovah said" or "Aaron and I were the ones speaking to Pharaoh."

Exodus 7:1 How was Moses made "God to Pharaoh"?

Exodus 7:1 Updated American Standard Version (UASV)

7 And Jehovah said to Moses, "See, I make you as **God to Pharaoh**, and your brother Aaron shall be your prophet.

The title *elohim* [God, god] draws attention to strength, might, power, and Jehovah God gave Moses divine power and authority over Pharaoh. Therefore, he had no reason to fear that Egyptian king. In other words, Moses had far greater power than Pharaoh did because his support came from Jehovah, while Pharaoh had his power and support from Satan.

Exodus 7:11 How could the wise men and sorcerers of Pharaoh Perform the same feats of power that God did through Moses?

Puzzled by this miracle, Pharaoh summoned his wise men and sorcerers. With the help of demon powers, these men were able to do something similar with their own rods. You can see from Revelation 16:14 below that Satan and his demonic spirit creatures have the power, because they are creatures above mankind in strength and power, to perform counterfeit miracles, in an effort to deceive.

Revelation 16:14 Updated American Standard Version (UASV)

¹⁴ for they are spirits of demons, performing signs, which go out to the kings of the whole inhabited earth, to gather them together for the war of the great day of God, the Almighty.

Exodus 7:19-20 How could the Israelites escape this plague when it affected the whole of Egypt?

Some commentators as well as other Bible difficulty books have tried to argue, "the Hebrew language the normal word for all is not necessarily absolute."[70] In other words, not all of the water of Egypt was affected. (See Exodus 9:25; 10:5.) However, there is another option that agrees with the facts. Exodus 7:24 says, "And all the Egyptians dug along the Nile for water to drink, for they could not drink the water of the Nile." Therefore, they still had access to unaffected water, by digging wells around the Nile. Moreover, this likely where the Egyptian wise men and sorcerers were able to get their waters to repeat the same miracle of turning water into blood, which discouraged Pharaoh from releasing the Hebrews.

Exodus 8:15 Is not the Bible critic always arguing that God hardened the heart of the Pharaoh?

Exodus 8:15 Updated American Standard Version (UASV)

¹⁵ But when **Pharaoh** saw that there was a relief, **he hardened**[71] **his heart** and would not listen to them, as Jehovah had said.

See Exodus 4:21 above

Exodus 8:26-27 Why did Moses say that Israel's sacrifices would be "an abomination to the Egyptians"?

Many different animals were venerated in Egypt. The reference of sacrifices therefore supplied force and persuasion to Moses' resolve that Israel be permitted to go away to sacrifice to Jehovah.

---

[70] Thomas Howe; Norman L. Geisler. Big Book of Bible Difficulties, The: Clear and Concise Answers from Genesis to Revelation (Kindle Locations 900-901). Kindle Edition.
[71] Lit *made heavy*

Exodus 9:6, 19-21 If all the livestock of the Egyptians died; then, how is that some survived?

In verse 6 of chapter nine, we are told "all the livestock of the Egyptians died" in the **fifth plague**. However, verse 19 of the same chapter instructs them concerning the **eighth plague**, to "get your livestock and all that you have in the field into safe shelter." If **all** the livestock died in the fifth plague, how could there be any left for the eighth plague?

First, it should be mentioned that, in both the Old and New Testament, the original language words for "all" is commonly used as hyperbole, an exaggeration to make a point, and seldom means a literal everything, but rather the vast majority. Second, the plague was limited to the livestock "in the field" (vs. 3), not what may have been in stalls.

Exodus 11:33 How Could Moses praise himself and still be considered meek?

First, it is obvious that Moses did not write every word of the Pentateuch. Why? The section that relates his death would be something that Joshua could have added after Moses' death. (Deuteronomy 34:1–8) In addition, to the critic, it would hardly seem very meek to pen these words about yourself: "Now the man Moses was very meek, more than all people who were on the face of the earth." (Numbers 12:3, ESV) Nevertheless, consider that Jesus said of himself: "I am gentle and lowly in heart" (Matthew 11:29, ESV), which no one would fault Jesus with as though he were boasting. Both Moses and Jesus were simply stating a fact. The amount of possible material that may have been added by Joshua, another inspired writer is next to nothing, and does not negate Moses' authorship.

Exodus 12:29 Who were actually the firstborn?

The firstborn would not include females. (Numbers 3:40-51) This is obvious from the fact that later, when an exchange was made by giving the Levites over to Jehovah, only the males were counted. (Numbers 3:40-51) Pharaoh, himself would have been a firstborn, yet he was not killed. The reason being, he had his own household (Ex 12:12). It was not to be the family head but the firstborn son of the household, who died as a result of the tenth plague.

Some would argue that because of the stamen in verse 30 "for there was not a house where someone was not dead," that there had to be daughters involved as well. Well, we need not take this statement as an absolute, but more as hyperbole, emphasizing and highlighting the extent and reach of the justice. Moreover, this applied to the whole household, which would include all people under the patriarchal head, even grandchildren.

Exodus 12:29 How are we to understand that God, who is the epitome of love, could slay every firstborn in Egypt?

Exodus 12:29-30 Updated American Standard Version (UASV)

²⁹ Now it came about at midnight that the Lord struck all the firstborn in the land of Egypt, from the firstborn of Pharaoh who sat on his throne to the firstborn of the captive who was in the dungeon, and all the firstborn of cattle. ³⁰ And Pharaoh rose up in the night, he and all his servants and all the Egyptians. And there was a great cry in Egypt, for there was not a house where someone was not dead.

When we consider that the Egyptian people had no control over Pharaoh's decision to not let Israel go, how are we to understand that God, could slay every firstborn in Egypt, who is the epitome of love? Part of the answer lays only a few verses away, 12:38, which states that "And a mixed multitude [of Egyptians] went up also with them; and flocks, and herds, even very much cattle."

The firstborn of the Egyptians, who, after the first nine plagues decided that they were with the only true God, Jehovah, were not slayed. Therefore, we cannot say that the other Egyptians were not responsible, because they still stubbornly chose to cling to Pharaoh as their god. Like others, at any given time, every Egyptian could have avoided the plagues, by siding with Moses' God. Moreover, those who sided with Pharaoh could have changed his mind on the issue by having a complete uprising, and causing him to alter his decision, or having him removed. Notice that after the tenth plague, the Egyptians chose to involve themselves, whereas they had not before.

Exodus 12:33 Updated American Standard Version (UASV)

³³ The Egyptians urged the people, to send them out of the land in haste, for they said, "We will all be dead."

There is nothing prior to this point that shows the Egyptians making it know to Pharaoh that they wanted the Israelites out of the land. They were likely more concerned with losing their slaves. Therefore, they are not as innocent as some would presume. The punishment was for the horrendous treatment of God's people, by the whole of Egypt, not just the Pharaoh and his household. Below is just one incident of the Egyptian effort to keep the Israelites powerless.

Exodus 1:16, 22 Updated American Standard Version (UASV)

[16] and he said, "When you are helping the Hebrew women to give birth and see them upon the birthstool, if it is a son, then you will put him to death; but if it is a daughter, then she will live." [22] And Pharaoh commanded all his people, saying, "Every son who is born you will throw into the Nile, and every daughter you will let live."

Exodus 12:14 By what internal evidence does the Bible fix the date of Israel's Exodus from Egypt?

Exodus 12:40-41 Updated American Standard Version (UASV)

[40] Now the time that the sons of Israel dwelled in Egypt was four hundred and thirty years. [41] And at the end of four hundred and thirty years, on that very day, all the armies of Jehovah[72] went out from the land of Egypt.

In looking at the expression "Who dwelt," the Hebrew verb is plural, and the relative pronoun 'asher´, 'who,' can apply to the 'sons of Israel' as opposed to the 'dwelling.' The Greek Septuagint renders 12:40, "But the dwelling of the sons of Israel which they dwelt **in the land of Egypt and in the land of Canaan** [was] four hundred and thirty years long." (Bold mine) In addition, the Samaritan *Pentateuch* reads, ". . . in the land of Canaan and in the land of Egypt." The first century Jewish Historian Josephus wrote in *Jewish Antiquities*, "They left Egypt in the month of Xanthicus, on the fifteenth day of the lunar month; four hundred and thirty years after our forefather Abraham came into Canaan, but two hundred and fifteen years only after Jacob removed into Egypt."[73] It is all too clear that the 430-year period encompasses 215 years from the time Abraham enters Canaan, and 215 years in Egypt, starting from the time Jacob moves to Egypt. We now turn to the Apostle Paul, who also shows that this 430-year period began when Abraham crossed the Euphrates and

---

[72] **Jehovah of armies**: (Heb. *jhvh tsaba*) literally means an army of soldiers, or military forces (Gen. 21:22; Deut. 20:9). It can also be used figuratively, "the sun and the moon and the stars, all the armies of heaven." (Deut. 4:19) **In the plural form, it is also used of the Israelites forces as well.** (Ex. 6:26; 7:4; Num. 33:1; Psa. 44:9) However, the "armies" in the expression "Jehovah of armies" is a reference to the angelic forces primarily, if not exclusively.

[73] Flavius Josephus and William Whiston, *The Works of Josephus: Complete and Unabridged* (Peabody: Hendrickson, 1987).

entered into the Promise Land, validating the Abrahamic covenant and ended at the Israelites Exodus out of Egypt.

Galatians 3:16-18 Updated American Standard Version (UASV)

[16] Now the promises were spoken to Abraham and to his seed. He does not say, "And to seeds," as referring to many, but rather to one, "And to your seed," that is, Christ. [17] What I am saying is this: the Law, which came four hundred and thirty years later [same year as the Exodus], does not invalidate a [the Abrahamic] covenant previously ratified by God, so as to nullify the promise. [18] For if the inheritance is based on law, it is no longer based on a promise; but God has granted it to Abraham by means of a promise.

Now, we simply measure chronologically from the time that Abraham entered the Land of Canaan, validating, until the Israelite exodus from Egypt.

- **Genesis 12:4-5** (ESV) [4] ... Abram was **seventy-five years old** when he departed from Haran. (At this time the Abrahamic covenant goes into effect.)

- **Genesis 21:5** (ESV) [5] Abraham was a hundred years old when his son Isaac was born to him. (**25 years**)

- **Genesis 25:26** (ESV) [26] ... Isaac was **sixty years old** when she bore them. (**60 years**)

- **Genesis 47:9** (ESV) [9] And Jacob said to Pharaoh, "The days of the years of my sojourning are **130 years** ..."

- Total (215 years) in the land of Canaan

- The other 215 years were spent in Egypt.

Exodus 14:21-29 How is it that 2-3 million people were able to cross the Red Sea in a mere 24 hours?

We need not always assume the most difficult setting when we are presented with a difficulty. First, the text is not absolute in the it was just that one day. Exodus 14:21 states that, "Moses stretched out his hand over the sea; and Jehovah caused the sea to go back by a strong east wind all the night, and made the sea dry land, and the waters were divided." Now, verse 22 of chapter 14 does seem to give the reader the impression that they crossed the next morning, "and the children of Israel went into the midst of the sea upon the dry ground: and the waters were a wall unto them on their right hand, and on their left." Thereafter, verse 24 states, "and it came to pass in the morning watch, that Jehovah looked forth upon the army of the Egyptians through the pillar of fire and of cloud, and threw the Egyptian army into a panic." Then, verse 26 states, "Then Jehovah said to Moses, 'Stretch out your hand over the sea, that the water may come back upon the Egyptians, upon their chariots, and upon their horsemen.'" The account does not offer an indication of time, so there is no need to assume that the Israelites crossed in that morning alone.

Second, we need not assume that they crossed in some single file line, even though much artwork suggest such. The crossing could have been 1-3 miles wide. Therefore, the Israelites could have crossed in as little as 3-6 hours. We can picture an organized type army march, with no panic, or trampling of people. The Israelites had entered the sea bed and were far into the crossing, when Jehovah moved the cloud that had been blocking them off from the Egyptians, to the front, allowing the Egyptians to see them. The size of the opening is highlighted here, because the very large Egyptian army entered the sea bed, bent on recapturing their slaves. Then, we are told that "in the morning watch [about **2:00 a.m. to 6:00 a.m.**], that Jehovah looked forth upon the army of the Egyptians through the pillar of fire and of cloud, and threw the Egyptian army into a panic." (14:24)

By the time of sunrise, the Israelites, were safely on the eastern side of the Red Sea. Then, 'Moses stretched out his hand over the sea, so that the water may come back upon the Egyptians, upon their chariots, and upon their horsemen.' (14:26) At this "the sea returned to its normal course when the morning appeared. And as the Egyptians fled into it, Jehovah threw the Egyptians into the midst of the sea." (14:27) Here again, we see another indicator of a wide opening into the Red Sea, because if it had been a narrow opening, there would be no need to mention any attempt at fleeing the sea caving in on them, because it would have been instantaneous.

The Bible critics argue that the Hebrew *yamsuph* ("Red Sea") literally means "sea of rushes, or, reeds, bulrushes," and as a result the Israelites crossed, not the arm of the Red Sea known as the Gulf of Suez, but a sea of reeds, a swampy place such as the Bitter Lakes region. However, the Septuagint renders *yamsuph* with the Greek *erythra thalassa*, meaning, literally, "Red Sea." Moreover, both Luke (quoting Stephen in Acts) and the Apostle Paul use this same Greek word in their referring to the Exodus account.—Ac 7:36; Heb. 11:29.

Additionally, the account would have been nothing special if they crossed in a marsh, not to mention the impossibility of how the Egyptian army could have been covered by the Red Sea. (Heb. 11:29; Ex 15:5) Thus, it is evident that such an overwhelming inundation would be impossible in a marsh. Besides, in a shallow marsh dead bodies would not wash up on the seashore, as actually took place, so that "Israel saw the Egyptians dead on the seashore." (Ex 14:22-31) Moses and Joshua wrote of this breathtaking miracle, but it was Paul, who said the Israelites had been baptized into Moses by way of the cloud and the Red Sea. This means that the waters that were held up on both sides had to be above their heads, with the cloud above them. (1 Corinthians 10:1-2)

Exodus 20:4 Why the command to not make carved images, when he had commanded them to make images at times?

(See comments on Ex. 25:18)

Exodus 20:5a Why is Almighty God Jealous?

Jehovah defines himself as "a jealous God."[74] (Ex 20:5; De 4:24; 5:9; 6:15) He also says: "for thou shall worship no other god: for Jehovah, whose name is Jealous, is a jealous God." (Ex 34:14, ASV) What would the Almighty God need to be jealous of and how are we to understand that Jealousy? He certainly does not need to be envious of any other, as they are created being by him. He is the owner of everything, and gives generously to all who love him, so it is no selfishly jealous, an imperfect human characteristic. His jealousy is a zeal or an enthusiastic passion for his holy name (personal name and reputation), to which he himself has said: "Therefore thus says the Lord Jehovah: Now will I bring back the captivity of Jacob, and have mercy upon the whole house of Israel; and I will be jealous for my holy name. Eze 39:25

Exodus 20:5b Does Jehovah God punish the guilt of the parents on the children on the third and on the fourth generations of those hating him?

We must consider the context. Jehovah instituted the Law covenant with the Israelite nation, to which they agreed to be obedient. They said as one,

Exodus 19:8 Updated American Standard Version (UASV)

8 All the people answered together and said, "All that Jehovah has spoken we will do!" And Moses brought back the words of the people to Jehovah.

---

[74] Or, "a God exacting exclusive devotion (zealous); a God not tolerating rivalry." Heb., 'El qanna''; Gr., Theos' zelotes'.

The whole nation of Israel entered themselves into this covenant with Jehovah God, where if they were obedient, Jehovah blessed the nation in many ways; however, if they disobeyed, he simply removed his special blessing, and they would be subject to the difficulties of life like any other nation. Thus, Exodus 20:5 is not directed to individuals, but the nation as a whole.

When the Israelite nation remained obedient to the covenant, they benefited by the blessings that Jehovah bestowed upon them. (Lev. 26:3-8) However, when they were disobedient, the opposite took place, as a result of his removing his extra blessings that he was bestowing on them (a protective hedge about them), they were subject to the elements that every other nation was subject too. (Judg. 2:11-18) When the nation as a whole disobeyed, there was undoubtedly a number that remained obedient to the Law, regardless of what the whole was doing. (1 Ki. 19:14, 18) However, the blessing came as a result of the nation's obedience, so when the majority lost that blessing, the few would feel the loss as well. However, Jehovah still expressed loving-kindness toward them. (Jer. 52:3-11, 27)

Furthermore, there were times that the Nation of Israel became not only disobedient, but unashamedly, grossly rebellious in the extreme in their violation of Jehovah's Law. At times they would be conquered by other petty nations that surrounded them, such as the days of the Judges. In another case, northern Israel was conquered by Assyria and taken captive, while Southern Judah was taken captive by Babylon for seventy years. Of course, this would have affect the individual as well. Thus, there was three to four generations that suffered because of the nation's gross sin, just as Exodus 20:5 said would happen.

In addition, the Scriptures contain moments where individual families suffered as a result of the parents disobedience. For example, you have the High Priest Eli, who offended Jehovah, because he failed to punish, or even remove his worthless, immoral sons as priests. (1 Sam. 2:12-16, 22-25) Clearly, Eli had "honored [his] sons more than [Jehovah] by making [themselves] fat from the best of all the offerings of [God's] people Israel." Thus, it was decreed that the family of Eli would be cut off from the high priesthood, which began with Eli's great-grand-son, Abiathar. (1 Sam. 2:29-36; 1 Ki. 2:27)

1 Kings 2:27 Updated American Standard Version (UASV)

27 So Solomon drove out Abiathar from being priest to Jehovah, thus fulfilling the word which Jehovah had spoken concerning the house of Eli in Shiloh.

Jehovah is the Creator and the designer of life, who has the right to exercise his authority over his creation. Moreover, he does so in according to his righteous and just standards. Just like anything else in this life that Adam and Eve helped us into, we are subject to the results of other's actions. Even so, those who remain obedient, Jehovah "hears the cry of distress from the needy." Yes, individuals, who remain faithful and look to Jehovah, will receive his favor by their being obedient to his Word, our guide through this wicked age. (Job 34:28) And there are times, when some that are being used by God to carry out his will and purposes, are afflicted by the actions of the many, to which he will miraculously bring relief. However, we must understand, this is the extreme exception to the rule of allowing man to walk on his own.

Exodus 20:8-11 Are Christians wrong for worshipping on Sunday?

Ex. 31:16, 17: "Therefore the people of Israel shall keep the Sabbath, observing the Sabbath throughout their generations, as a covenant forever. It is **a sign** forever **between me and the people of Israel** that in six days the Lord made heaven and earth, and on the seventh day he rested and was refreshed." (ESV)

You will notice that this a 'sign between God and the people of Israel.' This could not be the case if it involved all peoples keeping the Sabbath. The Hebrew word rendered "forever" in the ESV and other translations is ohlam, which carries the meaning of a period of time that, from the standpoint of the time it was uttered or penned, is indefinite or the end is out of sight but long-lasting. Therefore, it can carry the meaning of forever, but can also carry the meaning of an indefinite period of time. For example, you find ohlam at Numbers 25:13, where it is applied to the priesthood, and the ESV renders it "a perpetual priesthood." Now, it is commonly understand, as well as Scripturally understood that the priesthood ended, some 1,500 years later. (Heb. 7:12)

Romans 10:4 Updated American Standard Version (UASV)

⁴ For **Christ is the end of the law** for righteousness to everyone who believes.

Here you will notice that "Christ is the end of the law," and the Sabbath was a part of that law. The ransom sacrifice of Christ brought that law to an end. The Israelites were able to have a righteous standing before God by keeping the Mosaic Law as best they could, and offering animal sacrifices where they fell short. Christians maintain a righteous standing before God by their faith in Christ, not on keeping a weekly Sabbath. See also, Galatians 4:9-11 and Ephesians 2:13-16.

Colossians 2:13-16 Updated American Standard Version (UASV)

13 And you, who were dead in your trespasses and the uncircumcision of your flesh, God made alive together with him, having forgiven us all our trespasses, **14** having canceled out **the certificate of debt** consisting of decrees against us, which was hostile to us; and he has taken it out of the way, having nailed it to the cross.[75] **15** having disarmed the rulers and authorities, he made a public display of them openly, triumphing over them by it.[76]

Let no Man Pass Judgment on You Based on Misinterpretation

16 Therefore **let no man judge you about what you eat and drink** or about the observance of a festival or of the new moon **or of a sabbath day.**[77]

There is a bit of irony when you come across those that suggest we are obligated to keep the Sabbath. Usually, they are not aware that if you are going to follow it, you must keep all of its biblical nuances. If an Israelite under the Mosaic Law violated the Sabbath, and was found guilty, he was to be stoned to death by the whole community. (Exodus 31:14; Numbers 15:32-35) Once you disclose that fact to them, they generally start back tracking, suggesting that we do not have to follow all of its details. As you may also have noted from the text above, to have a righteous standing before God is no longer accomplished by observing the Sabbath that had been given to Israel.

How did Sunday come to be the day of worship?

Christ was resurrected on the first day of the week (now called Sunday), and the early Christians in the book of Acts, many times, they had a worship service on Sunday. (Acts 20:7; 1 Cor. 16:2) Also, there is the interpretation of Revelation 1:10, where John is describing the visions that he was having, and said he "was **in the Spirit on the Lord's day,** and I heard behind me a loud voice like a trumpet." Many reason that "on the Lord's Day" referred to the first day of the week, Sunday, in honor of Jesus' resurrection, by the time John penned the book of Revelation in 96 C.E. It should be noted that the New Testament gives no explicit instruction to set Sunday aside a sacred day.

Three options have been suggested for its meaning: (1) It may be a reference to the eschatological day of the Lord, so that John is transported to the time of the eschaton (so

---

[75] σταυρός **stauros**; from the same as *2476; an upright stake,* hence *a cross* (the Rom. instrument of crucifixion):—cross(27).–NASB Dictionaries

[76] i.e. the cross; it could also be rendered *through him*

[77] Or *days*

115

Bullinger 1909: 12; Walvoord 1966: 42); but neither the language here nor the contents of 1:12-20 make that likely, for the NT commonly uses the genitive [kuriou] (*kyriou*, Lord's) to designate the "day of the Lord," while John here has the adjective. (2) It may refer to Easter Sunday as the day of the parousia within the confines of Easter liturgy (M. Shepherd 1960; Strand 1966–67); but this is highly speculative, and this view did not arise until at least a century later. (3) Most likely this phrase refers to Sunday, chosen by the early church on the basis of the resurrection as the day of worship (Stott 1965–66; Bauckham 1982: 221–50). (Osborne 2002, 84)

Considering that there is no real clear command, only inference, the day should not be considered a sacred day. The rendering of John 1:10 can just as easily be he "was in the Spirit **in** the Lord's day," which would give credence to number one in the above commentary; he was transported to the Lord's Day, a future eschatological time. Having said all of that, there is nothing intrinsically wrong with Sunday, and serves just fine as a day of worship. In conclusion, the Sabbath Day of Saturday was set aside for Israel and Israel alone. Jesus Christ's ransom sacrifice ended that system, and we are now under the Law of Christ. Sunday is a great day for worship, but it should not be given a special sacred status, because the decision to go to this day is only based on inference, not an explicit command, as the Lord's Supper was.

Luke 22:19 Updated American Standard Version (UASV)

[19] And he [Jesus] took bread, and when he had given thanks, he broke it and gave it to them, saying, "This is my body, which is given for you. **Do this in remembrance of me**."[78]

1 Corinthians 11:24-25 Updated American Standard Version (UASV)

[24] and when he had given thanks, he broke it, and said, "This is my body, which is for you. **Do this in remembrance of me**."[79] [25] In the same way also he took the cup, after supper, saying, "This cup is the new covenant in my blood. **Do this**, as often as you drink it, **in remembrance of me**."[80]

---

[78] I.e., *as my memorial*

[79] I.e., *as my memorial*

[80] I.e., *as my memorial*

Exodus 20:13 Here we read do not "murder."[81] Yet, at Exodus 21:12, we are commanded "whoever strikes a man so that he dies shall be put to death."

Exodus 20:13 King James Version (KJV)	**Exodus 20:13** American Standard Version (ASV)
13 Thou shalt not kill.	13 Thou shalt not kill.
Exodus 20:13 English Standard Version (ESV)	**Exodus 20:13** New King James Version (NKJV)
13 "You shall not murder.	13 "You shall not murder.

The Problem arises in our older translations, such as the 1611 King James Version and the 1901 American Standard Version, as they **incorrectly** render the Hebrew word ratsach, as "kill." However, ratsach here clearly refers to deliberate and unlawful killing, murder. If it were **incorrectly** rendered "kill," this would be the taking of another life, which could be intentional and premeditative (murder), or it could be by accident (manslaughter), or it could be by negligence (negligent homicide). God was not regulating accidental or negligence in this command; he was regulating the willful premeditated taking of a life, murder. Therefore, the more correct rendering is found in the in the English Standard Version above, as well as the New King James Version, and other modern day translations. There is no contradiction here. Exodus 20:13 is a command to not deliberately, premeditatedly take the life of another, murder. Exodus 21:12 is the capital punishment for committing murder, and is not murder. From the days of Noah (Gen 9:6), humans had been authorized by God, to administer capital punishment for murder.

Exodus 21:22-23 Are unborn children worth less in the eyes of God?

Exodus 21:22-23 Updated American Standard Version (UASV)

22 "'And if men struggle with each other, and injure a pregnant woman, so that her child comes out [prematurely], and yet there is no **fatality** results [ason, Or "serious injury."]; he shall be surely fined, as the

---

[81] The Hebrew word also covers causing human death through carelessness or negligence

woman's husband shall lay upon him; and he shall pay as the judges determine. ²³ But if there is a **fatality** [*ason*], then he shall give life for life

Some translations like the *Revised Standard Version* below render the verses as though the woman is the main focus of the law. However, this just is not the case, as the Hebrew focuses on a serious injury or a fatality to either the mother or the child.

Exodus 21:22-23 Updated American Standard Version (UASV)

²² "If men should struggle with each other and they hurt a pregnant woman **and her children come out,**⁸² yet there is no injury, he shall **surely be fined** as the woman's husband lays on him, and he shall pay as the judges determine. ²³ And if **any harm follows**, you shall give **life for life,**

The picture that one could get from renderings like the RSV is that the only grave unease here is for the woman, not the unborn or premature child. Someone could determine from such a translation that if the hurt caused the death of a prematurely born child but no other harm to the woman, the guilty man was merely to receive a fine, as was the conclusion of Josephus of the first-century.

Here is how the first-century Jewish historian **Flavius Josephus** paraphrased these verses:

> He that kicks a woman with child, so that the woman miscarry, let him pay a fine in money, as the judges shall determine, as having diminished the multitude by the destruction of what was in her womb; and let money also be given the woman's husband by him that kicked her; but if she die of the stroke, let him also be put to death, the law judging it equitable that life should go for life.⁸³

> Philo and others appear to have understood this law (Exod. 21:22, 25) better than Josephus, who seems to allow, that though the infant in the mother's womb, even after the mother were quick, and so the infant had a rational soul, were killed by the stroke upon the mother, yet if the mother escaped, the offender should only be fined, and not put to death; while the law seems rather to mean, that if the infant in that case be killed, though the mother escape, the offender must be put to death; and not only when the mother is killed, as Josephus

---

⁸² I.e., *she gives birth prematurely*

⁸³ Flavius Josephus and William Whiston, The Works of Josephus: Complete and Unabridged (Peabody: Hendrickson, 1996), Book IV, Chapter viii, paragraph 33.

understood it. It seems this was the exposition of the Pharisees in the days of Josephus.[84]

Alternatively, the translators of the Greek Septuagint Version of the Old Testament saw things differently.

Exodus 21:22-23 Septuagint Version of the Old Testament (LXX)

[22] And if two men strive and smite a woman with child, and her child be born imperfectly formed [or, "she miscarry of an embryo"], he shall be forced to pay a penalty: as the woman's husband may lay upon him, he shall pay with a valuation. [23] But if it be perfectly formed, he shall give life for life.[85]

Therefore, these translators believed that if what was miscarried were too young to have developed recognizable human features, a monetary fine would suffice. However, if the fetus was "perfectly formed" the man who gave cause to the loss of life of the prematurely born child must pay life for life. With such disagreement going on, it is best that we go to the original Hebrew.

If you consider the possible outcomes, there are more than you may have thought. Let us look to the woman first. She could have suffered anything from a minor injury to a serious injury, even crippled, but no loss of life. Alternatively, she could have lost her life. Next, think of the child or children developing in her womb. If she was far enough along in her pregnancy, being struck could have brought about a premature birth. Then, there is the possible hurt of the unborn losing its life and the mother's hurt of having lost her child(ren). Clearly, the law had to cover a far range of outcomes.

Let us look at the law to see what it really said? Below is the literal rendering in the Hebrew-English Interlinear by Dr. G. R. Berry (read from right to left)

---

[84] Ibid., footnote

[85] Lancelot Charles Lee Brenton, *The Septuagint Version of the Old Testament: English Translation* (London: Samuel Bagster and Sons, 1870), Ex 21:22–25.

וְכִי־יִנָּצוּ	אֲנָשִׁים	וְנָגְפוּ
contend when And	,men	strike they and

אִשָּׁה	הָרָה	22	וְיָצְאוּ	יְלָדֶיהָ
²woman a	¹pregnant,		and goes forth	her child,

וְלֹא יִהְיֶה אָסוֹן	עָנוֹשׁ	יֵעָנֵשׁ
and not is injury;	surely	he shall be fined,

כַּאֲשֶׁר	יָשִׁית	עָלָיו	בַּעַל
as	put may	him upon	the husband of

הָאִשָּׁה	וְנָתַן	בִּפְלִלִים :
the woman,	and he shall give	with the judges.

וְאִם־אָסוֹן	יִהְיֶה	וְנָתַתָּה	נֶפֶשׁ
And if injury	is,	(and) thou shalt give	soul 23

תַּחַת	נֶפֶשׁ :
for	soul,

The Hebrew word here rendered "injury" ("harm," Revised Standard Version) is *ason*. According to *The Hebrew and Aramaic Lexicon of the Old Testament*, ason means "fatal accident."[86] Therefore, the rendering "fatality" in the Updated American Standard Version allows one to more fully understand what the law had to say.

The question that begs to be asked is, 'who is the term "fatality" applying to? It is to the mother alone, the child, or the mother and the child? The Jerusalem Bible reads:

Exodus 21:22-23 Jerusalem Bible (JB)

22 "'If, when men come to blows, they hurt a woman who is pregnant and she suffers a miscarriage, though *she* does not die of it, the man responsible must pay the compensation demanded of him, . . . **23** But should *she* die, you shall give life for life. (Italics added)

The Jerusalem Bible is correct in the choice rendering of "fatality," but they go beyond translation into the realms of interpretation when

---

[86] Ludwig Koehler, Walter Baumgartner, M.E.J Richardson and Johann Jakob Stamm, *The Hebrew and Aramaic Lexicon of the Old Testament*, electronic ed. (Leiden; New York: E.J. Brill, 1999), 73.

they insert "she," which will cause the reader to believe that if the woman lost the child in a premature birth, but lived, the offender would only receive a fine. Is this really, what the Hebrew text says?

The above-mentioned interlinear reading discloses that the Hebrew does not limit the application of "injury" (fatality) to just the mother. Therefore, the *Commentary on the Old Testament* says that a fine was satisfactory only when "no injury [fatal accident] was done either to the woman or the child that was born." The commentary goes on to show that if what the Law merely meant was, if the mother lived, regardless of the child, only a fine would be imposed; then, the Hebrew text would have had the ending lah, "to her." Therefore, the verse would have read, 'When men struggle and they strike a pregnant woman and her child goes forth and no injury [fatality] is done to her, a fine must be paid.' Yet, the commentary concluded, "The omission of lah, also, apparently renders it impracticable to refer the words to [an] injury done to the woman alone."[87]

Hebrew scholar U. Cassuto (A Commentary on the Book of Exodus [Jerusalem: Magnes Press, 1967]) asserts, "The passage does not deal with miscarriage" (but is speaking of premature birth), thus assuming that the lxx rendering was conjectural and that the Hb. must and can be comprehended on its own. N. L. Collins points out that the verb used in 21:22 to refer to men fighting (יִנָּצוּ from nṣh) always conveys the sense of two people fighting and thus the specificity in the lxx and Syriac translations (two men) is simply proper ancient translation and not the addition of a concept by periphrastic translators ("Notes on the Text of Exodus XXI:22," VT 43 [1993]: 289–301).

The verses are about the sacredness of life, the life of the woman, or her unborn child. If the woman or her unborn child was seriously injured by a premature birth, or either lost their life, the man would be punished to the degree of deliberateness and the circumstances. If there was no loss of life of either mother or child, there would be a fine. If there was a loss of life of either mother or child, there would be a death penalty.

The Hebrew word *yatsa*, has the following range of meaning, "to go out, come out; to bring out, lead forth; produce; to be brought out; emptied; by extension: to grow (of plants), to have offspring."[88] It is the word that is commonly used for giving birth in the Hebrew Old Testament, and "miscarriage" is a mistranslation. It should be noted that if

---

[87] Carl Friedrich Keil and Franz Delitzsch, Commentary on the Old Testament. (Peabody, MA: Hendrickson, 2002).

[88] William D. Mounce, Mounce's Complete Expository Dictionary of Old & New Testament Words (Grand Rapids, MI: Zondervan, 2006), 951.

Moses wanted to say "miscarriage," there was a Hebrew term for that, *shakol*. Finally, whether harm came to the child (*yeled*) or the mother, the punishment was the same.

Exodus 21:29-30 Why was the death penalty set aside for some murders?

At first glance, there seems to be an issue when we compare Numbers 35:31 and Exodus 21:30. Is there really a conflict between the two verses? Let us look.

Numbers 35:31 Updated American Standard Version (UASV)

³¹ Moreover, you shall not take ransom for the soul of a murderer who is guilty of death, but he shall surely be put to death.

Exodus 21:29-30 Updated American Standard Version (UASV)

²⁹ But if the ox has been accustomed to gore in the past, and its owner has been warned but has not kept it in, and it kills a man or a woman, the ox shall be stoned, and its owner also shall be put to death. ³⁰ If a ransom is laid on him,⁸⁹ then he shall give for the redemption of his soul whatever is laid on him.⁹⁰

There is no conflict here, as one was a willful, purposeful murder, while the other was what we would call a negligent homicide.⁹¹ In the case of the murder, there was the actual intention of taking the life of another, a malice act. In the negligent homicide, the offender did not intend to take the life of another, even if he was warned that someone could get hurt beforehand. (Ex 21:28-29) Even today, there is no death penalty for negligent homicide; there is jail time and a fine, restitution. The Israelites did not have jails and prisons.

---

⁸⁹ I.e. a ransom is *demanded of him*

⁹⁰ I.e. whatever is *demanded of him*

⁹¹ Negligent homicide is a criminal charge brought against people who, through criminal negligence, allow others to die. Negligent Homicide is a lesser included offense to first and second degree murder, in the sense that someone guilty of this offense can expect a more lenient sentence, often with imprisonment time comparable to manslaughter. Wikipedia.

Exodus 23:19 What would be the reason for God prohibiting the Israelites from boiling a kid (young goat) in its mother's milk?

This prohibition appears three times in the Mosaic Law. (Ex 23:19; 34:26; Deut. 14:21) This prohibition helps the reader to appreciate Jehovah God's decency, his concern for his created beings, and his sensitivity.

If we pause for a moment and consider what God created the milk for; to nourish the young goat and help it grow. Therefore, to boil a young goat in its mother's milk would be contrary to the arrangement that God had set in place.

There are other suggestions as to why God established this prohibition: (1) it was an idolatrous practice, (2) it was an occult practice to improve the productivity of the land, (3) the belief that milk and meat were difficult to digest, (4) it would be disrespectful to the feast of ingathering, (5) and so on.

In reality, the Law had a number of comparable restrictions against brutality toward animals and protections against working in opposition to the natural order of things. For example, the Law encompassed instructions that prohibited sacrificing an animal except when it had been with its mother for at least seven days, sacrificing both an animal and its young on the same day, and taking from a nest both a mother and her eggs or young.—Leviticus 22:27, 28; Deuteronomy 22:6, 7.

Exodus 24:9-11 Has God ever truly been seen or not, is it even possible?

Moses once expressed the desire to see God. At Exodus 33:18-20, we read:

Exodus 33:18-20 Updated American Standard Version (UASV)

[18] And he [Moses] said, "Please show me your glory." [19] And he said, "I will make all my goodness pass before your face and will proclaim before you my name 'Jehovah.' And I will be gracious to whom I will be gracious, and will show mercy on whom I will show mercy. [20] But he said, "You cannot see my face, for no man can see me and live!"

What did God permit Moses to see? It was his passing goodness or glory. Take note of what 33:21-23 states,

Exodus 33:21-23 Updated American Standard Version (UASV)

21 And Jehovah said, "Behold, there is a place by me where you shall stand on the rock, **22** and while my glory passes by I will put you in a cleft of the rock, and I will cover you with my hand until I have passed by. **23** Then I will take away my hand, and you shall see my back, but my face shall not be seen.

John 1:18 Updated American Standard Version (UASV)

18 No one has seen God at any time; the only begotten god**92** who is in the bosom of the Father,**93** that one has made him fully known.

When we consider what Jehovah Himself told Moses, and what the Apostle John said, it is all too clear that Moses merely saw the afterglow of God's glory pass by. Even then, Moses still needed divine protection to survive the event. Clearly Moses did not see God.

Exodus 33:11 says that Moses saw God "face to face." This expression of "face to face" is not meant to mean that Moses was in visual contact with Jehovah's face. It is an expression that is refers to the manner of the communication. The expression simply means a two-way conversation. It is easier understood today, as a person can carry on a two-way conversation with another person on the other side of earth with a cellphone, and not seeing each other.

Things were different with Moses when he communicated with God, as it was not by visions, as was true of other prophets. This is stated:

Numbers 12:6-8 Updated American Standard Version (UASV)

6 And he said, "Hear my words: If there is a prophet among you, I the Lord make myself known to him in a vision; I speak with him in a dream.
7 Not so with my servant Moses. He is faithful in all my house. **8** With him I speak mouth to mouth, clearly, and not in riddles, and he beholds the form of Jehovah. Why then were you not afraid to speak against my servant Moses?"

Moses beheld the "form of Jehovah" when he, Aaron his brother, as well as others were on Mount Sinai.

Exodus 24:10 Updated American Standard Version (UASV)

10 and they saw the God of Israel; and under his feet was what seemed like a sapphire pavement, as clear as the sky itself.

---

92 Jn 1:18: "only-begotten god", P⁶⁶ℵ*BC*Lsyrʰᵐᵍ·ᵖ; **[V1]** "the only-begotten god," P⁷⁵ℵ¹33copᵇᵒ; **[V2]** "the only-begotten Son." AC³(Wˢ)ΘΨf1·¹³ MajVgSyrᶜ

93 Or *at the Father's side*

However, in what sense did these men see "the God of Israel," because God had told him, "you cannot see my face, for man shall not see me and live." Verse 11 of Exodus 24 goes on to say, "He did not lay his hand on the chief men of the sons of Israel; they beheld God, and ate and drank." What exactly did they behold?

Jehovah God has no reason to come down from heaven itself in order to deliver messages to humans. This would be like the President of the United States, getting in Air force One, to go to some small town in the Mid-West, to deliver a message to one of his congressmen. It is almost nonsensical, and the press would make such a big deal if it ever happened. Now, imagine the Creator of everything, going to visit a human personally. There are only three incidents when God's voice was heard from heaven, all coming from the New Testament three and a half years of Jesus' ministry. (Matthew 3:17; 17:5; John 12:28)

Who were making the personal visits for God to the earth, from the time of Abraham forward? Jehovah God used his angels (messengers), as representatives of himself. Even when Moses received the Law, these angelic messengers transmitted it.

Galatians 3:19 Updated American Standard Version (UASV)

[19] Why, then, the Law? It was added because of transgressions, until the seed should arrive to whom the promise had been made; and it was transmitted through angels by the hand of a mediator.

Moses even spoke to an angel that came in the place of God. This angel was God's spokesperson, and he spoke to Moses as if it were Jehovah God himself speaking, because in a representative way it was.

Acts 7:38 Updated American Standard Version (UASV)

[38] This is the one who was in the congregation in the wilderness with the angel who spoke to him at Mount Sinai, and with our fathers; and he received living sayings[94] to give to us.

This holds true of the angel that visited Moses at the thorn bush as well, he was the mouthpiece of Jehovah God, speaking as though he were him. Exodus 3:2 tells us, "And the angel of Jehovah appeared unto him in a flame of fire out of the midst of a bush." However, when we look to verse 4 we get, "And when Jehovah saw that he turned aside to see, God called to him out of the midst of the bush." Then, in verse 6 this angelic representative says, "I am the God of thy father, the God of

---

[94] **Sayings**: (Gr. *logia*, *on* [only in the plural]) A saying or message, usually short, especially divine, gathered into a collection.–Acts 7:38; Romans 3:2; Hebrews 5:12; 1 Peter 4:11.

Abraham, the God of Isaac, and the God of Jacob." Thus, when Moses was speaking with an angelic representative of God, he addressed him as though he were Jehovah God himself, and the angel would speak as such too.—Exodus 4:10.

We find a similar experience in Judges chapter 6, verses 11-22 of Gideon speaking with an angelic representative as though the angel were God himself.[95] In verse 22 Gideon even says:

Judges 6:22 Updated American Standard Version (UASV)

[22] And Gideon realized that he was the angel of Jehovah; and Gideon said, "Alas, O, my lord Jehovah! For now I have seen the angel of Jehovah face to face."

Exodus 25:18 Are All Images Idols?

Exodus 25:18 Updated American Standard Version (UASV)

[18] And you will make two cherubim of gold; you will make them of hammered work at the two ends of the mercy seat.

While God's law forbade the making of images (Ex 20:4-5), it did not exclude making pictures of things, by embroidering, paintings or statues. This is indicated by the above text, where Jehovah commands them to make images of "two cherubim of gold." Moreover, he had also commanded that they embroider cherubs in the tabernacle cover. In addition they were to make a veil of blue and purple and scarlet yarns and fine twined linen. It was to be made with cherubim skillfully worked into it. (Ex 25:18; 26:1, 31, 33) In fact, there were representations of things all throughout the kingdom. In the inner sanctuary, they made two cherubim of olivewood. (1 Ki 6:23) In addition, around all the walls of the house they carved engraved figures of cherubim and palm trees and open flowers, in the inner and outer rooms. (1Ki 6:28-29) They had 12 copper bulls around the sea of cast metal (1 Ki 7:25, 28-29) Also, they had 12 lions that led up to the throne.—2 Chronicles 9:17-19.

These representations of things, were not used for idol worship. The images in the temple were only seen by the priests. Even so, the images were not worshiped, but were used pictorially of heavenly things (cherubs), as well as the throne of the king, and so on. (Heb. 9:24-25) Jehovah's worshipers were even forbidden to worship the real thing, the angels.—Colossians 2:18; Revelation 19:10; 22:8, 9.

---

[95] Also, consider the case of Manoah and his wife, the parents of Samson. (Judges 13:2-18)

Nevertheless, there were times when the Israelites fell off into image worship. Hezekiah, the King of Israel, removed the high places and broke the pillars and cut down the Asherah. And he broke in pieces the bronze serpent that Moses had made, for until those days the people of Israel had made offerings to it. (Num. 21:9; 2 Ki 18:1, 4) And Gideon made an ephod of it and put it in his city, in Ophrah. And all Israel whored after it there, and it became a snare to Gideon and to his family.–Judges 8:27

There is no place within Scripture, which authorizes using images to address God in prayer. In fact, this would be counter to Scripture itself, which says, "God is spirit, and those who worship him must worship in spirit and truth." (John 4:24; 2 Cor. 4:18; 5:6-7) God does not stand for idolatrous worship being mixed in with his pure worship. (Ex 32:3-10) His exact words are, "I am Jehovah, that is my name; and my glory will I not give to another, neither my praise unto graven images."–Isaiah 42:8

Exodus 31:18 Does God have fingers?

Exodus 31:18 Updated American Standard Version (UASV)

18 And he gave to Moses, when he had finished speaking with him on Mount Sinai, the two tablets of the testimony, tablets of stone, written with **the finger of God**.

While it is true that the above text says, God wrote the Ten Commandments with his finger, it is also true that Scripture says "God is spirit" (John 4:24), "For a spirit does not have flesh and bones." (Luke 24:39) Figuratively, God is spoken of as having fingers, not literally. In a nonliteral sense, it means that God is actively involved in carrying something out, like the Ten Commandments, performing miracles (Ex. 8:18-19), and creating the heavens (Psa. 8:3). It is called anthropomorphism, where an attribution of a human form, human characteristics, or human behavior is attributed to God in a nonliteral sense. God is said to have an "arm" [power] (Jer. 27:5; 32:17), "eyes" [watchfulness] (1 Pet. 3:12), and so on. While these anthropomorphism are not to be taken literally, we are expected to ascertain what they mean, and that is to be taken literally. It is literally true that God is actively involved in human affairs ("finger"), it is literally true that God is watching over us ("eyes), and it is true that He has the power to carry out his will and purposes toward us ("arm").

Exodus 32:14 Does God change his mind?

Exodus 32:14 Updated American Standard Version (UASV)	Genesis 6:6 Updated American Standard Version (UASV)
[14] And Jehovah began to feel regret[96] about the calamity which he said he would do to his people.	[6] And Jehovah regretted that he had made man on the earth, and it grieved him to his heart.

Genesis 6:6-7 Updated American Standard Version (UASV)

[6] And **Jehovah regretted that he had made man** on the earth, and it grieved him to his heart. [7] Jehovah said, "I will blot out man whom I have created from the face of the land, from man to animals to creeping things and to birds of the heavens;[97] for **I regret that I have made them**."

The English word "regret" means 'to feel sorry and sad about something previously done or said that **now appears wrong, mistaken,** or hurtful to others.' The Hebrew word (nacham) here translated "regretted" relates to a change of attitude or intention. This could not be used to suggest that God felt **that he had made a mistake** in creating man.

However, returning to our Hebrew word behind the English word, we find that Jehovah had changed his attitude or intention toward the pre-flood generation of which he said, "the wickedness of man was great in the earth, and that every intention of the thoughts of his heart was only evil continually. (Gen. 6:5) Since they had willfully rejected and disobeyed Him, it was now obligatory for Him to reject them in return. The change in their attitude mandated a resultant change in His attitude toward them. It is this change or altered situation that is conveyed by the Hebrew nacham ("repent," "be sorry about," "change one's mind about"). The Theological Wordbook of the Old Testament had this to say,

---

[96] **Feel regret over**: (nacham) Or feel regret over. The Hebrew word (nacham) translated "be sorry," "repent," "regret," "be comforted," "comfort," "reconsider" and "change one's mind" can pertain to a change of attitude or intention. God is perfect and therefore does not make mistakes in his dealings with his creation. However, he can have a change of attitude or intention as regards how humans react to his warnings. God can go from the Creator of humans to that of a destroyer of them because of his unrepentant wickedness and failure to heed his warnings. On the other hand, if they repent and turn from their wicked ways, he can be compassionate and merciful, slow to anger, and abounding in loyal love; and he will "reconsider" the calamity that he may have intended.—Genesis 6:6; Exodus 32:14; Joel 2:13.

[97] Or sky

128

Unlike man, who under the conviction of sin feels genuine remorse and sorrow, God is free from sin. Yet the Scriptures inform us that God repents (Gen 6:6–7: Ex 32:14; Jud 2:18; I Sam 15:11 et al.), i.e. he relents or changes his dealings with men according to his sovereign purposes. On the surface, such language seems inconsistent, if not contradictory, with certain passages which affirm God's immutability: "God is not a man ... that he should repent" (I Sam 15:29 contra v. 11); "The lord has sworn and will not change his mind" (Ps 110:4). When nāham is used of God, however, the expression is anthropopathic and there is not ultimate tension. From man's limited, earthly, finite perspective it only appears that God's purposes have changed. Thus the OT states that God "repented" of the judgments or "evil" which he had planned to carry out (I Chr 21:15; Jer 18:8; 26:3, 19; Amos 7:3, 6; Jon 3:10). Certainly Jer 18:7–10 is a striking reminder that from God's perspective, most prophecy (excluding messianic predictions) is conditional upon the response of men. In this regard, A. J. Heschel (The Prophets, p. 194) has said, "No word is God's final word. Judgment, far from being absolute, is conditional. A change in man's conduct brings about a change in God's judgment."[98]

The change in attitude and intention was going from the Creator of humanity to that of destroying them by means of an earth wide flood. He was very displeased with their wicked heart condition, but saved Noah and his family to continue with his plan of offering a future seed that would ransom humankind. (Gen 3:15' Matt 20:28) The evidence is that he only "regretted" those that had chosen to become so evil in their ways that they forced him to the course of destroying them. (2 Peter 2:5, 9) However, his choice to all some to survive means that his words are not applicable to His creation of mankind itself.

As a final thought, some may conclude that the "them" at the end of verse 7 is in reference to both animals and wicked mankind, but this is not the case. There is nothing in the text that would suggest that the animals had done anything to displease God. Therefore, it would be inappropriate to suggest that "them" is in reference to the animals as well. They were simply victims of man's sin, and the flood would result in their destruction as well. The antecedent of "them" need not be the immediate referent, but was to the preceding reference to "man" (Heb., ha adam), wicked mankind.

---

[98] Marvin R. Wilson, "1344 נחם" In , in Theological Wordbook of the Old Testament, ed. R. Laird Harris, Gleason L. Archer, Jr. and Bruce K. Waltke, electronic ed. (Chicago: Moody Press, 1999), 571.

APPENDIX A Defending Moses as Author of the Pentateuch

It was in the latter half of the nineteenth century that higher criticism began to be taken seriously. These critics rejected Moses as the writer of the Pentateuch, arguing instead that the accounts in Genesis, Exodus, Leviticus, Numbers, and Deuteronomy were based on four other sources [writers] written between the 10th and the 6th centuries B.C.E. To differentiate these sources one from the other, they are simply known as the "J," "E," "D," and "P" sources. The letters are the initial to the name of these alleged sources, also known as the Documentary Hypothesis.

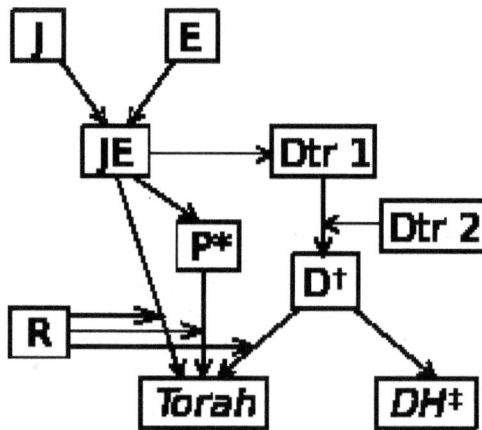

Image 1 Diagram of the Documentary Hypothesis.

*   **includes most of Leviticus**

†   **includes most of Deuteronomy**

‡   **"Deuteronomic history": Joshua, Judges, 1 & 2 Samuel, 1 & 2 Kings –**
Wikipedia

Source Criticism, a sub-discipline of Higher Criticism, is an attempt by liberal Bible scholars to discover the original sources that the Bible writer(s) [not Moses] used to pen these five books. It should be noted that most scholars who engage in higher criticism start with liberal presuppositions. Dr. Gleason L. Archer, Jr., identifies many flaws in the reasoning of those who support the Documentary Hypothesis; however, this one flaw being quoted herein is indeed the most grievous and lays the foundation for other irrational reasoning in their thinking. Identifying their problem, Archer writes, "The Wellhausen school started with the pure assumption (which they have hardly bothered to demonstrate) that Israel's religion was of merely human origin like any other, and that it was to be explained as a mere product of evolution."[99] In other words, Wellhausen and those who followed him begin with the presupposition that God's Word is *not* that at all, the Word of God, but is the word of mere man, and then they reason **into** the Scripture not **out of** the Scriptures based on that premise. As to the effect, this has on God's Word and those who hold it as such; it is comparable to having a natural disaster wash the foundation right out from under our home.

Liberal Christianity says that Moses did not pen every word from Genesis through Deuteronomy. They conclude that this is nothing more than a tradition that originated in the times that the Jews returned from their exile in Babylon in 537 B.C.E. and the destruction of Jerusalem in 70 C.E. These source critics reason that there was and is a misunderstanding of Deuteronomy 31:9, which says that Moses "[wrote] this law, and delivered it unto the priests the sons of Levi, that bare the ark of the covenant of Jehovah, and unto all the elders of Israel." They argue that Deuteronomy only implies that Moses wrote the laws of Deuteronomy chapters 12–28; moreover, this was extended into a tradition that encompassed the belief that the entire Pentateuch was *not* written by Moses.

In addition, these source critics put forth that the language of Deuteronomy chapters 12–18, as well as the historical and theological context, places the writing and completion of these five books centuries after Moses died. According to these critics, this alleged tradition of Moses being the author of the first five books of our Bible was completely accepted as fact by the time Jesus Christ arrived on the scene in the first-century C.E. These critics further argue that Jesus, the Son of God, was also duped by this tradition and simply perpetuated it when he referred to "the book of Moses" (Mark 12:26), which to the Jews at that time counted Genesis, Exodus, Leviticus, Numbers, and Deuteronomy as a book by Moses. In addition, at John 17:23, Jesus spoke of "the law of Moses," which he and all others Jews had long held to be the Pentateuch. Thus, for the critic, Jesus simply handed this misunderstood tradition off to first-century Christianity.

We have read much in previous chapters thus far about these critical scholars, but it will not hurt to review, before delving into discrediting their hypothesis. How has such extreme thinking as this Documentary Hypothesis come down to us, going from being a hypothesis to being

---

[99] 99. Gleason L. Archer, A Survey of Old Testament Introduction (Moody Publishers, Chicago, 2007), 98.

accepted as *law* in secular universities and most seminaries? What is the relationship between a hypothesis, theory, and law? In the physical sciences, there are several steps before a description of a phenomenon becomes law.

(1) **Observation:** "I noticed that objects fall to the earth."

(2) **Hypothesis:** "I think something must be pulling these objects to the earth. Let me call it gravity."

(3) **Experimentation:** "Let me put this to the test by releasing different objects from that cliff. Umm, it seems that everything I let go falls. My hypothesis seems to be right."

(4) **Theory:** "I have noticed that every time I release an object, and wherever I do it, over the sidewalk, from the 32nd floor of that office building and even from the cruise ship—they fall to the earth as if pulled by something. It happens often enough to be called a theory."

(5) **Law:** "Well, this has consistently been occurring over the years. It must be absolutely true and therefore a Law."

Where does the "Documentary Hypothesis" fit into this scheme? Wellhausen *et al.* made certain **Observations** and then produced a **Hypothesis** to explain what they saw. I would argue that is as far as they made it in following the formula for the scientific method.

The Forefathers of Source Criticisms

Abraham Ibn Ezra (1089–1164) Ibn Ezra was, by far, the most famous Bible scholar of medieval times. True enough, he may have questioned the idea that Moses wrote the entire Torah; however, he chose not to do this in an outward way; he chose to be more subtle in presenting such an idea. For Ibn Ezra, several verses seemed not to have come from Moses, but one verse stood out above the others. Deuteronomy 1:1 reads: "These are the words that Moses spoke to all of Israel beyond the Jordan." The east side of the Jordan would be "this" side with the west side being the "other side." (Numbers 35:14; Joshua 22:4) The point of his contention here being the fact that Moses was never on the other side of the Jordan, the west side, with the Israelite nation. Therefore, the question begs to be asked, Why would Moses pen "beyond," a seeming reference to the west side? This will be answered soon enough.

Thomas Hobbes (1588–1679) writes, "It is therefore sufficiently evident that the five books of Moses were written after his time, though how long after it be not so manifest." Is Hobbes a friend or foe of Christianity? Like Francis Bacon before him, he deepened the crack in the acceptance of the Bible being a source of divine authority.[100]

Benedict Spinoza (1632–1677) writes, "It is thus clearer than the sun at noon the Pentateuch was not written by Moses but by someone who lived long after Moses." Spinoza lays the groundwork for higher criticism based on logical or reasonable deduction, believing that thought and actions should be governed by reason, deductive rationalism.[101] He writes that because "There are many passages in the Pentateuch which Moses could not have written, it follows that the belief that Moses was the author of the Pentateuch is ungrounded and irrational."[102] Moses was not the only Biblical author to lose his writership at the chopping block of Spinoza. "I pass on, then, to the prophetic books ... An examination of these assures me that the prophecies therein contained have been compiled from other books ... but are only such as were collected here and there, so that they are fragmentary." Daniel did not fare so well either, he is only credited with the last five chapters of his book. Spinoza presents the notion that the 39 books of the Hebrew Old Testament were set down by none other than the Pharisees. Moreover, the prophets spoke not by God, being inspired, but of their own accord. As to the apostles, Spinoza wrote, "The mode of expression and discourse adopted by [them] in the Epistles show very clearly that the latter are not written by revelation and divine command, but merely by the natural powers and judgment of the authors." Did Matthew, Mark, Luke, and John, fare any better? Hardly! Spinoza states: "It is scarcely credible that God can have designated to narrate the life of Christ four times over, and to communicate it thus to mankind."

Spinoza had no respect for those he deemed fools because of their belief in miracles. He writes, "Anyone who seeks for the true causes of miracles and strives to understand natural phenomena as an intelligent being, and not gaze upon them like a fool, is set down and denounced as an impious heretic by those, whom the masses adore as the interpreters of nature and the gods. Such a person knows that, with the removal of ignorance, the wonder which forms their only available means for proving and preserving their authority would vanish also. . . . A miracle, whether a contravention to, or beyond nature is a mere absurdity."[103]

---

[100] Garrett, Don, *The Cambridge companion to Spinoza* (Cambridge: Cambridge University Press, 1996), 389.

[101] Richard Elliot Friedman, *Who Wrote The Bible* (San Francisco: Harper Collins, 1997), 21.

[102] R. H. M. Elwes, *A Theologico-political Treatise, and a Political Treatise* (New York, NY: Cosimo Classics , 2005), 126.

[103] Norman L. Geisler, *Inerrancy* (Grand Rapids, MI: Zondervan, 1980), 318.

Such a dogmatic disbelief in miracles is a contributing factor to Spinoza being the father of modern-day higher criticism.

Richard Simon (1638–1712). This French Catholic priest accepted Moses as the author for most of the Pentateuch, but he is the first to notice repetition with certain portions that would come to be known as doublets.

- two different creation stories

- two stories of the Abrahamic covenant

- two stories where Abraham names his son, Isaac

- two stories where Abraham claims Sarah as his sister

- two stories of Jacob's journey to Haran

- two stories where God revealed himself to Jacob at Bethel

- two stories where God changes Jacob's name to Israel

- two stories of when Moses got water from a rock at Meribah

Jean Astruc (1684–1766) This French physician and professor of medicine would, by a rather naïve observation, get the Documentary Hypothesis underway. While Astruc never denied Mosaic writership, he had observed that there seemed to be two sources for Moses' penning the early chapters of Genesis: one that favored the title God (Elohim), and another that favored the personal name of God (Jehovah). This theory seemed to carry even more support by duplicate material, as Astruc viewed Genesis chapter one as one creation account and Genesis chapter two as another. It should be kept in mind that Astruc credited Moses as the writer, but was simply looking for what Moses may have drawn on in penning the Pentateuch.[104]

David Hume (1711–1776) was an eighteenth-century Scottish philosopher whose influence on the denial of divine authority, miracles, and prophecy has had a major impact that has reached down to the twenty-first century! Hume has three major pillars that hold up his refutation of divine authority. First, he writes, "A miracle is a violation of the laws of nature."[105] The laws of nature have been with man since his start. If a person falls from a high place, he will hit the ground. If a rock is dropped into the sea, it will sink. Each morning our sun comes over the horizon and each night it goes down, and so on. Without a doubt, there

---

[104] Norman L. Geisler and William E. Nix, *A General Introduction to the Bible. Rev. and Expanded* (Chicago, IL: Moody Press, c.1986, 1996), 156.

[105] David Hume, *An Enquiry Concerning Human Understanding* (Boston, MA: Digireads.com, 2006), 65.

are laws of nature that never fail to follow their purpose. Therefore, for Hume, there is nothing that would ever violate the laws of nature. This 'conclusive evidence,' Hume felt, "is as entire as any argument from experience" that there could never be miracles.

Hume's second pillar is based on his belief that humankind is gullible. Moreover, he reasons that the masses of 'religious persons' want to believe in miracles. In addition, there have been many who have lied about so-called miracles, which have been nothing but a sham. For his third pillar, Hume argues that miracles have occurred only in the time periods of ignorance; as the enlightenment of man grew the miraculous diminished. Hume reported, "Such prodigious events never happen in our days." Hume rejected the inspiration of Scripture on two grounds: (1) he denied the possibility of miracles and prophecy, and (2) he rejected the Bible's divine authority as a whole because, to him, it was based upon perception or feeling, rather than upon fact, nor could it be proved by observation and experiment. Thus, for Hume, the result is that the Bible "contains nothing but sophistry and illusion."[106] As we can see, Hume's conclusion is obvious: Because the Bible is, in fact, not inspired, it could never be a true source of knowledge that it claims, and it is certainly not God's Word for humankind.

Johann Gottfried Eichhorn (1752–1827) took Jean Astruc's conjectures beyond Genesis to other books of the Pentateuch, arguing that the Pentateuch contained three primary sources that were distinct by vocabulary, style, and theological features. He also borrowed the phrase "higher criticism" from Presbyterian minister and scientist Joseph Priestly, and he was the first to name these alleged sources "E" (for Elohim) and "J" for Jehovah.[107]

Karl Heinrich Graf (1815–1869), aside from Julius Wellhausen, was the person we look to most for the modern documentary hypothesis. For Graf the "J" source was the earliest, composed in the ninth century B.C.E.;[108] the "E" source was written shortly thereafter. The author of Deuteronomy wrote shortly before Josiah's clearing away false worship in the seventh century B.C.E., and finally, the "P" source was written in the sixth century after the exile.

In 1878, the German Bible critic **Julius Wellhausen (1844–1918),** writing in *Prolegomena zur Geschichte Israels* (*Prolegomena to the History*

---

[106] Ibid., 90.

[107] Norman L. Geisler and William E. Nix, *A General Introduction to the Bible. Rev. and Expanded* (Chicago, IL: Moody Press, c.1986, 1996), 157.

[108] B.C.E. means "before the Common Era," which is more accurate than B.C. ("before Christ"). C.E. denotes "Common Era," often called A.D., for anno Domini, meaning "in the year of our Lord."

of Israel), popularized the ideas of the above scholars that the first five books of the Bible, as well as Joshua, were written from the 9th century into the 5th century B.C.E., over a millennium [1,000 years] after the events described.[109]

The capital letter "J" is used to represent an alleged writer. In this case it stands for any place God's personal name, Jehovah, is used. It is argued that this author is perhaps a woman as it is the only one of their presented authors who is not a priest. (Harold Bloom, *The Book of "J"*) They date the portion set out to "J" to c.850 B.C.E. Some scholars place this author in the southern portion of the Promised Land, Judah.[110]

Another writer is put forth as "E," for it stands for the portion that has Jehovah's title Elohim, God. Most higher critics place this author c.750–700 B.C.E. Unlike "J," this author "E" is said to reside in the northern kingdom of Israel. As stated earlier, this author is reckoned a priest, with his lineage going back to Moses. It is also proffered that he bought this office. In addition, it is argued that an editor combined "J" and "E" after the destruction of Israel by the Assyrians but before the destruction of Jerusalem by the Babylonians, which they date to about 722 BC.E.[111]

These same critics hold out that the language and theological content of "D," Deuteronomy, is different from Genesis, Exodus, Leviticus, and Numbers. Thus they have another author. They argue that the priests living in the northern kingdom of Israel gathered "D" over several hundred years; however, it was not until much later that "D" was combined with the earlier works. It is also said that the "D" writer (source) was also behind Joshua, Judges, 1 and 2 Samuel and 1 and 2 Kings (Dtr). It is suggested strongly that, in fact, this is the book found in the temple by Hilkiah the high priest and given to King Josiah. (2 Kings 22:8) It is further put forth that J/E/D were fused together as one document in about 586 B.C.E.[112]

The source critics use the capital letter "P" for Priestly. This is because this portion of the Pentateuch usually relates to the priesthood. For instance, things like the sacrifices would be tagged as belonging to this author. Many scholars suggest that "P" was written before the destruction of Jerusalem, which they date at 586 B.C.E. Others put forth that it was written during the exile of seventy years, the Priest(s) composing this holy

---

[109] Ernest Nicholson, *The Pentateuch in the Twentieth Century: The Legacy of Julius Wellhausen* (New York: Oxford University Press, 1998), 36–47.

[110] Mark F. Rooker, *Leviticus: The New American Commentary* (Nashville: Broadman & Holman, 2001), 23.

[111] Ibid., 23.

[112] Ibid., 23.

portion for the people who would return from exile, while others say it was written after the exile, about 450 B.C.E. These liberal scholars find no consensus on when this supposed author "P" wrote this portion of the first five books. The critics tell us that the final form of J/E/D/P was composed into one document about 400 B.C.E.[113]

The capital "R" represents the editor(s) who put it together and may have altered some portions to facilitate their social-circumstances of their day. The "R" comes from the German word *Redakteur* (Redactor), which is an editor or reviser of a work.

With all the focus on Wellhausen and the impetus he has given to the Documentary Hypothesis, one would conclude that he had made an enormous, critical investigation of the text, which, in essence, moved him to cosign with his predecessors. If that is your conclusion, you will have to regroup, for it was simply a feeling that something was not quite right that moved Wellhausen to accept a system of understanding without any evidence whatsoever. In his book *Prolegomena to the History of Israel*, first published in 1878, Wellhausen helps his readers to appreciate just how he came about his expressed interest in the Documentary Hypothesis:

> In my early student days I was attracted by the stories of Saul and David, Ahab and Elijah; the discourses of Amos and Isaiah laid strong hold on me, and I read myself well into the prophetic and historical books of the Old Testament. Thanks to such aids as were accessible to me, I even considered that I understood them tolerably, but at the same time was troubled with a bad conscience, as if I were beginning with the roof instead of the foundation; for I had no thorough acquaintance with the Law, of which I was accustomed to be told that it was the basis and postulate of the whole literature. At last I took courage and made my way through Exodus, Leviticus, Numbers, and even through Knobel's Commentary to these books. But it was in vain that I looked for the light which was to be shed from this source on the historical and prophetical books. On the contrary, my enjoyment of the latter was marred by the Law; it did not bring them any nearer me, but intruded itself uneasily, like a ghost that makes a noise indeed, but is not visible and really effects nothing. Even where there were points of contact between it and them, differences also made themselves felt, and I found it impossible to give a candid decision in favour of the priority of the Law. Dimly I began to perceive that throughout there was between them all the difference that separates two

---

[113] Ibid., 23–24.

wholly distinct worlds. Yet, so far from attaining clear conceptions, I only fell into deeper confusion, which was worse confounded by the explanations of Ewald in the second volume of history of Israel. At last, in the course of a casual visit in Göttingen in the summer of 1867, I learned through Ritschl that Karl Heinrich Graf placed the law later than the Prophets, and, almost without knowing his reasons for the hypothesis, I was prepared to accept it; I readily acknowledged to myself the possibility of understanding Hebrew antiquity without the book of the Torah.[114]

Martin Noth (1902–1968) A liberal twentieth-century German scholar who specialized in the pre-Exilic history of the Jewish people. Noth presented what he called the "Deuteronomic Historian." He argued that the language and theological outlook of Joshua, Judges, 1 and 2 Samuel and 1 and 2 Kings was the same as the book of Deuteronomy. Noth believed this writer lived during the exile because of a reference from 2 Kings to the exile. Modern critics, however, believed this writer lived before the exile, with 2 Kings 25:27 being a later addition.

Frank M. Cross, Jr., Hebrew and Biblical scholar' muddies the water even more with his proposition that there was not one Deuteronomistic history, but two. The first he proposed to be written during the reign of the Judean King Josiah to aid him in cleaning up the false worship going on within Judah. After the destruction of Jerusalem, Cross said the same writer or possibly another goes back to edit this work, to add in the destruction of Jerusalem and the exile to Babylon.

Redaction Criticism

I briefly address the Redaction Theory here because of its relationship to the Documentary Hypothesis. As stated above in our alphabet soup of alleged authors ("J," "E," "D," "P," and "R"), a redactor is an editor or reviser of a work. Redaction Criticism is another form of Biblical criticism that intends to investigate the Scriptures and draw conclusions concerning their authorship, historicity, and time of writing. This form of criticism as well as the others has really done nothing more than tear down God's Word. R. E. Friedman, the Documentary Hypothesis' biggest advocate, asserts that the "J" document was composed between 922–722 B.C.E. in the southern kingdom of Judah, while the northern kingdom of Israel was composing the "E" document during these same years. Friedman contends that sometime thereafter a compiler of history put these two sources together, resulting in "J/E," with the compiler being known as "RJE."

---

[114] Julius Wellhausen, *Prolegomena to the History of Israel* (1878), 3–4

Friedman states that shortly thereafter, the priesthood in Jerusalem put out yet another document, known today as "P," this being another story to be added to the above "J/E." Going back to their authors for the first five books of the Bible, Friedman and these critics claim a redactor, or editor put the whole Pentateuch together using "D," "P," and the combination of "J/E." For them this editor (Deuteronomist) used the written sources he had available to make his additions for dealing with the social conditions of his day. They claim this editor's express purpose was to alter Scripture to bring comfort and hope to those who were in exile in Babylon. Wellhausen's theories, with some adjustments, have spread like a contagious disease, until they have consumed the body of Christendom. However, the real question is, Do these higher critics have any serious evidence to overturn thousands of years of belief by three major religious groups (Jews, Christians, and Muslims) that the Pentateuch was written by Moses?

What these critics have are pebbles, each representing minute inferences and implications [circumstantial evidence at best] that they place on one side of a scale. These are weighed out against the conservative evidence of Moses' authorship of the Pentateuch. As unsuspecting readers work their way through the books and articles written by these critics, the scales seem to be tilted all to one side, as if there were no evidence for the other side. Thus, like a jury, many uninformed readers; conclude that there is no alternative but to accept the idea that there are multiple authors for the Pentateuch instead of Moses, who is traditionally held to be the sole author.

Just what impact has the Documentary Hypothesis had on academia? Let us allow R. Rendtorf, professor Emeritus of the University of Heidelberg, to answer:

> Current international study of the Pentateuch presents at first glance a picture of complete unanimity. The overwhelming majority of scholars in almost all countries where scholarly study of Old Testament is pursued, take the documentary hypothesis as the virtually uncontested point of departure for their work; and their interest in the most precise understanding of the nature and theological purposes of the individual written sources seems undisturbed.[115]

Let us take a moment to look at many of these pebbles and see which side of the scale they are to be placed on. As stated at the outset,

---

[115] R. Rendtorff, "The Problem of the Process of Transmission in the Pentateuch," *JSOT* (1990): 101.

we will address the major arguments as a case against the whole. Some of these pebbles are major obstacles for honest-hearted Christians.

Arguments of Higher Critics for the Documentary Hypothesis

We will address four areas of argumentation from the higher critics: (1) the divine names, (2) discrepancies, (3) repetition, known as "doublets," and (4) differences in language and style. We will give at least one example of each and address at least one example under the evidence for Moses' writership.

Divine Names

The higher critics argue that every Bible verse that contains the Hebrew word for God, (´Elohim´), set off by itself has its own writer, designated by the capital "E" ("Elohist"). On the other hand, any verse that contains the Tetragrammaton, (Jehovah, Yahweh), God's personal name, is attributed to yet another writer, "J" ("Jawist"). (Cassuto, 18-21) Let us see how they explain this. The critics argue that "God" (´Elohim´) is restricted in use exclusively in the first chapter of Genesis (1:1–31) in relation to God's creation activity, and that starting in Genesis 2:4 through the end of the second chapter we find God's personal name.

R. E. Friedman speaks of a discovery by three men: "One was a minister, one was a physician, and one was a professor. The discovery that they made ultimately came down to the combination of two pieces of evidence: doublets and the names of God. They saw that there were apparently two versions each of a large number of Biblical stories: two accounts of the creation, two accounts each of several stories about the patriarchs Abraham and Jacob, and so on. Then, they noticed that, quite often, one of the two versions of a story would refer to God by one name and the other version would refer to God by a different name." (R. E. Friedman, 50)

Different settings, however, require different uses. This principle holds true throughout the whole of the entire Old Testament. Moses may choose to use (´Elohim´) in a setting in which he wants to show a particular quality clearly, like power, creative activity, and so on. On the other hand, Moses may choose to use God's personal name (Jehovah, Yahweh) when the setting begs for that personal relationship between the Father and his children, the Israelites, or even more personable, a one-on-one conversation between Jehovah God and a faithful servant.

The Divine Names: The weakness of claiming multiple authors because of the different names used for God is quite evident when we look at just one small portion of the book of Genesis in the *American Standard Version* (1901). God is called "God Most High," "possessor (or maker) of heaven and earth," "O Lord Jehovah," "a God that seeth," "God Almighty," "God," "[the] God,"[116] and "the Judge of all the earth." (Genesis 14:18, 19; 15:2; 16:13; 17:1, 3; 18:25) It is difficult to believe that different authors wrote these verses. Moreover, let us look at Genesis 28:13, which says, "And, behold, Jehovah stood above it, and said, I am Jehovah, the God ["Elohim"] of Abraham thy father, and the God of Isaac: the land whereon thou liest, to thee will I give it, and to thy seed." Another scripture, Psalm 47:5, says, "God is gone up with a shout, Jehovah with the sound of a trumpet."[117] In applying their documentary analysis, we would have to accept the idea that two authors worked together on each of these two verses.

Many conservative scholars have come to realize that in a narrative format one will often find a ruler being referred to not only by name but also by a title, such as "king." M. H. Segal observes: "Just as those interchanges of human proper names and their respective appellative common nouns cannot by any stretch of the imagination be ascribed to a change of author or source of document, so also the corresponding interchanges of the divine names in the Pentateuch must not be attributed to such a literary cause."[118] If one were to look up "Adolf Hitler" using *Academic American Encyclopedia*, within three paragraphs he will find the terms "Führer," "Adolf Hitler," and simply "Hitler." Who is so bold as to suggest that there are three different authors for these three paragraphs?

Dr. John J. Davis[119] helps us to appreciate that there is "no other religious document from the ancient Near East [that] was compiled in such a manner; a documentary analysis of the Gilgameš Epic or Enūma Eliš would be complete folly. The author of Genesis may have selected divine names on the basis of theological emphasis rather than dogmatic preference. Many divine names were probably interchangeable; Baal and

---

[116] The title *'Elo·him'* preceded by the definite article *ha*, giving the expression *ha·'Elo·him'*.

[117] See also Psalm 46:11; 48:1, 8.

[118] See also Psalm 46:11; 48:1, 8.

[119] John J. Davis, *Paradise to Prison: Studies in Genesis* (Salem: Sheffield, 1975), 22–23.

Hadad were used interchangeably in the Hadad Tablet from Ugarit,[120] and similar examples could be cited from Egyptian texts."[121]

In fact, we now know that there were many deities in the ancient Near East that had multiple names. As stated above with the Babylonian Creation account, the Enuma Elish, the god Marduk (Merodach), chief deity of Babylon, also had some 50 different names.[122] It would not even be thinkable to apply any of the Documentary Hypothesis analysis to any of these works. Why? Not only because we can see that ancient writers are no different than modern writers and are able to use different names and titles interchangeably within their work, but they were written on stone, so to speak. If one has one clay tablet that has both a personal name and two different titles for the same king, it would be difficult to argue that there were two or three different authors for the one tablet. Bible scholar Mark F. Rooker has the following to say about the use of Elohim and Yahweh in the Old Testament:

> Moreover, it is clear that throughout the Old Testament that the occurrence of the names of God as Elohim or Yahweh is to be attributed to contextual and semantic issues, not the existence of sources. This conclusion is borne out by the fact that the names consistently occur in predictable genre. In the legal and prophetic texts the name Yahweh always appears, while in wisdom literature the name for God is invariably Elohim. In narrative literature, which includes much of the Pentateuch, both Yahweh and Elohim are used.[123] Yet consistently the names do not indicate different sources but were chosen by design. The name Elohim was used in passages to express the abstract idea of Deity as evident in God's role as Creator of the universe and the Ruler of nature. Yahweh, on the other hand, is the special covenant name of God who has entered into a relationship with the Israelites since the name reflects God's ethical character. (Cassuto, 31) Given the understanding of the meaning of these names for God, it is no wonder that the source which contains the name Yahweh

---

[120] G. R. Driver, *Canaanite Myths and Legends* (New York: T. & T. Clark, 1971), 70-72.

[121] For example, see the "Stele of Ikhernofret" in James B. Pritchard, ed., *Ancient Near Eastern Texts*, 2nd ed. Princeton: Princeton University Press, 1955, pp. 329–30.

[122] K. A. Kitchen, *On the Reliability of the Old Testament* (Grand Rapids: Eerdmans, 2003), 424–5.

[123] Similarly, Livingston has pointed out that the cognate West Semitic divine names il and ya(w) appear to be interchangeable in the Eblaite tablets. (*The Pentateuch in Its Cultural Environment*, 224.)

would appear to reflect a different theology from a selected group of texts which contained the name Elohim."[124]

Let us, on a small scale, do our own analysis of the divine names in the first two chapters of Genesis. The Hebrew word ('*elohim*´) is most often agreed upon to be from a root meaning "be strong," "mighty," or "power."[125] It should be said too that by far, most Hebrew scholars recognize the plural form (*im*) of this title '*elo·him*´ to be used as a plural of "majesty," "greatness," or "excellence." The Hebrew word ('*elo·him*´) is used for the Creator 35 times from Genesis 1:1 to 2:4a. Exactly what is the context of this use? It is used in a setting that deals with God's power, his greatness, his excellence, his creation activity, all of which seems appropriate, does it not?

Moving on to Genesis 2:4b–25, we find God now being referred to by his personal name, the Tetragrammaton (YHWH, JHVH), which is translated "Jehovah" (KJV, ASV, NW, NEB, etc.) or "Yahweh" (AT, NAB, JB, HCSB, etc.). It is found in verses 4b–25 eleven times; however, it comes before his title ('*elohim*´).[126] Why the switch, and what is the context of this use? This personal name of God is used in a setting that deals with his personal relationship with man and woman. This is not a second creation account; it is a more detailed account of the creation of man, which was only briefly mentioned in chapter one in passing, as each feature of creation was ticked off. In chapter two, the Creator becomes a person as he speaks to his intelligent creation, giving them the prospect of an perfect eternal life in a paradise garden, which is to be cultivated earth wide, to be filled with perfect offspring. Therefore, we see a personal interchange between God and man as He lays out His plans to Adam, which seems very appropriate, does it not when switching from using a title in chapter one to using a personal name in chapter two? In chapter two, we have the coupling of the personal name "Jehovah" with the title "God," to show that we are still talking about this 'great,' 'majestic,' 'all powerful' Creator, but personalized as he introduces himself to his new earthly creation.

Thus, there is no reason to assume that we are talking about two different writers. No, it is two different settings in which a skilled writer would make the transition just as Moses did. It would be no different than if a modern-day news commentator was giving as a report about the United States President visiting Russia to meet with Dmitry Anatolyevich Medvedev, in which he used the title President predominately. The

---

[124] Mark F. Rooker, *Leviticus: The New American Commentary* (Nashville: Broadman & Holman, 2001), 26–27.

[125] Ibid., 27.

[126] "Jehovah God." Heb., Yehwah´ 'Elohim´.

following week the same news commentator may be covering the President visiting a hospital with injured children who had survived a tornado, and refer to the President as President Obama. It isn't difficult to see that one is an official setting where the President needs to be portrayed as powerful, while in the other setting; he needs to be portrayed as personable. The same principles used herein apply to the rest of the Pentateuch and the Old Testament as a whole.

Discrepancies

Discrepancies, or should I say "perceived" discrepancies, are the critic's favorite pebble. These perceived discrepancies set off an alarm for the critic, and then he rushes off with his pebble like a child to add it to the multiple-authors side of the scale. To differentiate between the supposed different sources texts, I will lay them out as follows:

("**J**") will be used to represent an alleged writer. In this case, it stands for any place God's name Jehovah is used.

("**E**") will be for the portion that has Jehovah's title, *Elohim*, God.

("**P**") will be for the portion of priestly activities.

("**D**") Deuteronomy is different from Genesis, Exodus, Leviticus, and Numbers. Thus, it has another author.

("**RJE**") will represent the compiler who put "J" and "E" together.

("**R**") will represent the editor(s), who put it all together and may have altered some portions to express their social circumstances of their day.

("**U**") will represent the alleged "unknown independent texts."

"**Narrative Discrepancy**" (Genesis 12:1, ASV) Now Jehovah said unto Abram, Get thee out of thy country, and from thy kindred, and from thy father's house, unto the land that I will show thee: ("J") (after Terah, Abram's father, died, Abram is commanded to leave Haran)

> **(Genesis 11:26, ESV)** When Terah had lived 70 years, he fathered Abram, Nahor, and Haran ("U"). (When Terah was 70, Abram was born.)

144

(Genesis 11:32, ESV) The days of Terah were 205 years ("U"): and Terah died in Haran ("R"). (Terah died at the age of 205, which would make Abraham 135 when he left Ur.)

(Genesis 12:4, ASV) So Abram went, as Jehovah had spoken unto him; and Lot went with him ("J"): and Abram was seventy and five years old when he departed out ("P") of Haran ("R"). (12:4 has Abram being only 75 when he leaves Haran.)

Discrepancy: According to 11:32, Terah died at the age of 205; hence, Abram must have been 135 when he was called to leave Haran. However, 12:4 says that he was only 75 when he left Haran. The Source Critic informs us that this seeming contradiction is resolved if Genesis chapter 12 is of a different source from the genealogy of Genesis chapter 11.

The above need not be a contradiction at all. True enough, it was at the age of 70 that Terah began having children (Genesis 11:26), but does Abraham have to be the firstborn child simply because he is listed first? Consider, what weight does the names Nahor and Haran play in the Bible account? Now consider, what about the name Abraham? He is considered the father and founder of three of the greatest religions on this planet: Judaism, Christianity, and Islam. He is the third most prominent person named in God's Word. This practice, that of placing the most prominent son first in a list of sons even though they are not the firstborn is followed elsewhere in God's Word with other prominent men of great faith, for example, Shem and Isaac. (Genesis 5:32; 11:10; 1 Chronicles 1:28) Therefore, let us keep it simple. Genesis 11:26 does not say that Abram was the firstborn; it simply says that Terah began fathering children, and then it goes on to list his three sons, listing the most prominent one first. Thus, it is obvious that Terah fathered Abram at the age of 130. (Genesis 11:26, 32; 12:4) In addition, it is true that Sarah was Abram's half-sister, not by the same mother, but by having Terah as the same father. (Genesis 20:12) Therefore, in all likelihood, it is Haran who is the firstborn of Terah, whose daughter was old enough to marry Nahor, another of Terah's three sons. – Genesis 11:29.

"Narrative Discrepancy" (Genesis 37:25–28, 36; 38:1; 39:1, YLT)

(Genesis 37:25–28, YLT) And they sit down to eat bread ("E"), and they lift up their eyes, and look, and lo, a company of Ishmaelites coming from Gilead, and their camels bearing spices, and balm, and myrrh, going to take [them] down to Egypt. 26 And Judah saith unto his brethren, 'What gain when we slay our brother, and have concealed his blood? 27 Come, and we sell him to the Ishmaelites, and our hands are not on him, for he [is] our brother—our flesh;' and his brethren hearken ("J"). 28 And Midianite merchantmen pass by and they draw out and bring up Joseph out of the pit ("E"), and sold him to the Ishmaelites for twenty shekels of silver. They took Joseph to Egypt ("J"). (Genesis 37:36) And the Medanites have sold him unto Egypt, to Potiphar, a eunuch of Pharaoh, head of the executioners ("E"). (Genesis 38:1) And it cometh to pass, at that time, that Judah goeth down from his brethren, and turneth aside unto a man, an Adullamite, whose name [is] Hirah ("J"). (Genesis 39:1) And Joseph hath been brought down to Egypt, and Potiphar, a eunuch of Pharaoh, head of the executioners, an Egyptian man, buyeth him out of the hands of the Ishmaelites who have brought him thither ("J").

Discrepancy: In Genesis 37:25 the Ishmaelites are passing by at the opportune time mentioned in verses 26 and 27, with Judah suggesting that instead of killing Joseph they sell him to the Ishmaelites. Yet, verse 28 switches in midstride to the Midianites, as they drew Joseph from the pit, selling him to the Ishmaelites. In verse 36, the Medanites (likely a scribal error; almost every translation has Midianites, so we will accept that as so) are selling Joseph to Potiphar in Egypt. Yet, the discrepancy pushes the envelope even further, for Genesis 39:1 says, it was the Ishmaelites who delivered and sold Joseph to Potiphar in Egypt. Was Joseph sold to Ishmaelites or to Midianites? In addition, who delivered and sold Joseph to Potiphar in Egypt? It seems that the higher critics are bent on using ambiguous passages (ambiguous at first glance to the casual reader) to facilitate their Documentary Hypothesis. You might say that these discrepancies are fuel for the engine that drives their Documentary Hypothesis locomotive. E. A. Speiser writes:

> The narrative is broken up into two originally independent versions. One of these (J) used the name Israel, featured Judah as Joseph's protector, and identified the Ishmaelites as the traders who bought Joseph from his brothers. The other (E) spoke of Jacob as the father and named Reuben as Joseph's friend; the slave traders in that version were Midianites who discovered Joseph by accident and sold him in Egypt to Potiphar.[127]

For Speiser, it is time to slice up the text and divide it up between our alleged "J"-Text and "E"-Text writers. It is also hypothesized that our "R"-Redactor edits the two and slips in some additional information as

---

[127] E. A. Speiser, *Genesis*, Anchor Bible (Garden City, N.Y.: Doubleday, 1964), 293–4.

well, suggesting that the Midianites are the ones who were actually passing by, selling Joseph later to the Ishmaelites. Thus, it would be the Ishmaelites, who would deliver and sell Joseph to Potiphar in Egypt. Yes, at first glimpse, this would appear to make it all well, but we still have a problem: Genesis 37:36 states that it was the Midianites, who sold Joseph to Potiphar in Egypt.

Actually, when one looks below the surface reading, there is no discrepancy here at all. Ishmael (son of Hagar and Abraham) and Midian (son of Keturah and Abraham) were half-brothers. It is highly likely that there was intermarriage between the descendants of these two, allowing for an interchangeable use of the expression "Ishmaelites" and "Midianites." (Genesis 25:1–4; 37:25–28; 39:1) We see this in the days of Judge Gideon when Israel was being attacked, with both terms "Ishmaelites" and "Midianites" being used to describe the attackers. (Judges 8:24; 7:25; 8:22, 26) Alternatively, even still we could have an Ishmaelite caravan encompassing Midianite merchants that were passing by, with the Midianites brokering the deal and delivering Joseph from the pit to the Ishmaelite caravan, where Joseph would be under the Ishmaelites' custody even if he was being *detained* by the Midianites. Once they arrived at Potiphar's place in Egypt, it would be the Midianites to broker the deal with Potiphar. Thus, it can be stated either way, the Ishmaelites or the Midianites delivered and sold Joseph to Potiphar in Egypt.

Repetitions (Doublets)

What are doublets? It is the telling of the same story twice, making the same events appear to happen more than once. For example,

(1) there are two stories of the creation account,

(2) two stories of God's covenant with Abraham,

(3) two stories where Abraham names his son Isaac,

(4) two stories where Abraham claims Sarah is his sister, two stories of Jacob's journey to Haran,

(5) two stories where God revealed himself to Jacob at Bethel,

(6) two stories where God changes Jacob's name to Israel,

(7) two stories of when Moses got water from the rock at Meribah, and a detailed description in Exodus 24–29 of how to build the tabernacle, then within five chapters a retelling of how they did it, repeating the details again in chapters 34–40.

The critic goes on to point out that, there is more to this "doublet" story than meets the eye; they argue that one of the doublets will contain the title for the Creator, God (*Elohim*); while the other doublet of the same story will contain the personal name for the Creator, Jehovah. Moreover, they argue that there are other defining features that are only within one side or the other.

> **(Genesis 1:27, ESV)** So God created man in his own image, in the image of God he created him; male and female he created them.

> **(Genesis 2:7, ASV)** And Jehovah God formed man of the dust of the ground, and breathed into his nostrils the breath of life; and man became a living soul.

Within two chapters, we have two verses where the writer, if one person, informs us of the creation of man twice, the second as though the first was never mentioned at all. Again, the source critic will argue that there were two sources of the same information on the creation of man and the compiler allowed both to remain. What the source critic fails to tell his reader is that there are sense breaks within the various accounts in these first three chapters. Genesis 1:1–2:3 is the basic creation account. Genesis 2:4–25 is the restating of day three (verses 5, 6) and the subsequent preparation of the earth for the settling of man and woman in the Garden of Eden. Genesis 3:1–24 is specifically about the temptation, the entry of sin and death into the world, the promise of a seed to save humankind, a description of the conditions of imperfection and of man's loss of the Garden of Eden.

Bible scholar Leon Kass, who supports the Documentary Hypothesis, had this to say about the creation account of Genesis chapters 1 and 2:

> Once we recognize the independence of the two creation stories, we are compelled to adopt a critical principle of reading if we mean to understand each story on its own terms. We must scrupulously avoid reading into the second story any facts or notions taken from the first, and vice versa. Thus, in reading about the origin of man in the story of the Garden of Eden, we must not say or even think that man is here created in God's image or that man is to be the ruler over the animals. Neither, when we try to understand the relation of man and woman in the Garden, are we to think about or make use of the first story's account of the coequal coeval creation of man and woman. Only after we have read and interpreted each story entirely on its own should we try to integrate the two disparate teachings. By proceeding in this way, we will discover why

these two separate and divergent accounts have been juxtaposed and how they function to convey a coherent, noncontradictory teaching about human life.[128]

Let us look at another example in which the critic has argued that one source says forty days while the other speaks of 150 days:

(Gen 7:12, NET) And the rain fell on the earth forty days and forty nights.

(Gen 7:24, NET) The waters prevailed over the earth for 150 days.

Genesis 7:24 and 8:3 say the floodwaters lasted for 150 days, yet; Genesis 7:4, 12 and 17 say it was only forty days. Once again, the difference is solved with a simple explanation. Each is referring to two different time periods. Let us look at these verses again (italics mine):

(Gen 7:12, NET) And the rain fell on the earth forty days and forty nights. [Notice that the 40-days refer to how long the rain fell—"the rain fell."]

(Gen 7:24, NET) The waters prevailed over the earth for 150 days. [Notice that the 150-days refer to how long the flood lasted—"waters prevailed."]

(Gen 8:3, NET) The waters kept receding steadily from the earth, so that they had gone down by the end of the 150 days.

(Gen 8:4, NET) On the seventeenth day of the seventh month, the ark came to rest on one of the mountains of Ararat.

(Gen 7:11; 8:13, 14, NET) In the *six hundredth year of Noah's life*, in *the second month*, on the seventeenth day of the month, on that day all the fountains of the great deep burst open and the floodgates of the heavens were opened. *In Noah's six hundred and first year*, in the first day of the first month, *the waters had dried up* from the earth, and Noah removed the covering from the ark and saw that *the surface of the ground was dry*. And *by the twenty-seventh day of the second month the earth was dry.*

By the end of the 150 days, the water had gone down [Gen 8:3]. Five months from the beginning of the rain, the ark comes to rest on

---

[128] Leon R. Kass, *The Beginning of Wisdom: Reading Genesis* (New York: Free Press, 2003), 56.

Mount Ararat [8:4]. Eleven months later the waters dried up [7:11; 8:13]. Exactly 370 days from the start (lunar months), Noah and his family left the ark and were on dry ground.

Yet another example is found in 2 Kings 24:10-16. Verses 10-14 say, "At that time the servants of Nebuchadnezzar king of Babylon came up to Jerusalem, and the city was besieged. And Nebuchadnezzar king of Babylon came to the city while his servants were besieging it, and Jehoiachin the king of Judah gave himself up to the king of Babylon, himself and his mother and his servants and his officials and his palace officials. The king of Babylon took him prisoner in the eighth year of his reign and carried off all the treasures of the house of the LORD and the treasures of the king's house, and cut in pieces all the vessels of gold in the temple of the LORD, which Solomon king of Israel had made, as the LORD had foretold. He carried away all Jerusalem and all the officials and all the mighty men of valor, 10,000 captives, and all the craftsmen and the smiths. None remained, except the poorest people of the land."

Verses 15-16 say, "And he carried away Jehoiachin to Babylon. The king's mother, the king's wives, his officials, and the chief men of the land he took into captivity from Jerusalem to Babylon. And the king of Babylon brought captive to Babylon all the men of valor, 7,000, and the craftsmen and the metal workers, 1,000, all of them strong and fit for war."

Here we have a repetition of the same events back-to-back. Why? Is it multiple sources and the redactor simply keeping both? In an attempt to stave off the conservative view of Moses' writership, scholar, and critic Richard Elliot Friedman writes:

> Those who defended the traditional belief in Mosaic authorship argued that the doublets were always complementary, not repetitive, and that they did not contradict each other, but came to teach us a lesson by their 'apparent' contradiction. But another clue was discovered that undermined this traditional response. Investigators found that in most cases one of the two versions of a doublet story would refer to the deity by the divine name, Yahweh . . . , and the other version of the story would refer to the deity simply as 'God.' That is, the doublets lined up into two groups of parallel versions of stories. Each group was almost always consistent with the name it used. Moreover, the investigators found that it was not only the names of the deity that lined up. They found various other terms and characteristics that regularly appeared in one of the other group. This tended to support the hypothesis that someone had taken two different old source documents, cut

150

them up, and woven them together to form the continuous story in the Five Books of Moses.[129]

Ancient Semitic literature has other similar examples of repetition. Moreover, the use of Elohim in one instance and Jehovah in another is due to context and semantic issues. Notice Friedman's use of the phrases "in most cases" and "almost always." Which is it? And as we will see, he is overstating his case to the point of exaggeration. Let us look at the most popular example in the "Matriarch in Danger." It has three occurrences in Genesis: Sarah in Egypt with Pharaoh (Genesis 12:10–20), Sarah in Gerar with Abimelech (Genesis 20:1–18), and Rebekah in Gerar with Abimelech (Genesis 26:7–11). Friedman would argue that we simply have one story with three different sources that had been maintained over time. The personal name of God, Jehovah, is used in the account of Sarah in Egypt with Pharaoh (vs. 17). The title Elohim is used in the account about Sarah in Gerar with Abimelech (vs. 3), but so is Jehovah (vs. 18). In the account of Rebekah in Gerar with Abimelech, neither Elohim nor Jehovah is used. Therefore, Friedman's case is really no case at all, because both Jehovah and Elohim appear in one account with Sarah in Gerar with Abimelech and neither Jehovah nor Elohim appear in the account with Rebekah in Gerar with Abimelech. It should be noted that all three occurrences are in reference to Abimelech and Pharaoh, but both times that the name Jehovah is used, it is in reference to Jehovah executing a punishment of these rulers. If their best example does not even come close to their claims, then what are we to think of the others? Before moving on to the differences in language and style, we should close with one last point about the literature of the Ancient Near East (ANE). One of the features of ANE literature, which includes Hebrew, is its parallelism, repetition, the telling of stories that are similar to stress patterns that are important. Even in the book of Acts, you have three different accounts of Paul's conversion (Ac 9:3-8; 22:6-11; 26:12-18). It is repetition for emphasis. At the outset of this section, we mentioned that chapters 24-29 of Exodus give a detailed description of how the tabernacle was built, and chapters 34-40 repeat the very same information. Chapters 24-29 contain the directions, and chapters 34-40 show how they did it; thus, the repetition is emphasizing that they did exactly what Jehovah had asked them to do.

Differences in Language and Style

Supporters of the Documentary Hypothesis would argue that within the Pentateuch we see such things as preferences for certain words, differences in vocabulary, reoccurring expressions in Deuteronomy that

---

[129] Richard Elliot Friedman, *Who Wrote The Bible* (San Francisco: Harper Collins, 1997), 22.

are not found in Genesis, Exodus, Leviticus, and Numbers, all evidence for the higher critics and their multiple source theory. Also, there are individual characteristics in grammar and syntax. Further, the critic describes "P" as being very boring, completely lacking in interest or excitement, dry; while the writers of "J" and "E" are very vivid and lively, holding the reader's interest in their storytelling. Additionally, "D" uses expressions like 'with all your heart and all your soul,' which the rest of the Pentateuch lacks in those types of expressions. Their conclusion is that there is no alternative but to have multiple writers as the differences in language and style dictate.

If the alleged writers of the Pentateuch were so narrow in their vocabulary and writing abilities that they would use only one given word for a given idea and never use another when dealing with that idea, it would be easy to suggest a division of actual sources. Yet this is not the case at all. The writers of the Hebrew Scriptures throughout ancient Israel actually expressed a great variety of words in their work. Douglas K. Stuart (Ph.D., Harvard University), Professor of Old Testament at Gordon–Conwell Theological Seminary, is of the same opinion:

> In fact, the contrary situation appears to be true. In ancient Israel there were four demonstrable indications of a preference for variety in written expression rather than for desire for stylistic consistency. (1) If there were two different ways of spelling a word the Israelites chose to preserve both spellings as valid and to include both of them frequently in any document. Thus with regard to spelling (orthography), ancient Israelites had no commitment to consistency to style, but the free use of alternative spellings was regarded as not only proper, but desirable. (2) In the case of common expressions, a similar phenomenon can be observed. Where variation was possible, it apparently was not avoided, but preferred. Alternative ways of forming a given multiword expression were employed commonly so that both alternatives were preserved. Thus, in the case of repeated phraseology in prose contexts, there was no commitment to consistency of style, but rather the alternative formulation was regarded not only proper, but desirable. (3) With regard to variation in grammatical forms, a similar phenomenon is observed. If there existed two different ways of saying something, even in the case of a common verb form, both ways were used so as to preserve both in the common discourse. Again, the preference appears to have been for inclusion of variety rather than for consistency of one form if two existed. (4) The Masoretic system of *Kethib-Qere* represents a fourth indicator of the tendency in past times to

preserve variance rather than to select one option and to employ it consistently, a tendency that extended into the medieval period when the Masoretes worked. This system arose from a desire to include, not merely side-by-side, but actually within the same word, two variant readings rather than two select ones. The Masoretes provide the consonants of one text option in the vowels of another. They indicated their preferred reading, but did not omit the reading they regarded as inferior, they simply did not localize it.[130]

Differences in Style and Vocabulary: An investigator would not be honest if he were simply to reject these differences out of hand, as though they did not exist. Therefore, rightly, we need to investigate these differences, giving an answer that has substance. I will cite one of their pillar examples, to demonstrate the principle that if they are so far off base here, then we can conclude their foundation in this area is really no foundation at all. Before we get started, let us do a little review of Biblical Hebrew, to be better able to address our example.

(Qal): Qal is the simple form of the verb, meaning "light" or "easy." This is the simple active stem of the verb.

(Hiphil): This is generally called the "*causative*" form because it reveals the *causative* action of the qal verb. The "*h*" is prefixed to the stem, which modifies the root.

QAL   yalad (to give birth)

HIPHIL   holid (he caused to give birth)

Examples:

Gen. 14:18: Irad begat (*yalad*) Mehujael

Gen. 5:4: Adam after he begat (*holid*) Seth

The advocates of the Documentary Hypothesis argue that to find *yalad* in the genealogy of Cain in Genesis chapter 4, the Table of Nations in Genesis chapter 10, and Nahor's family line in Genesis chapter 22 (all being of the "J" author), while finding *holid* in Adam's history down to Noah in Genesis chapter 5 as well as the genealogy of Shem found in

---

[130] Douglas K. Stuart, *The New American Commentary: An Exegetical Theological Exposition of Holy Scripture: EXODUS* (Nashville: Broadman & Holman, 2006). See pp. 30–31 for examples of the above four points.

Genesis chapter 11 (being of the "P" author) is nothing more than proof positive that there are two authors: "J" and "P."

In short, we are not dealing with a word or phrase that is peculiar to an individual writer like "J" or "P." No, this is nothing more than an example of following the basic rules of Hebrew grammar and syntax. In many cases, it could not have been written in any other way, because it is the socially accepted usage of the Hebrew language. When those who support the Documentary Hypothesis pull Hebrew words or even phrases out of their setting (as I have done above), looking at them in isolation, their reasoning becomes based solely on personal wishes, feelings, or perceptions, rather than on linguistic rules, reasons, or principles of the language itself. Hebrew, like any other language, conforms to the socially accepted style, with the regular and specific order, or arrangement. The Hebrew language has its own rules and allowable combinations of how words are joined together to make sense to the Hebrew mind. Umberto Cassuto, also known as Moshe David Cassuto, (1883–1951), who held the chair of Biblical studies at the Hebrew University of Jerusalem had this to say concerning the usage of *yalad* and *holid*:

> It will suffice to note the fact that the verb *yaladh* occurs in the signification of *holidh* only in the *past tense* [perfect] and the *present* [participle]. We say, "so-and-so *yaladh* [mas. sing. perfect] so-and-so," and we say *yoledh* [participle mas. Sing.: "is begetting"]; but we do not say in the *future tense* [imperfect] so-and-so *yeledh* [to signify: "he will beget"] (or *wayyeledh* [imperfect with *waw* conversive, to connote: "and he begot"]) so-and-so." In the imperfect, the *Qal* is employed only with reference to the mother, for example, so-and-so *teledh* ["will give birth to"] (*watteledh* ["and gave birth to"]) so and so." In connection with the father one can only say, *yolidh* [*hiphil* imperfect; "he will beget"] or *wayyoledh* [*hiphil* imperfect with *waw* conversive; "and he begot"] (although we find in Prov. xxvii 1: what a day may bring forth ["*yeledh*"; *Qal* imperfect] the verb is used there not in connotation of "begetting" but actually in the sense of "giving birth"). Similarly, we do not say, using the infinitive, Aajare *lidhto* [to signify: "after his begetting"] but only Aajare *lidhtah* ["after her giving birth"]; with regard to the father we can only say Aajare *holidho* ["after his begetting"]. This is clear to anyone who is sensitive to the Hebrew idiom. In the genealogies from Adam to Noah and from Noah to Abraham, it would have been impossible to write anything else but *wayyoledh* and Aajare *hoilidho*; every Hebrew author would have had no option but to write thus and not

otherwise. It is not a question of sources but of the general usage of the Hebrew tongue.[131]

Professor K. A. Kitchen, one of the leading experts on Biblical history, notes in his book *Ancient Orient and Old Testament:* "Stylistic differences are meaningless, and reflect the differences in detailed subject-matter." He says that similar style variations can also be found "in ancient texts whose literary unity is beyond all doubt."[132]

A 1981 news report relates to this debate and provides some interesting facts.[133]

> TEL AVIV, Israel (UPI)—A five-year long computer study of the Bible strongly indicates that one author—and not three as widely held in modern criticism—wrote the book of Genesis.
>
> "The probability of Genesis' having been written by one author is enormously high—82 percent statistically," a member of the research team said in an article published in Wednesday's *Jerusalem Post.*
>
> Professor Yehuda Radday, a Bible scholar from the Technion, a Haifa university, said more than 20,000 words of Genesis were fed into a computer which conducted a painstaking analysis of its linguistic makeup.
>
> Bible critics widely hold that Genesis had three authors— the Jawhist or "J" author, the Elohist or "E" author and a priestly writer, dubbed "P."
>
> "We found the J and E narratives to be linguistically indistinguishable," Radday told a news conference today. But the P sections differ widely from them.
>
> "This is only to be expected, since dramatic tales and legal documents must necessarily display different 'behavior,'" he said. "If you compared love letters and a telephone directory written by the same person, linguistic analysis would point to different authors."
>
> The team combined statistical and linguistic methods with computer science and Bible scholarship to reach their conclusions. They used 54 analysis criteria, including word

---

[131] Umberto Cassuto, *The Documentary Hypothesis* (New York, NY: Shalem Press, 2006), 55-56.

[132] K. A Kitchen, *Ancient Orient and Old Testament* (Downers Grove, IL: InterVarsity Press, 1975), 125.

[133] As published in the *St. Petersburg Times:* http://tinyurl.com/noke4m

length, the use of the definite article and the conjunction "and," richness of vocabulary and transition frequencies between word categories.

"These criteria are a reliable gauge of authorship because these traits are beyond an author's conscious control and furthermore are countable," Radday said.

A mathematics expert on the team ran a computer check against classical German works by Goethe, Herder and Kant and found that the statistical probability of their being the sole authors of their own work were only 22 percent, 7 percent and 9 percent respectively.

As mentioned above, Jewish and Christian conservatives accept one writer for the first five books of the Bible, namely, Moses. The critics, however, argue that although Moses is definitely the main character of the Pentateuch because they are unable to find any *direct mention* within it of Moses having written these five books, it is for them simply a tradition that Moses is the writer. This author is certain that is not the impression you will have after reading the next chapter.

Internal and External Evidence for Moses Authorship

First, it is obvious that Moses did *not* write *every word* of the Pentateuch. Why? The section that relates his death would be something that Joshua could have added after Moses' death. (Deuteronomy 34:1–8) In addition, the critic would argue, it would hardly seem very meek to pen these words about oneself: "Now the man Moses was very meek, more than all people who were on the face of the earth." (Numbers 12:3, ESV) Nevertheless, consider that Jesus said of himself: "I am gentle and lowly in heart" (Matthew 11:29, ESV), which no one would fault Jesus with as though he were boasting. Both Moses and Jesus were simply stating a fact. The amount of possible material that may have been added by Joshua, another inspired writer is next to nothing and does not negate Moses' authorship.

What Does the Biblical Evidence from the Old Testament Report?

Exodus 17:14 (ASV)	Exodus 24:4 (ASV)	Exodus 34:27 (ASV)
14 And Jehovah said unto Moses, Write this	4 And Moses wrote all the words of Jehovah,	27 And Jehovah said unto Moses, Write

for a memorial in a book, and rehearse it in the ears of Joshua: that I will utterly blot out the remembrance of Amalek from under heaven.

and rose up early in the morning, and builded an altar under the mount, and twelve pillars, according to the twelve tribes of Israel.

thou these words: for after the tenor of these words I have made a covenant with thee and with Israel.

Leviticus 26:46 (ASV)

46 These are the statutes and ordinances and laws, which Jehovah made between him and the children of Israel in mount Sinai by Moses.

Leviticus 27:34 (ASV)

34 These are the commandments, which Jehovah commanded Moses for the children of Israel in mount Sinai.

Numbers 33:2 (ASV)

2 And Moses wrote their goings out according to their journeys by the commandment of Jehovah: and these are their journeys according to their goings out.

Numbers 36:13 (ASV)

13 These are the commandments and the ordinances which Jehovah commanded by Moses unto the children of Israel in the plains of Moab by the Jordan at Jericho.

Deuteronomy 1:1 (ASV)

1 These are the words which Moses spake unto all Israel beyond the Jordan in the wilderness, in the Arabah over against Suph, between Paran, and Tophel, and Laban, and Hazeroth, and Di-zahab.

Deuteronomy 31:9 (ASV)

9 And Moses wrote this law, and delivered it unto the priests the sons of Levi, that bare the ark of the covenant of Jehovah, and unto all the elders of Israel.

Deuteronomy 31:22 (ASV)

22 So Moses wrote this song the same day, and taught it the children of Israel.

Deuteronomy 31:24 (ASV)

24 And it came to pass, when Moses had made an end of writing the words of this law in a book, until they were

Joshua 1:7 (ASV)

7 Only be strong and very courageous, to observe to do according to all the law, which Moses my servant commanded thee:

finished,

Joshua 8:31 (ASV)

31 as Moses the servant of Jehovah commanded the children of Israel, as it is written in the book of the law of Moses, an altar of unhewn stones, upon which no man had lifted up any iron: and they offered thereon burnt-offerings unto Jehovah, and sacrificed peace-offerings.

1 Kings 2:3 (ASV)

3 and keep the charge of Jehovah thy God, to walk in his ways, to keep his statutes, and his commandments, and his ordinances, and his testimonies, according to that which is written in the law of Moses, that thou may prosper in all that thou does, and whithersoever thou turn thyself.

2 Kings 14:6 (ASV)

6 but the children of the murderers he put not to death; according to that which is written in the book of the law of Moses, as Jehovah commanded, saying, The fathers shall not be put to death for the children, nor the children be put to death for the fathers; but every man shall die for his own sin.

2 Kings 21:8 (ASV)

8 neither will I cause the feet of Israel to wander any more out of the land which I gave their fathers, if only they will observe to do according to all that I have commanded them, and according to all the law that my servant Moses commanded them.

Ezra 6:18 (ASV)

18 And they set the priests in their divisions, and the Levites in their courses, for the service of God, which is at Jerusalem; as it is written in the book of Moses.

Nehemiah 13:1 (ASV)

1 On that day they read in the book of Moses in the audience of the people; and therein was found written, that an Ammonite and a Moabite should not enter into the assembly of God for ever,

Daniel 9:13 (ASV)

13 As it is written in the law of Moses, all this evil is come upon us: yet have we not entreated the favor of Jehovah our God, that …

Malachi 4:4 (ASV)

4 Remember ye the law of Moses my servant, which I commanded unto him in Horeb for all Israel, even statutes and ordinances.

To reject Moses as the writer of the Pentateuch is to reject these inspired writers and suggest they are not reliable; moreover, this would mean they were not inspired, because those under inspiration would not make such errors. If these critics are correct, then all the above is merely a great conspiracy. This author hardly thinks so!

What Does the Biblical Evidence from Jesus Christ Report?

Matthew 8:4 (ESV)	Matthew 11:23-24 (ESV)
4And Jesus said to him, "See that you say nothing to anyone, but go, show yourself to the priest and offer the gift that Moses commanded, for a proof to them."	23And you, Capernaum, will you be exalted to heaven? You will be brought down to Hades. For if the mighty works done in you had been done in Sodom, it would have remained until this day. 24 But I tell you that it will be more tolerable on the day of judgment for the land of Sodom than for you."
Matthew 19:4-5 (ESV)	**Matthew 19:8 (ESV)**
4He answered, "Have you not read that he who created them from the beginning made them male and female, 5and said, 'Therefore a man shall leave his father and his mother and hold fast to his wife, and the two shall become one flesh'?	8He said to them, "Because of your hardness of heart Moses allowed you to divorce your wives, but from the beginning it was not so.
Matthew 24:37 (ESV)	**Mark 10:5 (ESV)**
37 For as were the days of Noah, so will be the coming of the Son of Man.	5And Jesus said to them, "Because of your hardness of heart he wrote you this commandment.
Mark 12:26 (ESV)	**Mark 1:44 (ESV)**
26And as for the dead being raised, have you not read in the book of Moses, in the passage about the bush, how God spoke to him, saying, 'I am the God of Abraham,	44and said to him, "See that you say nothing to anyone, but go, show yourself to the priest and offer for your cleansing what Moses

and the God of Isaac, and the God of Jacob'?	commanded, for a proof to them."

Mark 7:10 (ESV)	**Luke 5:14 (ESV)**
¹⁰For Moses said, 'Honor your father and your mother'; and, 'Whoever reviles father or mother must surely die.'	¹⁴And he charged him to tell no one, but "go and show yourself to the priest, and make an offering for your cleansing, as Moses commanded, for a proof to them."

Luke 11:51 (ESV)	**Luke 17:32 (ESV)**
⁵¹from the blood of Abel to the blood of Zechariah, who perished between the altar and the sanctuary. Yes, I tell you, it will be required of this generation.	³² Remember Lot's wife.

Luke 24:27, 44 English Standard Version (ESV)	**John 5:46 English Standard Version (ESV)**
²⁷And beginning with Moses and all the Prophets, he interpreted to them in all the Scriptures the things concerning himself. ⁴⁴Then he said to them, "These are my words that I spoke to you while I was still with you, that everything written about me in the Law of Moses and the Prophets and the Psalms must be fulfilled."	⁴⁶For if you believed Moses, you would believe me; for he wrote of me.

John 7:19 English Standard Version (ESV)	**John 8:58 (UASV)**
¹⁹ Has not Moses given you the law? Yet none of you keeps the law. Why do you seek to kill me?"	Jesus said to them, "Truly, truly, I say to you, before Abraham came to be I have been in existence."[134]

How does one ignore the strongest evidence of Moses' writership of these five books, which is specifically referred to by Jesus Christ and numerous other inspired writers? Being on trial by the modern day critic, I

---

[134] K. L. McKay, A New Syntax of the Verb in New Testament Greek (New York: Peter Lang, 1994), p. 42.

am certain Moses would appreciate the numerous witnesses that can be called to the stand on his behalf.[135]

What Does the Biblical Evidence from the Apostles Report?

Acts 2:32 (ESV)	Acts 6:14 (ESV)	Acts 15:5 (ESV)
[32]This Jesus God raised up, and of that we all are witnesses.	[14]for we have heard him say that this Jesus of Nazareth will destroy this place and will change the customs that Moses delivered to us."	[5]But some believers who belonged to the party of the Pharisees rose up and said, "It is necessary to circumcise them and to order them to keep the law of Moses."
Acts 26:22 (ESV)	**Acts 28:23 (ESV)**	**Romans 10:5 (ESV)**
[22] To this day I have had the help that comes from God, and so I stand here testifying both to small and great, saying nothing but what the prophets and Moses said would come to pass:	[23]When they had appointed a day for him, they came to him at his lodging in greater numbers. From morning till evening he expounded to them, testifying to the kingdom of God and trying to convince them about Jesus both from the Law of Moses and from the Prophets.	[5]For Moses writes about the righteousness that is based on the law, that the person who does the commandments shall live by them.
1 Corinthians 9:9 (ESV)	**Hebrews 9:19 (ESV)**	**Hebrews 10:28 (ESV)**
[9]For it is written in the	[19]For when every commandment of the	[28] Anyone who has set

---

[135] Old Testament witnesses to Moses' writership of the Pentateuch: Joshua 1:7; 8:32–35; 14:10; 1 Kings 2:3; 1 Chronicles 6:49; 2 Chronicles 33:8; 34:14; 35:12; Ezra 3:2; 6:18; 7:6; Nehemiah 1:7, 8; 8:1, 14, 15; Daniel 9:11, 13; Malachi 4:4. New Testament witnesses to Moses' writership of the Pentateuch: Matthew 8:2–4; 19:7; Mark 1:44; 12:26; Luke 2:22; 16:29, 31; 24:27, 44; John 1:45; 7:22; 8:5; 9:29; 19:7 [Leviticus 24:16]; Acts 3:22; 6:14; 15:5; 26:22; 28:23; Romans 10:5; 1 Corinthians 9:9; Hebrews 9:19; 10:28.

Law of Moses, "You shall not muzzle an ox when it treads out the grain." Is it for oxen that God is concerned?	law had been declared by Moses to all the people, he took the blood of calves and ...	aside the law of Moses dies without mercy on the evidence of two or three witnesses.

What Does the Internal Evidence Report?

If the writer(s) of the Pentateuch were, in fact, living from the ninth century into the fifth century B.C.E., more than a millennium [1,000 years] after the events described, they would have had to be thoroughly familiar with, even an expert in geology, geography,[136] horticulture, archaeology, toponymy, onomatology (Archer, 1974), botany, zoology,[137] climatology,[138] and history. **Alternatively**, he would have to have been an eyewitness who walked through the events and situations detailed in the Pentateuch; thus, the writer. Here is how I defend these affirmations:

- He would need to have a thorough knowledge of Egyptian names and titles that match inscriptions.

- He would need to have been an expert in toponymy, the study of place-names.

- He would need to have been an expert in onomatology, the study of proper names of all kinds and the origin of names.

- He would need to be aware of the customs and cultures and religious practices of Egypt, desert dwellers, and life in Canaan 1,000 years into the past.

- He would need to have a thorough knowledge of the environment, climate, and the physical features of three regions.

- He would need to have a thorough knowledge of botany, being aware of naturally occurring plant life in three regions 1,000-years before his time.

- He would need to have a thorough knowledge of the environment, climate, and the physical features of three regions.

---

[136] Genesis 13:10; 33:18; Numbers 13:22.

[137] Leviticus 11 and Deuteronomy 14.

[138] Exodus 9:31, 32; Exodus 16–Deuteronomy.

This internal evidence deals with the proof within the Pentateuch about Moses: the customs and culture of some 3,500 years ago, literary forms used as well as the language itself, and the unity of these five books. As to dating the Pentateuch based on literary forms, one needs look no further than the titles by which God is referred to within the Hebrew Scriptures. From the years of 850–450 B.C.E., we find the Hebrew expression Yehowah´ tseva'ohth´, "Jehovah of armies," being used in a significant way. It is found 243 times, with variations, in the Scriptures: 62 times in Isaiah, 77 in Jeremiah, 2 in Micah, 4 in Nahum, 2 in Habakkuk, 2 in Zephaniah, 15 in Haggai, 54 in Zechariah, and 25 in Malachi. This is the same time period, in which higher criticism places the writing of the books of the Pentateuch. If they were penned or constructed during this time period, one would expect to find a high number of occurrences of the expression "Jehovah of armies." Yet, we find just the opposite: there is not one occurrence of this expression to be found in the five books of the Pentateuch. This evidence demonstrates that these books were written prior to the book of Isaiah, before 800 B.C.E., which invalidates the Documentary Hypothesis. Moreover, many aspects of the priesthood that had been adjusted over the centuries, under inspiration, would have been evident if the Pentateuch were written after David[139] and others had made such adjustments.

The building of the tabernacle at the foot of Mount Sinai fits in with the environment of that area. F. C. Cook stated, "In form, structure, and materials, the tabernacle belongs altogether to the wilderness. The wood used in the structure is found there in abundance."[140] The external evidence validates names, customs, and culture, religious practices, geography, places and materials of the book of Exodus, which would have been privy only to an eyewitness. The geographical references by this writer are so vast, detailed, and tremendously precise that it is almost impossible to have him be anyone other than an eyewitness.

Deuteronomy reads, "Then we . . . went through all that great and terrifying wilderness." This region in which the annual rainfall is less than 25 cm./10 in. is not different even today, which puts the nomadic traveler on a constant search for water and pasture. In addition, we have meticulous directions as to the encampment of the Israelites (Numbers 1:52, 53), the marching orders (Numbers 2:9, 16, 17, 24, 31), and the signals of the trumpet (Numbers 10:2–6) that directed their every move as evidence that these accounts were written in the "great and terrifying

---

[139] David organized the tens of thousands of Levites into their many divisions of service, including a great chorus of singers and musicians.—1 Chronicles 23:1–29:19; 2 Chronicles 8:14; 23:18; 29:25; Ezra 3:10.
[140] F. C. Cook, Exodus (1874), 247.

wilderness." Numbers 13:22 makes reference to the time Hebron was built, using the city of Zoan as a reference point: "They went up into the Negeb and came to Hebron. Ahiman, Sheshai, and Talmai, the descendants of Anak, were there. (Hebron was built seven years before Zoan in Egypt.)" Moses "was instructed in all the wisdom of the Egyptians" (Acts 7:22); thus, he would have knowledge of the building of Zoan, an Egyptian city, and of Hebron, a city on one of the trade routes between Memphis in Egypt and Damascus in Syria.

From the internal evidence, it is clearly obvious that the writer must have had an intimate knowledge of the desert, being an eyewitness to that environment. (See Leviticus 18:3; Deuteronomy 12:9; 15:4, 7; Numbers 2:1; Leviticus 14:8; 16:21; 17:3, 9.) The evidence is such because it is something that cannot be retained for a thousand years, but must come from an eyewitness. The details are extremely exact, and some would not have existed hundreds of years later: "Then they came to Elim, where there were twelve wells of water and seventy palm trees, and they camped there by the water," and "ram skins dyed red, fine leather, acacia wood." – Exodus 15:27; 25:5

Again, it should be noted that Moses "was instructed in all the wisdom of the Egyptians." (Acts 7:22) It is also obvious that the writer was quite familiar with Egyptian names: Pithom, meaning "House of Atum;" On, meaning "City of the Pillar" (the Greeks called the city Heliopolis); Potiphera,[141] meaning "He Whom Ra Has Given;" and Asenath, her name deriving from Egyptian, meaning: "Holy to Anath."

In addition, the writer used Egyptian words generously. "He had Joseph ride in his second chariot, and [servants] called out before him, 'Abrek!' So he placed him over all the land of Egypt." (Genesis 41:43) The exact meaning of this expression transliterated from Egyptian into Hebrew has not yet been determined. Some feel that it is an Egyptian word meaning (Attention!) while others see it as a Hebrew word meaning Kneel or Bow down! One misstep and the writer will lose credibility. However, this is never the case with the writer of the Pentateuch. He mentions the acacia tree, which is found in Egypt and Sinai but not in the land of Canaan. Moreover, this writer refers to numerous animals that are to be found primarily in Egypt or Sinai. – See Deuteronomy. 14:5; Leviticus 16:11.

The old form of words in the Pentateuch are of the time frame of the fifteenth century B.C.E. as well, and had no longer been in use for centuries by the time of the supposed writer(s) and redactor(s) of the

---

[141] A funeral pillar (stele) discovered in 1935 and now in the Cairo Museum refers to a personage named Potiphare.

ninth to the sixth centuries B.C.E. Dr. John J. Davis gives us the most widely recognized example, "The pronoun *she*, which appears as *hiw'* instead of *hî'*. Another example is the word *young girl*, spelled *na'ar* instead of *na'ărâ*, the feminine form."[142]

All who engaged in idolatry or prophesying falsely were to be stoned to death, no exceptions. (Deuteronomy 13:2–11) This included not only individuals but also entire communities, every person within a city (verses 12–17). One has to ask, why would a writer include this if it were penned during the time period of 850–450 B.C.E. when most of the time Israel was shoulder deep in idolatry and false prophets abounded? This would mean certain destruction for every city in the kingdom. It would have been mere foolishness to incorporate these laws, which could never be enforced and would cause nothing but resistance to the law. However, it makes perfectly good sense for laws such as these to be given to people living in the time of Moses who had just exited an idolatrous nation and who was preparing to go in and conquer a number of other nations who lived and breathed idolatry.

What Does the External Evidence Report?

"The book of the law of Moses," as Joshua called the Pentateuch, was accepted by Jews, Christians, and Muslims as containing evidence of inspiration. The fact that Moses is the writer of these five books is **not** something that grew up out of tradition; it is something Moses himself claims, saying he wrote under the divine command of Jehovah God. Moreover, the Jewish communities throughout the Roman empire were in total harmony with the fact that Moses was the writer of the Pentateuch, this being supported by the Samaritan Pentateuch, the Palestinian Talmud, the Babylonian Talmud, the Apocrypha, Philo Judaeus (a contemporary of Jesus and Paul and the first century), and by Jewish historian Flavius Josephus (37–100 C.E.).[143] What about the early Christian writers, who wrote about Christianity between 150 C.E. and 400 C.E.?

> Moses, the servant of God, recorded, through the Holy Spirit, the very beginning of the creation of the world. First he spoke of the things concerning the creation and genesis of the world, including the first man and everything that happened afterwards in the order of events. He also indicated the number

---

[142] John J. Davis, *Paradise to Prison: Studies in Genesis* (Salem: Sheffield, 1975), 26.

[143] See Ecclesiasticus 45:5; 2 Maccabees 7:30; Philo (*On the Life of Moses* II; III, 12–14; IV, 20; VIII, 45–48, pp. 93–95); Josephus (*The Antiquities of the Jews*, 3.8.10); Exodus 17:14; 24:4.

of years that elapsed before the Deluge.—*Theophilus* (c. 180, E), 2.118.[144]

The origin of that know ledge should not, on that account, be considered as originating with the Pentateuch. For knowledge of the Creator did not begin with the volume of Moses. Rather from the very first it is traced from Adam and paradise.—*Tertullian* (c. 207, W), 3.278.[145]

What portion of scripture can give us more information concerning the creation of the world than the account that Moses has transmitted?--*Origen* (c. 225, E), 4.341.[146]

The destruction of Sodom and Gomorrah by fire on account of their sins is related by Moses in Genesis.--*Origen* (c. 248, E), 4.505.[147]

Moses said, "And the Lord God saw that the wickedness of men was overflowing upon the Earth" [Gen. 6:5–7].--*Novatian* (c. 235, W), 5.658.[148]

It is contained in the book of Moses, which he wrote about creation, in which is called Genesis.--*Victorinus* (c. 280, W), 7.341.[149]

If you will look at the books of Moses, David, Solomon, Isaiah, or the Prophets who follow . . . . You will see what offspring they have left.--*Methodious* (c. 290, E), 6.333.[150]

Let the following books be considered venerable and holy by you, both of the clergy and the laity. Of the Old Testament: The five books of Moses—Genesis, Exodus, Leviticus, Numbers, and Deuteronomy. . . .--*Apostolic Constitutions* (compiled c. 390, E), 7.505.[151]

---

[144] David W. Bercot, *A Dictionary of Early Christian Beliefs* (Peabody: Hendrickson, 1998), 599.
145. Ibid., 600.
146. Ibid., 600.
147. Ibid., 600.
148. Ibid., 601.
149. Ibid., 601.
150. Ibid., 601.
151. Ibid., 602.

Archaeology and the Bible

Unlike higher criticism, archaeology is a field of study that has a solid foundation in physical evidence, instead of presenting only hypotheses, inferences, and implications. Within archaeology, one has both explicit and direct evidence as well as implicit evidence. There are many great publications that will undoubtedly go into this area in much greater detail, but suffice it to say that the Biblical events, the characters, geography, agriculture, plants and trees and settings are all in harmony with and accessible through archaeology.

While archaeology is not a total vindicator, it has defended God's Word. No one can argue against the fact that our understanding of ancient times has increased tremendously over the past 150 years and is being continuously refined. At present, one could list thousands of events within the Scriptures that are in complete harmony with the archaeological record. In fact, Wellhausen had nothing like what is available to the modern scholar. If he had, one would have to wonder if he would have come to the same conclusions. Conveying this exact point, Dr. Mark F. Rooker, Professor of Old Testament and Hebrew, stated:

> Regarding the issue of differing divine names, it is now clear from archaeological data not available to Wellhausen and early critical scholars that deities in the ancient Near East often had multiple names. This fact is especially clear in the conclusion to the Babylonian Creation account, the *Enuma Elish*, where the god Marduk is declared to be preeminent and his fifty different names are mentioned in celebration of his conquest.[22] No one has suggested that each name represents a different source, as was done in biblical studies. On the contrary, it would have been impossible to attribute these different names to different sources that have been pasted or joined together in the literary account because the Mesopotamian writing system involved inscription in stone! Moreover, it is clear that throughout the Old Testament the occurrence of the names of God as Elohim or Yahweh are to be attributed to contextual and semantic issues, not the existence of sources. This conclusion is borne out by the fact that the names consistently occur in predictable genre. . . . Thus through scientific discovery and analysis the criterion of the differing divine names, which gave rise to the Documentary Hypothesis, has been found wanting. If this information would have been known in the last years of the

nineteenth century, it is safe to assume that the critical approach to the Pentateuch would never have seen the light of day.[152]

Much archaeological evidence as well as other forms of evidence has been uncovered to reveal the accuracy of the record. The ziggurat located at Uruk (Erech) was found to be built with clay, baked bricks for stone, and asphalt (bitumen) for mortar.[153] The Egyptian names and titles that Moses penned in the book of Exodus match Egyptian inscriptions. The book of Exodus shows that the Hebrew people were allowed to live in the land of Egypt as foreigners, as long as they kept separate from the Egyptians. Archaeology supports this custom. Likely, you will recall that Pharaoh's daughter bathed in the Nile (Exodus 2:5), which "was a common practice in ancient Egypt," according to Cook's *Commentary*. "The Nile was worshipped as an emanation . . . of Osiris, and a peculiar power of imparting life and fertility was attributed to its waters."

> The fact that a king's daughter should bathe in the open river is certainly opposed to the customs of the modern, Mohammedan East, where this is only done by women of the lower orders, and that in remote places (Lane, *Manners and Customs*); but it is in harmony with the customs of ancient Egypt,[154]* and in perfect agreement with the notions of the early Egyptians respecting the sanctity of the Nile, to which divine honours even were paid (vid., Hengstenberg's *Egypt*, etc. pp. 109, 110), and with the belief, which was common to both ancient and modern Egyptians, in the power of its waters to impart fruitfulness and prolong life (vid., *Strabo*, xv. p. 695, etc., and Seetzen, *Travels* iii. p. 204).[155]

In addition, history also testifies to the fact that magicians were a well-known feature of Egyptian life during the period of Moses.--Genesis 11:1-9; Exodus 8:22; 2:5; 5:6, 7, 18; 7:11.

Bricks have been found made with and without straw. The painting below was found in the private tomb of Vizier Rekhmire (the highest official under Pharaoh) on the west bank of ancient Thebes. Archaeology also supports "taskmasters--Egyptian overseers, appointed to exact labor

---

152. Mark F. Rooker, *Leviticus: The New American Commentary* (Nashville: Broadman & Holman, 2001), 26–27.

[153] (Genesis 11:3, *ESV*) "And they said to one another, 'Come, let us make bricks, and burn them thoroughly.' And they had brick for stone, and bitumen for mortar."

[154] Wilkinson gave a picture of a bathing scene in which an Egyptian woman of rank is introduced, attended by four female servants.

155. Carl Friedric Keil and Franz Delitzsch, *Commentary on the Old Testament* (Peabody, MA: Hendrickson, 2002), S. 1:278.

of the Israelites,"[156] as well as strictly controlled or enforced quotas that had to be met. (Exodus 5:6) Moreover, Egyptian papyri express serious concern for the needed straw (which was lacking at times) to be mixed with the mud to make these bricks. (Exodus 1:13, 14) The Papyri Anastasi, from ancient Egypt, reads, "There was no one to mould bricks, and there was no straw in the neighbourhood."[157]

Furthermore, the historical conditions and surroundings are in accord precisely with the occasions and assertions in the book of Numbers. We have references to Edom, Egypt, Moab, Canaan, Ammon, and Amalek, which are true to the times, and the names of places are free from error.[158] Archaeology is never absolute proof of anything, but it continues to add evidence, weighty at times to the fact that Moses had to be the writer of the Pentateuch. *Halley's Bible Handbook* writes, "Archaeology has been speaking so loudly of late that it is causing a decided reaction toward the conservative view. The theory that writing was unknown in Moses' day is absolutely exploded. And every year there are being dug up in Egypt, Palestine and Mesopotamia, evidences, both in inscriptions and earth layers, that the narratives of the Old Testament are true historical records. And 'scholarship' is coming to have decidedly more respect for the tradition of Mosaic authorship."[159]

The Silver Amulet is one of many archaeological nails in the coffin of the Documentary Hypothesis. Why? This portion of Numbers is argued by the critics to be part of the "P" document that was supposedly penned between 550 and 400 B.C.E. However, initially, it was dated to the late seventh / early sixth centuries B.C.E.

Of course, this dating was subsequently challenged by Johannes Renz and Wolfgang Rollig (*Handbuch der Althebraischen Epigraphik*, 1995) because the silver was cracked and blemished to the point of making many words and a few lines unreadable. This allowed these critics to argue for a date in the third to second centuries B.C.E. period, which would remove this stain on the lifeless body of their Documentary Hypothesis.

Then it was shipped to the University of Southern California to be examined under photographic and computer imaging. The results? The

---

156. Robert Jamieson, A. R. Fausset, and David Brown. *A Commentary, Critical and Explanatory, On the Old and New Testaments* (Oak Harbor: Scranton & Company, 1997), 51.

157. Adolf Erman and H. M. Tirard. *Life in Ancient Egypt* (Whitefish: Kessinger, 2003), 117.

158. "Sirion . . . Senir." These names appear in the Ugaritic texts found at Ras Shamra, Syria, and in the documents from Bogazköy, Turkey.

159. Henry Halley, *Halley's Bible Handbook* (Grand Rapids: Zondervan, 1988), 56.

researchers stated that they could "read fully and [had] analyzed with far greater precision," which resulted in the final analysis of being yet another vindication for Moses—the original dating stands: late seventh century B.C.E.

Exodus 14:6, 7 (*ESV*) reads, "So he [the Pharaoh] made ready his chariot and took his army with him, and took six hundred chosen chariots and all the other chariots of Egypt with officers over all of them." Pharaoh, being the god of the world and the supreme chief of his army, personally led the army into battle. Archaeology supports this custom.

Why are there no Egyptian records of the Exodus of the Israelites from Egypt? The critics may also ask why is there no archaeological evidence to support the Israelite's 215-year stay in Egypt (some of which was in slavery) and the devastation that was executed on the gods of Egypt. There is, in fact, one simple answer that archaeology has provided us: Any new Egyptian dynasty would erase any unflattering history prior to their dynasty, if such even existed, as it was their custom never to record any defeats that might be viewed as embarrassing or critical, which could damage the dignity of their people, for they were an extremely prideful empire.[160]

For example, Thutmose III ordered others to chisel Queen Hatshepsut out of the history books when he removed the name and representation of Queen Hatshepsut on a monumental stone record later uncovered at Deir al-Bahri in Egypt as well as from any other monuments she had built. Hatshepsut, daughter of Thutmose I, would eventually gain the throne upon her father's death even though Thutmose II (husband and half-brother to Hatshepsut) technically ascended the throne in name only. At best, Thutmose II lasted only three or four years before dying of a skin disease. Thutmose III was too young to rule, thus, Queen Hatshepsut simply held her own as the first female Pharaoh. Embarrassing for Thutmose III, indeed! Thus, as he grew, his hatred mounted for Hatshepsut and Senmut (her lover). After her death, Thutmose III worked vigorously to remove her name and the name of her lover from Egyptian history. If this was embarrassing, how much more so would be the ten plagues that had humiliated numerous gods of Egypt, including the Pharaoh himself? The exodus of 600,000 male slaves and their families, plus Egyptians who had chosen Jehovah as God instead of the Pharaoh of Egypt would have been quite embarrassing, indeed!

In 1925, discoveries of clay tablets were made at the ancient town of Nuzi in northeastern Mesopotamia; it was here that archaeologists found

---

160. Joseph P. Free, *Archaeology and Bible History* (Grand Rapids, MI: Zondervan Publishing, 1964).

a tremendous number of legal contracts dating to the fifteenth-century B.C.E. These actually shed much light on the life of people of that time. Due to the slow-moving life condition of the ancient Near East, they reflect life conditions for many years on both sides of the fifteenth century. Thus, what we now possess and know from studies of these Nuzi Tablets is that there are numerous customs in the Patriarchal period that were very much in common practice among the ancient Hurrians who lived in northern Mesopotamia, encompassing Haran, which was the home of Abraham after he left Ur and where Isaac later found his wife Rebekah.

Abraham's Contract. Eliezer was to be the legal inheritor of childless Abraham's property and position after Abraham's death. In fact, Abraham referred to Eliezer when he said, "a slave born in my house will be my heir." (Genesis 15:2, 3) Tablets from Nuzi discovered by archaeologists help the modern-day reader understand how a servant could become heir to his master's household. Mesopotamian records from the time of Abraham (2018–1843 B.C.E.); makes mention of the tradition of a childless couple adopting a son in their old age to have him take care of them up unto their death, and thereafter inheriting the household property. But if for some reason the couple would end up having a child, the child would become the primary heir instead, with the adopted servant or son getting a minor portion of the property as well. (Wood, 1996) In a culture that passed history down orally through its generations, we find Moses being only three generations removed from Abraham's great-grandson Levi (Levi, Kohath, Amram, and Moses) while our alleged "J" was a thousand years removed from Abraham, and the redactor even further. It is only by means of modern-day archaeology that we are aware of just how accurate the Genesis account is with minor details such as the legal system of adoption rights in Mesopotamia from 2000 B.C.E. (time of Abraham) to 1500 B.C.E. (time of Moses), knowledge that would not be available to our alleged composers. Thus, archaeology puts the Genesis account right back into the hands of its true writer, Moses.

The Price of a Slave. Joseph was the son of Jacob by Rachel, the grandson of Isaac, and the great-grandson of Abraham, and was sold as a slave to some Midianite merchants for a mere 20 pieces of silver by his jealous brothers in about 1750 B.C.E. (Genesis 37:28; 42:21) Throughout the stream of time, we find inflation in the slave trade, and the Biblical account of the price for Joseph falls exactly where it should to be in harmony with secular archaeology, as you can see in chart 1. Again, our alleged "J," "E," "D," and "P" composers would be a thousand years removed from Abraham, and "R" (the redactor) even further; thus they would have no access to this information so as to have gotten it correct.

Only the actual writer, Moses, would be aware of this information by family records or oral tradition.

The Inflation of the Slave Trade in Biblical Times (Wood, 1996)

SOURCE	DATE	PRICE OF A SLAVE IN SILVER
Akkad and 3rd Ur Dynasties	2000 B.C.E.	8–10 pieces of silver
Joseph (Genesis 37:2, 28)	1750 B.C.E.	20 pieces of silver
Hammurabi Code	1799–1700 B.C.E.	20 pieces of silver
Old Babylonian Tablets	B.C.E.	15–30 pieces of silver
Mari tablets	1799–1600 B.C.E.	20 pieces of silver
Exodus 21:32	1520–1470 B.C.E.	30 pieces of silver
Nuzi tablets	1499–1400 B.C.E.	30 pieces of silver
Ugarit tablets	1399–1200 B.C.E.	30–40 pieces of silver
Assyria	First millennium B.C.E.	50–60 pieces of silver
2 Kings 15:20	790 B.C.E.	50 pieces of silver
Persia	750–500 B.C.E.	90–120 pieces of silver

Seti I began much like his father Ramses, as a military commander. His military prowess led to many triumphs that are recorded on the walls of the temple of Amon-Ra at Karnak. Here Seti I recorded his military triumphs; captives are shown being seized by their hair. As was expressed earlier, victories were proudly recorded on Egyptian monuments, but embarrassing or critical events were ignored, that is, never chiseled into their annals of history.

Concluding Thoughts

I had given much thought to a conclusion that contained quotations from many reputable scholars who use thought-provoking points to support the writership of Moses for the Pentateuch, but what would that prove? Certainly, if you quote a reputable scholar you would add weight to an argument, but it does not make the case. It only validates that you are not alone in your reasoning. Therefore, I have added quotations of only two scholars to make just that point. One does not count the number of people who believe one thing as opposed to another and those with the most votes win. No, the results should be based on

172

evidence. In fact, the higher critics will infer that they are in the right by saying, 'Today, you will hardly find one scholar in the world who will argue for the writership of Moses for the Pentateuch.' If that makes them in the right, it also makes them in the wrong. Why? Because for centuries, for millenniums, the majority of Bible scholars—in the Jewish world, the Christian world, and the Islamic world—accepted Moses' writership; that is, until the Age of Reason within the eighteenth and nineteenth centuries when people started to question not only the writership of Moses but the very existence of God.

Would any Christian living in 1700 C.E. have ever doubted the writership of Moses? Hardly! So how did the Documentary Hypothesis become Documentary Fact? All it took was for some leading professors at major universities to plant seeds of doubt within their students. Being at the entrance of the era of higher criticism and skepticism of the nineteenth century, this Documentary Hypothesis had a well-cultivated field in which to grow. It created a domino effect as a few scholars produced a generation of students, who would then be the next generation of scholars, and so on.

As we moved into the twentieth century, these questions had become "facts" in the eyes of many; in fact, it became in vogue to challenge the Bible. Leading schools and leading scholars of higher criticism were the norm, and soon the conservative Christian was isolated. The twentieth-century student received a lean diet from those few scholars who still accepted God's Word as just that, the Word of God, fully inerrant, with 40 writers of 66 books over a period of about 1,600 years. No, these students would now be fed mostly liberal theology, and any who disagreed were portrayed as ignorant and naïve. This planting of uncertainty or mistrust, with question after question bringing Moses' writership into doubt, with most literature focusing on this type of propaganda, would create the latest generation of scholars, and today they dominate the world of scholarship.

How did this progressive takeover come off without a hitch? The conservative scholarship of the early twentieth century saw these liberal naysayers as nothing more than a fly at a picnic. Most did not even deem it necessary to address their questions, so by 1950–1970, the Documentary Hypothesis machine was in full throttle. It was about this same time that the sleeping giant finally awoke to find that conservative scholarship had taken a backseat to this new creature, liberal scholarship. It is only within the last 30–40 years that some very influential conservative scholars have started to publish books in a move to dislodge this liberal movement.* Is it too little, too late?

*This is not to say that the 19th and early 20th century did not have any apologist defending against biblical criticism. There were some giants in this field, like R. A. Torrey.

It is possible to displace higher criticism, but many factors stand in the way. For one, any opposition is painted as uninformed and inexperienced regarding the subject matter. Moreover, the books that tear down the Bible with all their alleged critical analysis sell far better than those do that encourage putting faith in God's Word. In addition, many conservative scholars tend to sit on the sideline and watch as a few leading scholars attempt to do the work of the many. In addition, there are liberal scholars continually putting out numerous articles and books, dominating the market. Unlike the conservative scholars in the first part of the twentieth century, these liberal scholars in the first part of the twenty-first century are not slowing down. Moreover, they have become more aggressive.

The book *Introduction to the Bible*, by John Laux, explains just what the Documentary Hypothesis would have meant for the Israelites if it were true:

> The Documentary Theory is built up on assertions which are either arbitrary or absolutely false. . . . If the extreme Documentary Theory were true, the Israelites would have been the victims of a clumsy deception when they permitted the heavy burden of the Law to be imposed upon them. It would have been the greatest hoax ever perpetrated in the history of the world.[161]

It goes much further than that; it would mean that the Son of God was either fooled by what these higher critics argue, that there was a tradition of Moses being the writer of the Pentateuch, which developed through time and was accepted as reality during Jesus' day, or that Jesus was a liar, because he had lived in heaven prior to his coming down to earth and was aware of the deception but had continued a tradition that he knew to be false. The truth is that the Son of God was well aware that Moses was, in fact, the writer of the Pentateuch and he presented Moses as such because he was there at the time!

So again, because Jesus taught that Moses was, in fact, the writer of the Pentateuch, we have three options:

- Jesus knew Moses was the writer because Jesus was there, in heaven, prior to his Virgin birth and observed Moses as the writer; or

---

161. John Laux, *Introduction to the Bible* (Chicago: Tan Books & Pub., 1992), 186.

- Jesus knew that Moses was not the writer and simply perpetuated a Jewish tradition that Moses was the writer; or

- Jesus possessed a limited knowledge and simply believed something that was a tradition because he was unaware of it being such.

So if Jesus knew Moses was *not* the writer and purposely conveyed misinformation for the sake of Jewish tradition, this makes Jesus a liar and therefore a sinner, which would contradict what Hebrews 4:15 says of him, that "he was without sin." If he was simply in ignorance and was mistakenly conveying misinformation, this certainly does away with Jesus having a prehuman existence. (John 1:1–2; 3:13; 6:38, 62; 8:23, 42, 58; Colossians 1:15–18; Revelation 3:14; Proverbs 8:22–30) Based on the scriptures and other evidence presented, we can conclude that Jesus was well aware that Moses was the writer, and that is what he truthfully taught.

Duane Garrett makes the following observation concerning the Documentary Hypothesis:

> The time has long passed for scholars of every theological persuasion to recognize that the Graf-Wellhausen theory, as a starting point for continued research, is dead. The Documentary Hypothesis and the arguments that support it have been effectively demolished by scholars from many different theological perspectives and areas of expertise. Even so, the ghost of Wellhausen hovers over Old Testament studies and symposiums like a thick fog. . . . One wonders if we will ever return to the day when discussions of Genesis will not be stilted by interminable references to P and J. There are indications that such a day is coming. Many scholars are exploring the inadequacies of the Documentary Hypothesis and looking toward new models for explaining the Pentateuch.[162]

These world-renowned scholars who have gone left of center are witty and able to express thoughts, ideas, and feelings coherently, having conviction that leads unsuspecting ones who are not aware of the facts to accept ideas that are made to appear as smooth-fitting pieces in a large puzzle, thinking that they are nothing more than long-awaited answers. Sadly, many unsuspecting readers have taken their words as absolute truth.

Jesus quotes or alludes to 23 of the 39 books of the Hebrew Scriptures. Specifically, he quotes all five of the books attributed to

---

[162] Garrett, Duane. *Rethinking Genesis: The Sources and Authorship of the First Book of the Pentateuch* (Grand Rapids: Baker Books, 1991), 13.

Moses—the book of Deuteronomy 16 times alone, this obviously being one of his favorites. As we close this chapter, we are going to let our greatest witness take the stand. As you read Jesus' references to Moses and the Law you will undoubtedly notice that he viewed Moses' writership as historically true, completely authoritative, and inspired of God. If one does not accept, Moses, as the writer of the Pentateuch as Jesus did, is that not calling Jesus a liar.

As Christians, we accept what the Bible teaches as true. By way of common sense and sound reasoning, the vast majority of the issues of higher criticism's Social Progressive Christian and Christian Modernists have been answered quite easily by the conservative scholar in absolute terms: for example, F. David Farnell, Gleason L. Archer Jr., C. John Collins, K. A. Kitchen, Norman L. Geisler, and others. For the handful of issues left, we still have reasonable answers, which are not beyond a reasonable doubt at this time; we are quite content to wait until we are provided with the concrete answers that will make these few issues beyond all reasonable doubt. The last 150 years of evidence that has come in by way of archaeological discoveries, a better understanding of the original language, historical-cultural and contextual understanding, as well as manuscripts has answered almost all those doubtful areas that have been called into question by the higher critics. Therefore, because we lack the complete answers for a few remaining issues means nothing.

Consider this: A critic raises an issue, but it is answered by a new archaeological discovery a few years later. The critic runs to another issue, and it is later answered by an improved understanding of the original languages. Then he runs to look for yet another issue, and it is answered by thousands of manuscripts that are uncovered over a period of two decades. This has been the case with thousands of issues. What are we to think the agenda is of those who continue scouring God's Word looking for errors, discrepancies, and contradictions? How many times must they raise objections and be proven wrong before we stop listening to their cries? If that is the case, why do their books still outsell those that expose their erroneous thinking? Does that say something about the Christian community and their desire for tabloid scholarship (sensationalized stories)? Would the average Christian rather read an article or book by Dan Brown on how Jesus allegedly married and had sexual relations with Mary Magdalene and fathered children (false, of course), or read an article or book on the actual, even more fascinating account of Jesus' earthly life, based on the four Gospels?

For today's Christian, there is no more important study than the life and ministry of the real, historical Jesus Christ. The writer of the book of Hebrews exhorts us to **"fix our eyes on** Jesus," to **"consider him** who endured such opposition from sinful men." Moreover, Jehovah God himself commanded: "This is my Son, whom I love; with him I am well pleased. **Listen to him!**" (*NIV*, bolding added) While an apologetic of the study of the "*Historical Jesus*," or "*The Case for the Resurrection of Jesus*"[163] is certainly fine, the primary source of the four Gospels accounts of Matthew, Mark, Luke, and John should be first place, the starting point of any real investigation of Jesus' life and ministry. A life and ministry that viewed the Old Testament as historically true and of the greatest importance to his followers that he would leave behind after his ascension back to heaven.

We return to Wellhausen, who investigated his documentary hypothesis under the worldview of Israelite religion from an evolutionary model: (1) at the beginning it was animistic and spiritistic, (2) gradually developing into polytheism, (3) moving eventually into henotheism (choosing one god out of many), and finally (4) gravitating to monotheism. Wellhausen could not accept that this development took place in a short period, but was an evolution that took more than a millennium. This evolutionary process is no longer held among today's critical scholarship.

Another obstacle was that Wellhausen did not believe in the miraculous and could not accept prophetic statements (for example, Genesis 49) happening before the actual events. This mindset was the catalyst behind his research.[164] Consequently, Wellhausen investigated the text with this way of thinking and that state of mind contributed to his discovering the Documentary Hypothesis issues of different uses of the divine name, discrepancies, repetitions (doublets), and differences in style and language, reading his views into the text (eisegesis).

The above facts of this book have easily demonstrated that the evidence of the documentary hypothesis is really no evidence at all. The modern-day critic has to deal with the lack of consensus on the part of his colleagues, who lack in agreement for the explanation of the sources.

> This failure to achieve consensus is represented by the occasional division of source strata into multiple layers (see Smend's J1 and J2) that often occasions the appearance of new

---

[163.] **Recommended**: Gary R. Habermas, *The Historical Jesus: Ancient Evidence for the Life of Christ* (Joplin, MO: College Press, 1996); Gary R. Habermas, *The Case for the Resurrection of Jesus* (Grand Rapids, MI: Kregel, 2004); Craig A. Evans, *Fabricating Jesus: How Modern Scholars Distort the Gospels* (Downers Grove, IL: IVP Books, 2006); Timothy Paul Jones, *Misquoting Truth: A Guide to the Fallacies of Bart Ehrman's Misquoting Jesus* (Downers Grove, IL: IVP Books, 2007).

[164] Tremper Longman III, and Raymond B. Dillard, *An Introduction to the Old Testament* (Grand Rapids: Zondervan, 2006), 43–44.

sigla (for instance, Eissfeldt's L [*aienquelle*], Noth's G[*rundschrift*], Fohrer's N [for Nomadic], and Pfeiffer's S [for Seir]. A further indication of the collapse of the traditional documentary hypothesis is the widely expressed doubt that E was ever an independent source (Voz, Rudolph, Mowinckel; cf. Kaiser, IOT, 42 n. 18). Similar disagreements are also found in the dating of the sources. J has been dated to the period of Solomon by Von Rad, though Schmidt would argue for the seventh century, and Van Seters (1992, 34) has advocated an exile date. While most scholars believe P is postexilic, Haran has argued that it is to be associated with Hezekiah's reforms in the eighth century BC.[165]

While the lack of consensus is not in and of itself capable of disproving the proposition of sources other than Moses for the writing of the Pentateuch, it does cast even more doubt on the critical scholar's proposal that the new school of the Documentary Hypothesis has any more to offer than the old school of Wellhausen.

As this book has clearly demonstrated, Moses is the inspired author of the Pentateuch. At best, we can accept that it is likely that Joshua may have updated the text in Deuteronomy chapter 34, which speaks of Moses' death, and it is possible that Joshua may have made the reference in Numbers 12:3 that refer to Moses as being 'the humblest man on the face of the earth.'[166] In addition, we can accept that a later copyist [or even possibly Ezra, another inspired author] updated Genesis 11:28, 31 to read "of the Chaldeans," a name of a land and its inhabitants in the southern portion of Babylonia that *possibly* was not recognized as Chaldea until several hundred years after Moses.

> The origin of the Chaldeans is uncertain but may well be in the west, or else branches of the family may have moved there (cf. Job 1:17). The general name for the area in the earliest period is unknown, since it was part of Sumer (*see* SHINAR); so it cannot be argued that the qualification of Abraham's home city UR as "of the Chaldeans" (Gen. 11:28, 31; 15:7; as later Neh. 9:7; cf. Acts 7:4) is necessarily a later insertion in the text.[167]

The same would hold true of a copyist updating Genesis 36:31, which reads: "Now these are the kings who reigned in the land of Edom before *any king reigned over the sons of Israel*." Moses and Joshua were

---

[165] Ibid., 49–50.

[166] For the possibility of Moses penning these words, see my comments in the first paragraph of section four.

[167] Geoffrey W. Bromiley, vol. 1, *The International Standard Bible Encyclopedia, Revised* (Wm. B. Eerdmans, 1988; 2002), 630.

long gone for hundreds of years before Israel ever had a king over them.[168] The same would hold true again for Genesis 14:14, which reads: When Abram heard that his relative had been taken captive, he led out his trained men, born in his house, three hundred and eighteen, and went in pursuit *as far as Dan*. Dan was an area settled long after Moses death, after the Israelites had conquered the Promise Land. This too is obviously an update as well, making it contemporary to its readers.[169]

Reference to "Ur of the Chaldeans"[170] (11:28) identifies the native land of Haran but not necessarily of Terah and his sons Abram and Nahor. In fact, the inclusion of this information for Haran may suggest the ancestral home was elsewhere (for this discussion see comments on 12:1). "Ur of the Chaldeans" occurs three times in Genesis (11:28, 31; 15:7) and once elsewhere (Neh 9:7). Stephen identified the place of God's revelation to Abram as "Mesopotamia" from which he departed: "So he left the land of the Chaldeans and settled in Haran" (Acts 7:3–4). The "land [*chōra*] of the Chaldeans" rather than "Ur of the Chaldeans" is the Septuagint translation, as reflected in Stephen's sermon, which can be explained as either a textual slip due to the prior phrase "land of his birth" or the ancient translator's uncertainty about the identity of the site. J. W. Wevers proposes that due to the apposition of "land of his birth," the translator interpreted "Ur" as a region.[171, 172]

As we have already stated, the critic is fond of finding portions of the text that lack secular support, and then summarily dismissing it as not being a real historical account. Once evidence surfaces to support their dismissal as being wrong and premature, they simply never mention this section again, but move on to another. The question that begs to be

---

[168] It should be noted that even this statement could belong to Moses, even though there were no kings in Israel at this time. How? He would be aware that Jehovah had promised Abraham that he would be so great that kings would come out of him (Gen 17:6) and the preparation for such is mentioned at Deuteronomy 17:14-20.

[169] It should be noted that this author does not accept higher criticisms unending desire to find source(s) for a book, because they have dissected it to no end. While there are a few details that may have been updated by a copyist, or even the inspired writer Ezra (writer of Chronicles and the book that bears his name), this does not mean that we accept the update, if it is such, as the inspired material that was originally written, unless it was done by another inspired writer like Joshua, Ezra, or Nehemiah, or even possibly Jeremiah. It is also possible that it could be an explanatory addition.

[170] Hb. "Chaldeans" כַּשְׂדִּים is *kaldu* (Akk.) in Assyrian texts, and the Gk. has καλδαιοι; the original *sd* has undergone a change to *ld* (see R. S. Hess, "Chaldea," *ABD* 1.886–87).

[171] J. W. Wevers, *Notes on the Greek Text of Genesis*, Septuagint and Cognate Studies 35 (Atlanta: Scholars Press, 1993), 158.

[172] K. A. Mathews, vol. 1B, *Genesis 11:27-50:26*, electronic ed., Logos Library System; The New American Commentary (Nashville: Broadman & Holman Publishers, 2007), 99–100.

asked by the logical and reasonable mind is, how many times must this take place before they stop and accept the Bible as sound and reliable history? Let us look at the historicity of the above account of Abraham's men defeating the Mesopotamian kings, for it is historically sound. Information had become known in the 20th century that vindicates this account as being historically true, and removes yet another arguing point from those supporters of the documentary hypothesis:

> The name of Chedorlaomer, King of Elam, contains familiar Elamite components: *kudur* meant "servant," and *Lagamar* was a high goddess in the Elamite pantheon. Kitchen (Ancient Orient, p. 44) generally prefers the vocalization Kutir instead of Kudur and gives the references for at least three Elamite royal names of this type. He equates tidal with a Hittite name, Tudkhaliya, attested from the nineteenth century B.C. As for Arioch, one King of Larsa ("El-Larsa") from this era was Eri-aku ("Servant of the Moon-god"), whose name in Akkadian was *Arad-Sin* (with the same meaning). The Mari tablets refer to persons by the name of Ariyuk. The cuneiform of the original of Amraphel, formerly equated with Hammurabi of Babylon, is not demonstrable for the twentieth century (Hammurabi himself dates from the eighteenth century, but there may possibly be a connection with Amorite names like *Amud-pa-ila*, according to H. B. Huffman. . . . It should be added that according to G. Pettinato, the leading epigraphist of the Ebla documents dating from 2400–2250 B.C., mention is made in the Ebla tablets of Sodom (spelled *Si-da-mu*), Gomorrah (spelled in Sumerian cuneiform *I-ma-ar*), and Zoar (*Za-e-ar*). He feels that quite possibly these may be the same cities mentioned in the Abrahamic narrative.[173]

> W. F. Albright comments: In spite of our failure hitherto to fix the historical horizon of this chapter, we may be certain that its contents are very ancient. There are several words and expressions found nowhere else in the Bible and now known to belong to the second millenium. The names of the towns in Transjordania are also known to be very ancient.[174]

In the final analysis, based on both the internal and external evidence, we can absolute confidence that Moses was the author of the Pentateuch. The minor additions of Joshua, who was himself an inspired

173. Gleason L. Archer, *Encyclopedia of Bible Difficulties* (Grand Rapids: Zondervan, 1982), 90–91.
174. H. C. Alleman and E. E. Flack, *Old Testament Commentary* (Philadelphia: Fortress, 1954), 14.

writer, as well as the handful of updates in the text to make it clearer to the then-current reader does no harm to the inspired message that God wished to convey.

Bibliography

Akin, Daniel L. *The New American Commentary: 1, 2, 3 John.* Nashville, TN: Broadman & Holman , 2001.

Aland, Kurt and Barbara. *The Text of the New Testament.* Grand Rapids: Eerdmans, 1987.

Alden, Robert L. *Job, The New American Commentary, vol. 11 .* Nashville: Broadman & Holman Publishers, 2001.

Aldrich, C Joseph. *Lifestyle Evangelism.* Portland, OR: Multnoma Press, 1981.

Alleman, H. C., and E. E. Flack. *Old Testament Commentary.* Philadelphia: Fortress Press, 1954.

Anders, Max. *Holman New Testament Commentary: vol. 8, Galatians-Colossians .* Nashville, TN: Broadman & Holman Publishers, 1999.

—. *Holman New Testament Commentary: vol. 8, Galatians, Ephesians, Philippians, Colossians.* Nashville, TN: Broadman & Holman Publishers, 1999.

—. *Holman Old Testament Commentary - Proverbs .* Nashville: B&H Publishing, 2005.

Anders, Max, and Trent Butler. *Holman Old Testament Commentary: Isaiah.* Nashiville, TN: B&H Publishing, 2002.

Andrews, Edward D. *THE COMPLETE GUIDE TO BIBLE TRANSLATION: Bible Translation Choices and Principles.* Cambridge: Christian Publishing House, 2012.

—. *THE EVANGELISM HANDBOOK: How All Christians Can Effectively Share God's Word in Their Community.* Cambridge: Christian Publishing House, 2013.

Andrews, Edward D. *AN INTRODUCTION TO BIBLE DIFFICULTIES So-Called Errors and Contradictions.* Cambridge: Christian Publishing House, 2011.

—. *An Introduction to Bible Difficulties: So-called Errors and Contradictions.* Cambridge, OH: Christian Publlishing House, 2012.

—. *BIBLE DIFFICULTIES: Debunking the Documentary Hypothesis.* Cambridge: Christian Publishing House, 2011.

—. *BOOKS OF 2 JOHN 3 JOHN and JUDE CPH New Testament Commentary*. Cambridge: Christian Publishing House, 2013.

—. *CHRISTIAN THEOLOGY: The Evangelism Study Tool*. Cambridge, OH: Christian Publishing House, 2016.

—. *CONVERSATIONAL EVANGELISM: Defending the Faith, Reasoning from the Scriptures, Explaining and Proving, Instructing in Sound Doctrine, and Overturning False Reasoning*. Cambridge, OH: Christian Publishing House, 2015.

—. *THE CHRISTIAN APOLOGIST: Always Being Prepared to Make a Defense* . Cambridge: Christian Publishing House, 2014.

—. *The Text of the New Testament: A Beginner's Guide to New Testament Textual Criticism*. Cambridge, OH: Bible-Translation.Net Books, 2012.

Archer, Gleason L. *A Survey of Old Testament Introduction (Revised and Expanded)*. Chicago: Moody, 1994.

—. *A Survey of Old Testament Introduction*. Chicago: Moody, 1994.

—. *Encyclopedia of Bible Difficulties*. Grand Rapids: Zondervan, 1982.

Arndt, William, Frederick W. Danker, and Walter Bauer. *A Greek-English Lexicon of the New Testament and Other Early Christian Literature*. 3rd ed. . Chicago: University of Chicago Press, 2000.

Arnold, Clinton E. *Zondervan Illustrated Bible Backgrounds Commentary Volume 2: John, Acts*. . Grand Rapids, MI: Zondervan, 2002.

—. *Zondervan Illustrated Bible Backgrounds Commentary Volume 3: Romans to Philemon*. Grand Rapids: Zondervan, 2002.

—. *Zondervan Illustrated Bible Backgrounds Commentary Volume 4: Hebrews to Revelation*. Grand Rapids, MI: Zondervan, 2002.

—. *Zondervan Illustrated Bible Backgrounds Commentary: Matthew, Mark, Luke, vol. 1*. Grand Rapids, MI: Zondervan, 2002.

Baer, Daniel. *The Unquenchable Fire*. Maitland, FL: Xulon Press, 2007.

Bahnsen, Greg, and Van Til. *Apologetic* . (Phillipsburg, NJ: Presbyterian and Reformed, 1998.

Barbour, R. S. *Traditio-Historical Criticism of the Gospels*. London: SPCK, 1972.

Barclay, William. *The Letter to the Hebrews (New Daily Study Bible)*. Louisville, KY: Westminster John Knox Press, 2002.

Barnett, Paul. *The Birth of Christianity: The First Twenty Years (After Jesus, Vol. 1)* . Grand Rapids, MI: Wm. B. Eerdmans , 2005.

Barton, John. *The Nature of Biblical Criticism*. Louisville: Westminster John Knox Press, 2007.

Barton, S.C. "'The Communal Dimension of Earliest Christianity'." *JTS 43*, 1992: 399–427.

—. *Discipleship and Family Ties in Mark and Matthew*. Cambridge: Cambridge University Press, 1994.

Bercot, David W. *A Dictionary of Early Christian Beliefs*. Peabody: Hendrickson, 1998.

Berkhof, Louis. *New Testament Introduction*. Grand Rapids: Eerdman-Sevensma, 1915.

—. *Principles of Biblical Interpretation*. . Grand Rapids, MI: Baker House, 1992.

Black, Allen, and Mark C Black. *THE COLLEGE PRESS NIV COMMENTARY 1 & 2 PETER*. Joplin: College Press Publishing Company, 1998.

Blenkinsopp, Joseph. *Isaiah 56-66: A New Translation with Introduction and Commentary*. New York: Anchor Bible, 2003.

Blomberg, Craig L. *Historical Reliability of the Gospels*. Downer Groves, IL: IVP Academic, 2007.

Blomberg, Craig L. "New Testament miracles and Higher Criticism: Climbing Up the Slippery Slope." *JETS 27/4*, December 1984: 436.

Blomberg, Craig L, and Stanley E., Stovell, Beth M Porter Jr. *Biblical Hermeneutics Five Views*. Downers Grove: InterVarsity Press, 2012.

Blomberg, Craig. *The New American Commentary: Matthew* . Nashville, TN : Broadman & Holman Publishers, 2001.

Boa, Kenneth, and Kruidenier. *Holman New Testament Commentary: Romans*. Nashville: Broadman & Holman, 2000.

Bock, Darrell L. *"Form Criticism,"* in *New Testament Criticism and Interpretation. Edited by David A. Black and David S. Dockery.* Grand Rapids: Zondervan, 1991.

—. *Studying the Historical Jesus: A Guide to Sources and Methods*. Grand Rapids, MI: Baker, 2002.

—. *The Missing Gospels: Unerthing the Truth Behind Alternative Christianities*. Nashville, TN: Thomas Nelson, 2006.

Borchert, Gerald L. *The New American Commentary: John 1-11* . Nashville, TN: Broadman & Holman Publishers, 2001.

Borchert, Gerald L. *The New American Commentary vol. 25B, John 12–21.* Nashville: Broadman & Holman Publishers, 2002.

Bradley, Anthony B. *Liberating Black Theology: The Bible and the Black Experience in America.* Wheaton: Crossway, 2010.

Brand, Chad, Charles Draper, and England Archie. *Holman Illustrated Bible Dictionary: Revised, Updated and Expanded.* Nashville, TN: Holman, 2003.

Bratcher, Robert. "Inerrancy: Clearing Away Confusion." *Christianity Today*, May 29, 1981: 12.

Bray, Gerald. *Biblical Interpretation: Past and Present.* Downers Grove, IL: InterVarsity Press, 1996.

Bridges, Jerry. *The Practice of Godliness* . Colorado Springs, CO: : NavPress, 1983.

Briley, Terry R. *The College Press NIV Commentary: Isaiah.* Joplin, MO: ollege Press Pub, 2000.

Bromiley, Geoffrey W. *The International Standard Bible Encyclopedia (Vol. 1-4).* Grand Rapids, MI: William B. Eerdmans Publishing Co., 1986.

Bromiley, Geoffrey W., and Gerhard Friedrich. *Theological Dictionary of the New Testament, ed. Gerhard Kittel, vol. 4.* Grand Rapids, MI: Eerdmans, 1964-.

Brotzman, Ellis R. *Old Testament Textual Criticism.* Grand Rapids: Baker Academic, 1994.

Bruce, F. F. *The New International Commentary on the New Testament: The Epistle to the Hebrews (Revised).* Grand Rapids, MI: William B. Eermans Publishing Company, 1990.

Bucher, Christina. "New Directions in Biblical Interpretation Revisited." *Bretheren Life and Thought 60, no. 1,* Spring 2015: 36.

Bultmann, Rudolf. *The History of the Synoptic Tradition.* Peabody: Hendrickson, 1990.

—. *The History of the Synoptic Tradition. Translated by John Marsh. Revised Edition.* Peabody, MA: Hendrickson, 1963.

Bultmann, Rudolf. "The New Approach to the Synoptic Problem." *Journal of Religion*, July, 1926: 345.

Bultmann, Rudolf, and Frederick C. Translated by Grant. *"The Study of the Synoptic Gospels," in Form Criticism, Two Essays on New Testament Research.* . New York: Harper & Brothers, 1932.

Burge, Gary M. *Interpreting the Fourth Gospel, Guides to New Testament Exegesis, vol. 3.* Grand Rapids, MI: Baker Book House, 1992.

Buter, Trent C. *Holman New Testament Commentary: Luke.* Nashville, TN: Broadman & Holman Publishers, 2000.

Byrne, James M. *Religion and the Enlightenment from Descartes to Kant.* Louisville: Westminster John Knox Press, 1996.

Caba, Tedl et al.,. *The Apologetics Study Bible: Real Questions, Straight Answers, Stronger Faith.* Nashville: Holman Bible Publishers, 2007.

Caird, George B. "The Study of the Gospels: II. Form Criticism." *Expository Times LXXXVII*, February 1976: 139.

Carson, D. A, and Douglas J Moo. *An Introduction to the New Testament.* Grand Rapids, MI: Zondervan, 2005.

Carson, D. A. *New Bible Commentary: 21st Century Edition.* 4th ed. Downers Grove: Inter-Varisity Press, 1994.

Cassuto, Umberto. *The Documentary Hypothesis: And The Composition of the Pentateuch.* Jerusalem: Shalem Press, 2006.

Coleman, E. Robert. *The Master Plan of Evangelism.* Westwood, NJ: Fleming H. Revell Company, 1964.

Collins, John. *Genesis 1-4: A Linguistic, Literary, and Theological Commentary.* Philipsburg: P&R, 2006.

Comfort, Philip. *Encountering the Manuscripts: An Introduction to New Testament Paleography and Textual Criticism.* Nashville: Broadman & Holman, 2005.

—. *Encounterring the Manuscripts: An Introduction to New Testament Paleography and Textual Criticism.* Nashville: Broadman & Holman, 2005.

Comfort, Philip W. *New Testament Text and Translation Commentary.* Carol Stream: Tyndale House Publishers, 2008.

Comfort, Philip, and David Barret. *The Text of the Earliest New Testament Greek Manuscripts.* Wheaton: Tyndale House Publishers, 2001.

Cook, Stephen L. "Introduction: Case Studies from the Second Wave of Research in the Social World of the Hebrew Bible," ed. Ronald Simkins and Athalya Brenner." *Semeia 87*, 1999: 1-2.

Cooper, Lamar Eugene. *The New American Commentary, Ezekiel, vol. 17.* Nashville, TN: Broadman & Holman Publishers, 1994.

Cottrell, Peter, and Maxwell Turner. *Linguistics and Biblical Interpretation.* Downers Grove: InterVarsity Press, 1989.

Cruse, C. F. *Eusebius' Eccliatical History.* Peabody, MA: Hendrickson, 1998.

Daly, Mary. *Beyond God the Father: Toward a Philosophy of Liberation.* Boston: Beacon Press, 1973.

Davies, William D. *Invitation to the New Testament, A Guide to Its Main Witnesses.* Garden City, N.Y.: Doubleday, 1966.

Davis, John J. *Paradise to Prison: Studies in Genesis.* Salem: Sheffield, 1975.

Dayton, Donald W. "The Battle for the Bible: Renewing the Inerrancy Debate." *The Christian Century* , Nov 10, 1976: 976-80.

Delahaunty, R. J. *Spinoza: Arguments of the Philosophers.* London: Routledge & Kegan Paul Books, 1985.

Dockery, David S., Kenneth A. Matthews, and Robert B. Sloan. *Foundations for Biblical Interpretation.* Nashville: Broadman & Holman Publishers, 1994.

Dodd, C. H. *History and the Gospel.* London: Nisbet, 1938.

Donald A. Hanger, The Jewish Reclamation of Jesus. Eugene: Wipf and Stock, 1997.

Driver, G R. *Canaanite Myths and Legends.* New York: T. & T. Clark, 1971.

Dunn, James D. G. *"The Messianic Secret in Mark," in The Messianic Secret Edited by Christopher Tuckett.* Philadelphia: Fortress, 1983.

Easley, Kendell H. *Holman New Testament Commentary, vol. 12, Revelation.* (Nashville, TN: Broadman & Holman Publishers, 1998.

Eims, LeRoy. *One to One Evangelism.* Wheaton, IL: Victor Books, 1974, 1990.

Ellingworth, Paul. *The Epistle to the Hebrews: A Commentary on the Greek Text.* Grand Rapids, MI: W.B. Eerdmans, 1993.

Elliott, J.H. *A Home for the Homeless: A Sociological Exegesis of I Peter: Its Situation and Strategy* . London: SCM Press, 1982.

Elliott, John H. "Social-Scientific Criticism of the New Testament: More on Methods and Models." *Semeia 35*, 1986: 6-7.

—. *What is Social Scientific Criticism?* . Minneapolis: Fortress Press, 1993.

Elwell, Walter A. *Evangelical Dictionary of Theology (Second Edition)*. Grand Rapids: Baker Academic, 2001.

Elwes, R H M. *A Theologico-political Treatise, and a Political Treatise* . New York, NY: Cosimo Classics , 2005.

Erickson, Millard J. "Biblical Inerrancy: the last twenty-five years." *Journal of the Evangelical Theological Society*, 1982: 387-394.

Erickson, Milliard J. *Christian Theology*. Grand Rapids, MI: Baker Academic, 1998.

Erickson, Richard J. *A Beginner's Guide to New Testament Exegesis*. Downers Grove: InterVarsity Press, 2005.

Esler, Philip F. *The First Christians in their Social Worlds* . New York: Taylor & Francis, 2007.

—. *The First Christians in their Social Worlds*. New York: Routledge, 1994.

Farmer, William R. *The Synoptic Problem*. Macon, Ga: Mercer University, 1976.

Farnell, F. David. "Historical Criticism vs. Grammatico-Historical Criticism?" *The Jesus Quest*, Quo Vadis Evangelicals: 503-520.

Fasold, Ralph, Jeff Connor-Linton, and ed. *An Introduction to Language and Linguistics*. Cambridge: Cambridge University Press, 2006.

Fee, Gordon D. *New Testament Exegesis: A Handbook for Studemts and Pastors*. Louisville: Westminister John Knox Press, 2002.

Ferguson, Everett. *Backgrounds of Early Christianity*. Grand Rapids, MI: Wm. B. Eerdmans, 2003.

Frame, John M. *Apologetics to the Glory of God*. Phillipsburg: P&R Publishing, 1994.

Frampton, Travis L. *Spinoza and the Rise of Historical Criticism of the Bible*. New York: T&T Clark, 2006.

Free, J. P. *Archaeology and Bible History (Revised amnd Expanded Edition)*. Grand Rapids: Zondervan, 1992.

Friedan, Betty. *The Feminist Mistique* . New York: Dell Publishing, 1963.

Friedman, Richard Elliot. *Who Wrote The Bible*. San Francisco: Harper Collins, 1997.

Friedman, Richard Elliott. *The Bible With Sources Revealed*. Northampton: Harper Collins, 2005.

Gangel, Kenneth O. *Holman New Testament Commentary: Acts*. Nashville, TN: Broadman & Holman Publishers, 1998.

Gangel, Kenneth O. *Holman New Testament Commentary, vol. 4, John* . Nashville, TN: Broadman & Holman Publishers, 2000.

—. *Holman Old Testament Commentary: Daniel*. Nashville: Broadman & Holman Publishers, 2001.

Garrett, Don. *The Cambridge companion to Spinoza*. Cambridge: Cambridge University Press, 1996.

Garrett, Duane. *Rethinking Genesis: The Sources and Authorship of the First Book of the Pentateuch* . Grand Rapids: Baker Books, 1991.

Geisler, Norman L. *Defending Inerrancy: Affirming the Accuracy of Scripture for a New Generation*. Grand Rapids, MI: Baker Books, 2012.

—. *Inerrancy*. Grand Rapids, MI: Zondervan, 1980.

Geisler, Norman L, and William E Nix. *A General Introduction to the Bible*. Chicago: Moody Press, 1996.

Geisler, Norman L. *"Inductivism, Materialism, and Rationalism: Bacon, Hobbes, and Spinoza," in The Biblical Errancy: An Analysis of Its Philosophical Roots. Edited by Norman Geisler*. Grand Rapids: Zondervan, 1981.

—. *Baker Encyclopedia of Christian Apologetics*. Grand Rapids: Baker Books, 1999.

—. *Biblical Errancy: An Analysis of Its Philosophical Roots*. Eugene, OR: Wipf and Stock Publisher, 1981.

Geisler, Norman L., and Thomas Howe. *The Big Book of Bible Difficulties*. Grand Rapids: Baker Books, 1992.

Geisler, Norman, and David Geisler. *CONVERSATION EVANGELISM: How to Listen and Speak So You Can Be Heard*. Eugene: Harvest House Publishers, 2014.

—. *CONVERSATION EVANGELISM: How to Listen and Speak So You Can Be Heard*. Eugene: Harvest House Publishers, 2009.

Geisler, Norman, and Ron Brooks. *When Skeptics Ask* . Grand Rapids, MI: Baker Books, 1996.

George, Timothy. *The New American Commentary: Galatians* . Nashville, TN: Broadman & Holman Publishers, 2001.

Gilson, Etienne, and Thomas Langan. *Modern Philosophy: Descartes to Kant.* New York: Random House, 1963.

Goodspeed, Edgar J. *Matthew, Apostle and Evangelist.* Philadelphia: John C. Winston, 1959.

Goodspeed, J. *Matthew, Apostle and Evangelist.* Philadelphia: John C. Winston, 1959..

Gorman, Michael J. *Elements of Biblical Exegesis: A Basic Guide for Students and Ministers.* Peabody: Hendrickson, 2001.

Green, Joel B, Scot McKnight, and Howard Marshall. *Dictionary of Jesus and the Gospels.* Downers Grove, IL: InterVarsity Press, 1992.

Greenlee, J Harold. *Introduction to New Testament Textual Criticism.* Peabody: Hendrickson, 1995.

Grenz, Stanley J., and Roger E Olsen. *20th Century Theology: God & the World in a Transitional Age.* Downers Gove: Intervarsity Press, 1992.

Grudem, Wayne, Leland Ryken, John C Collins, Vern S Poythress, and Bruce Winter. *Translating Truth: The Case for Essentially Literal Bible Translation.* Wheaton: Crossway Books, 2005.

Guelich, Robert A. *The Sermon on the Mount, A Foundation for Understanding.* Waco, TX: Word, 1982.

Gundry, Robert H. *The Use of the Old Testament in St. Matthew's Gospel.* Leiden: E. J. Brill, 1967.

Gundry, Robert H. "The Language Milieu of First-Century Palestine." *Journal of Biblical Literature 83*, 1964: 408.

Gunkel, Hermann (Translated by Scullion, John J. Edited by Scott, William R.). *The Stories of Genesis.* Berkeley: BIBAL, 1994.

Gunkel, Hermann. *The Stories of Genesis. Translated by John J. Scullion. Edited by William R. Scott.* Berkeley: BIBAL, 1994.

Guthrie, Donald. *Introduction to the New Testament (Revised and Expanded).* Downers Grove, IL: InterVarsity Press, 1990.

Guthrie, George H. *The NIV Application Commentary: Hebrews.* Grand Rapids, MI: Zondervan, 1998.

Gutierrez, Gustavo. *A Theology of Liberation: History, Politics, and Salvation.* Maryknoll, NY: Orbis Books, 1988.

Habib, M. A. R. *A History of Literary Criticism and Theory from Plato to the Present.* Malden: Blackwell Publishing, 2008.

Hagner, Donald. *The New Testament, History, and the Historical Critical Method, in New Testament Criticism and Interpretation.* Grand Rapids: Baker, 2013.

Hanson, K. C., and Douglas E. Oakman. *Palestine in the time of Jesus .* Minneapolis: : Augsburg Press, 1998.

Harris, Robert Laird, Gleason Leonard Archer, and Bruce K Waltke. *Theological Wordbook of the Old Testament.* Chicago: Moody Press, 1999, c1980.

Harrison, Everett F. *Introduction to the New Testament.* Grand Rapids: Eerdmans, 1971.

Harrison, R. K. *Introduction to the Old Testament.* Massachusetts: Hendrickson, 2004.

Hasel, Gerhard F. *Understanding the Living Word of God. .* Mountain View, CA: Pacific Press, 1980.

Hayes, John H, and Carl R Holladay. *Biblical Exegesis: A Beginner's Handbook.* Lousiville, KY: Westminister John Knox Press, 2007.

Hill, Jonathan. *Zondervan Handbook to the History of Christianity.* Oxford: Lion, 2006.

Hindson, Ed, and Ergun Caner. *The Popular Encyclopedia of Apologetics: Surveying the Evidence for the Truth of Christianity.* Eugene: Harvest House, 2008.

Hoerth, Alfred. *Archaeology and the Old Testament.* Grand Rapids: Baker, 1998.

Holbert, John C, and Alyce M McKenzie. *What Not to Say: Avoiding the Common Mistakes that Can Sink Your Sermon.* Lousiville: Westminster Knox Press, 1972.

House, Paul R. *The New American Commentary: 2 Kings .* Nashville: Broadman & Holman Publishers, 2001.

—. *The New American Commentary: Vol. 8., 2 Kings.* Nashville: Broadman & Holman Publishers, 2001.

House, Paul R., and Eric Mitchell. *Old Testament Survey (2nd Edition).* Nashville, TN: B&H Publishing Group, 2007.

Howe, Thomas A. *Objectivity in Biblical Interpretation*. North Charleston: CreateSpace, 2015.

Hume, David. *An Enquiry Concerning Human Understanding (vol. 35)*. Chicago: Great Books of the Western World, 1952.

Hume, David, and Adam Smith. *An Enquiry Concerning Human Understanding: And Selections from a Treatise of Human Nature*. New York: Barnes & Noble Library of Essential Reading, 2004.

Hutchison, John C. "Darwin's Evolutionary Theory and 19th-Century Natural Theology." *Bibliotheca Sacra 152*, July-September 1995: 334.

Huxley, Thomas H. *Science and Christian Tradition*. New York: D. Appleton, 1899.

Jeremias, Joachim. *New Testament Theology*. New York: Charles Scribner's Sons, 1971.

John, Robert H. *Evangelicals at an Impasse: Biblical Authority in Practice*. Atlanta: John Knox, 1979.

Johnson, Phillip E. *Darwin on Trial. Second Edition*. Downers Grove: InterVarsity, 1993.

Johnson, S. Lewis. *The Old Testament in the New: An Argument for Biblical Inspiration Contemporary Evangelical Perspectives*. Grand Rapids: Zondervan, 1980.

Kaiser Jr., Walter C. *The Old Testament Documents: Are They Reliable & Relevant?* Downer Groves: InterVarsity Press, 2001.

Kaiser, Christopher B. *Creational Theology and the History of Physical Science: The Creationist Tradition from Basil to Bohr*. Leiden: Brill, 1997.

Kaiser, Walter C, and Moises Silva. *Introduction to Biblical Hermeneutics: The Search for Meaning*. Grand Rapids: Zondervan, 1994, 2007.

Käsemann, Ernst. *"The Problem of the Historical Jesus," in Essays on New Testament Themes. Translated by W. J. Montague*. Philadelphia: Fortress Press, 1982.

Kass, Leon R. *The Beginning of Wisdom: Reading Genesis*. New York: Free Press, 2003.

Kassian, Mary A. *The Feminist Mistake*. Wheaton, IL: Crossway Books, 2005.

Keener, Craig S. *The IVP Bible Background Commentary: New Testament.* Downer Groves, IL: InterVarsity Press, 1993.

Keil, Carl Friedrich, and Franz Delitzsch. *Commentary on the Old Testament.* Peabody, MA: Hendrickson, 1996.

—. *Commentary on the Old Testament.* Peabody, MA: Hendrickson, 2002.

Kelber, Wegner H. *The Oral and the Written Gospel.* Philadelphia: Fortress, 1983.

Keller, Werner. *Archaeology & Science Delve 4,000 Years into the Past to Document THE BIBLE AS HISTORY (2nd Revised ed.).* New York: Hodder and Stoughton, 1980.

Kennedy, D. James. *Evangelism Explosion.* Wheaton, IL: Tyndale House Publishers, 1977.

Kenneth, Boa., and Kruidenier. *Holman New Testament Commentary: Romans, Vol. 6.* Nashville, TN: Broadman & Holman, 2000.

Kimel Jr., Alvin F. Kimel Jr., and ed. *This Is My Name Forever: The Trinity & Gender Language for God.* Downers Grove: InterVarsity Press, 2001.

Kissling, Paul J. *The College Press NIV commentary: Genesis.* Joplin, MO: College Press Pub. Co., 2004.

Kistemaker, Simon J, and William Hendriksen. *New Testament Commentary: vol. 15, Exposition of Hebrews.* Grand Rapids: Baker Book House, 1953-2001.

Kitchen, K A. *On the Reliability of the Old Testament.* Grand Rapids: Eerdmans, 2003.

—. *The Ancient Orient and the Old Testament.* Chicago: Tyndale Press, 1966.

Kitchen, K. A. *Ancient Orient and Old Testament.* Downers Grove, IL: InterVarsity Press, 1975.

—. *The Ancient Orient and Old Testament.* Downers Grove, IL: InterVarsity Press, 1975.

Koehler, Ludwig. "Problem in the Study in the Language of the Old Testament." *Journal of Semitic Studies,* 1956: 3-24.

Koehler, Ludwig, Walter Baumgartner, M E J Richardson, and Johann Jakob Stamm. *The Hebrew and Aramaic Lexicon of the Old Testament.* Leiden; New York: E. J. Brill, 1999.

Krentz, Edgar. *The Historical-Critical Method.* Philadelphia: Fortress Press, 1975.

—. *The Historical-Critical Method.* Philadelphia: Fortress Press, 1975.

Kümmel, Werner Georg. *The New Testament: The History of the Investigation of Its Problems,* trans. S. McLean Gilmour and Howard C. Kee. Nashville: Abingdon Press, 1970.

Kugel, James L. *How to Read the Bible: A Guide to Scripture, Then and Now.* New York: Free Press, 2008.

Ladd, George Eldon. *The New Testament and Criticism.* Grand Rapids: Eerdmans, 1967.

Language, John Peter. *A Commentary on the Holy Scriptures: Genesis.* Bellingham: Logos Research Systems, 1939, 2008.

Lantz, Charles Craig. *Hermeneutics: The Art and Science of Biblical Interpretation.* Seattle, WA: Create Space, 2012.

Larsen, L. David. *The Evangelism Mandate.* Wheaton: Crossway Books, 1992.

Larson, Knute. *Holman New Testament Commentary, vol. 9, I & II Thessalonians, I & II Timothy, Titus, Philemon.* Nashville, TN: Broadman & Holman Publishers, 2000.

Lasor, William Sanford, David Allan Hubbard, and Frederic Williams Bush. *The Message, Form, and Background of the Old Testament: Old Testament Survey (2nd ed.).* Grand Rapids: Wm. B. Eerdmans, 1996.

Lawrence, Paul, and Alan Millard. *The IVP Atlas of Bible History.* Downers Grove, IL: Intervarsity Press, 2006.

Lea, Thomas D. *Holman New Testament Commentary: Hebrews, James.* Nashville, TN: Broadman & Holman Publishers, 1999.

—. *Holman New Testament Commentary: Vol. 10, Hebrews, James.* Nashville, TN: Broadman & Holman Publishers, 1999.

Lea, Thomas D., and Hayne P. Griffin. *The New American Commentary, vol. 34, 1, 2 Timothy, Titus.* Nashville: Broadman & Holman Publishers, 1992.

Legaspi, Michael C. *The Death of Scripture and the Rise of Biblical Studies.* Oxford: Oxford University Press, 2010.

Lemche, Niels Peter. *The Old Testament Between Theology and History: A Critical Survey.* Louisville: Westminster John Knox Press, 2008.

Lenski, R. C. H. *Interpretation of the I & II Epistles of Peter the Three Epistles of John, and the Epistle of Jude.* Minneapolis: Augsburg Fortress, 1945, 2008.

—. *The Interpretation of The Acts of the Apostles.* Minneapolis, MN: Ediciones Sigueme, 1961.

Licona, Michael R. *The Resurrection of Jesus, A New Historiographical Approach.* Downers Grove: InterVarsity Press, 2010.

Lightfoot, J. B. *Essays on the Work Entitled Supernatural Religion.* London: Macmillan and Co., 1889.

Lightfoot, Neil R. *How We Got the Bible.* Grand Rapids, MI: Baker Books, 1963, 1988, 2003.

Lightfoot, Richard H. *History and Interpretation in the Gospels.* New York and London: Harper and Brothers, 1934.

Lightfoot, Robert H. *History and Interpretation of the Gospels.* (New York and London: Harper and Brothers, 1934.

Lindsell, Harold. *The Battle for the Bible.* Grand Rapids: Zondervan, 1976.

Linnemann. *Is There A Synoptic Problem? Rethinking the Literary Dependance of the First Three Gospels.* Grand Rapids, MI: Baker Book House, 1992.

Linnemann, Eta. *Biblical Criticism on Trial: How Scientific is "Scientific Theology"?* Grand Rapids: Kregel, 2001.

—. *Historical Criticism of the Bible: Methododology or Ideaology?* Grand Rapid, MI: Kregel Publications, 1990.

Longman III, Tremper. *How to Read Genesis.* Downers Groves, IL: Intervarsity Press, 2005.

Longman, III, Tremper. *Literary Approaches to Biblical Interpretation.* Grand Rapids: Zondervan Publishing House, 1987.

Longman, Tremper III. *Reading the Bible: With Heart & Mind.* Colorado Springs: NavPress, 1997.

Longman, Tremper III, and Raymond B Dillard. *An Introduction to the Old Testament.* Grand Rapids: Zondervan, 2006.

MacArthur, John. *The MacArthur Bible Commentary.* Nashville: Thomas Nelson, 2005.

Machen, J. Gresham. "Christianity and Culture." *Princeton Theological Review*, 1913: 7.

—. *The Christian Faith in the Modern World*. Grand Rapids: Eerdmans, 1965 [1936].

Maier, Gerhard. *The End of the Historical-Critical Method. Translated by Edwin W. Leverenz and Rudolf F. Norden*. St. Louis: Concordia, 1977.

Maier, Herhard. *The End of the Historical-Critical Method*. St. Loius, MO: Concordia Publishing House, 1974.

Malina, Bruce.J. *The Social Gospel of Jesus: The Kingdom of God in Mediterranean Perspective*. Minneapolis: Fortress Press, 2001.

Marshall, I. Howard. *A Critical and Exegetical Commentary on the Pastoral Epistles*. New York, London: T&T Clark LTD, 2004.

—. *Historical Criticism, Iin New Testament Interpretation*. Grand Rapids: Eerdmans, 1977.

Martin, D Michael. *The New American Commentary 33 1, 2 Thessalonians* . Nashville, TN: Broadman & Holman, 2001, c1995 .

Mathews, K. A. *The New American Commentary vol. 1A, Genesis 1-11:26* . Nashville: Broadman & Holman Publishers, 2001.

Matthews, K. A. *The New American Commentary Vol. 1B, Genesis 11:27-50:26*. Nashville: Broadman and Holman Publishers, 2001.

Mayers, Mark K. *Christianity Confronts Culture: A Strategy for Crosscultural Evangelism*. Grand Rapids : Zondervan, 1987.

McCue, Rolland. *Promises Unfulfilled: The Failed Strategy of Modern Evangelism*. Greenville, SC: Ambassador Group, 2004.

McGrath, Alister. "Why Evangelicalism is the Future of Protestantism." *Christianity Today*, June 19, 1995: 18-23.

McKay, K. L. *A New Syntax of the Verb in New Testament Greek*. New York: Peter Lang, 1994.

McKenzie, Stephen L, and Stephen R Hayes. *An Introduction to Biblical Criticism and Their Application: To Each its Own Meaning*. Louisville: John Knox Press, 1999.

McKnight, Edgar V. *Postmodern Use of the Bible: The Emergence of Reader-Oriented Criticism*. Nashville: Abingdon Press, 1988.

—. *What is Form Criticism?* Philadelphia: Fortress, 1969.

McKnight, Edgar V. *"Form and Redaction Criticism." The New Testament and Its Modern Interpreters*. Philadelphia: Fortress Press, 1989.

McRaney, William. *The Art of Personal Evangelism*. Nashville: Broadman & Holman, 2003.

McRay, John. *Archaeology and the New Testament*. Grand Rapids: Baker House Books, 1991.

Melick, Richard R. *The New American Commentary: vol. 32, Philippians, Colissians, Philemon*. Nashville, TN : Broadman & Holman Publishers, 2001.

Metzger, Bruce M. *The Text of the New Testament: Its Transmission, Corruption, and Transmission*. New York: Oxford University Press, 1964, 1968, 1992.

Metzger, Bruce M. *A Textual Commentary on the Greek New Testament*. New York: United Bible Society, 1994.

Mirriam-Webster, Inc. *Mirriam-Webster's Collegiate Dictionary. Eleventh Edition*. Springfield: Mirriam-Webster, Inc., 2003.

Morgan, Robert. *"Rudolf Bultmann," in The Modern Theologians, vol. 1 in An Introduction to Christian Theology in the Twentieth Century. Edited by David F. Ford*. New York: Basil Blackwell, 1989.

Morgenthaler, Sally. *Worship Evangelism*. Grand Rapids: Zondervan Publishing House, 1995.

Morris, Henry M. *The Genesis Record: A Scientific and Devotional Commentary on the Book of the Beginnings*. Grand Rapids: Baker Books, 2007, 1976.

Morris, Leon. *The Gospel According to Matthew*. Grand Rapids, MI: Inter-Varsity Press, 1992.

·Mounce, Robert H. *Matthew, vol. 1 in the New International Biblical Commentary. Edited by W. Ward Gasque*. Peabody, MA: Hendrickson, 1991.

Mounce, William D. *Mounce's Complete Expository Dictionary of Old & New Testament Words*. Grand Rapids, MI: Zondervan, 2006.

Mounce, William D. *Basics of Biblical Greek Grammar*. Grand Rapids: Zonervan, 2009.

Myers, Allen C. *The Eerdmans Bible Dictionary* . Grand Rapids, Mich: Eerdmans, 1987.

Nagel, Thomas. *The View from Nowhere*. New York: Oxford University Press, 1986.

Neil, Stephen, and Tom Wright. *The Interpretation of the New Testament, 1861-1986. Second Edition.* Oxford: Oxford University, 1988.

Nicholson, Ernest. *The Pentateuch in the Twentieth Century: The Legacy of Julius Wellhausen.* New York: Oxford University Press, 1998.

Niessen, Richard. "The virginity of the `almah in Isaiah 7:14." *Bibliotheca Sacra 137* , 1980: 133-50.

Nineham, D. E. "Eyewitness Testimony and the Gospel Tradition—I." *Journal of Theological Studies 9* , April 1958: 13.

Oden, Thomas C. *Ministry Through Word and Sacrament, Classic Pastoral Care.* New York: Crossroad, 1989.

Orchard, Bernard. *J. J. Griesbach: Synoptic and Text - Critical Studies .* Cambridge: Cambridge University Press, 1776-1976, 2005.

Orchard, Bernard, and Thomas R. W. Longstaff. *J. J. Griesbach: Synoptic and text-critical studies 1776-1976.* Cambridge: Cambridge University, 1978.

Osborne, Grant R. *THE HERMENEUTICAL SPIRAL A Comprehensive Introduction to Biblical Interpretation (2nd Edition).* Downers Grove, IL: InterVarsity Press, 2006.

Osborne, Grant R. *BAKER EXEGETICAL COMMENTARY ON THE NEW TESTAMET: REVELATION.* Grand Rapids, MI: Baker Academic, 2002.

Oswalt, John N. *The NIV Application Commentary: Isaiah.* Grand Rapids, MI: Zondervan, 2003.

Outlaw, W. Stanley. *The Book of Hebrews .* Nashville, TN: Randall House, 2005.

Packer, J. I. *Evangelism and Sovereignty of God.* Downers Grove, Il: InterVarsity Press, 1961.

Packer, J. I. *Evangelism and the Sovereignty of God.* Downers Grove, IL: InterVarsity Press, 1979.

Perrin, Norman. *Rediscovering the Teaching of Jesus.* New York: Harper and Row, 1976.

—. *What is Redaction Criticism?* Philadelphia: Fortress, 1969.

Pink, Arthur Walkington. *An Exposition of Hebrews.* Swengel, PA: Bible Truth Depot, 1954.

—. *Objections to God's Sovereignty Answered.* Bellingham: Logos Bible Software, 2005.

Polhill, John B. *The New American Commentary 26: Acts.* Nashville: Broadman & Holman Publishers, 2001.

Porter, Stanley E. *Handbook to Exegesis of the New Testament.* Leiden, NY: Koninklijke, 1997.

Posterski, C. Donald. *Reinventing Evangelism.* Downers Grove, IL: InterVarsity Press, 1989.

Powell, Doug. *Holman QuickSource Guide to Christian Apologetics.* Nashville, TN: Holman Reference, 2006.

Pratt Jr, Richard L. *Holman New Testament Commentary: I & II Corinthians, vol. 7.* Nashville: Broadman & Holman Publishers, 2000.

Pratt Jr, Richard L. *I & II Corinthians, vol. 7, Holman New Testament Commentary* . Nashville, TN: , 2000: Broadman & Holman Publishers, 2000.

Rainer, S. Thomas. *Evangelism in the Twenty-First Century.* Wheaton, IL: Harold Shaw Publishers, 1989.

Rainer, Thom S. *Surprising Insights From the Unchurched and Proven Ways to Reach Them.* Grand Rapids, MI: Zondervan, 2001.

Ramm, Bernard. *Protestant Biblical Interpretation: A Textbook of Hermeneutics, 3rd rev. ed.* Grand Rapids, MI: Baker, 1999.

Rast, Walter E. *Tradition History and the Old Testament.* Philadelphia: Fortress Press, 1972.

Reginald H. Fuller, The New Testament in Current Study. New York: Charles Scribner's Sons, 1962.

Reid, Alvin. *Introduction to Evangelism.* Nashville: Boardman & Holmes , 1998.

Reid, Alvin L. *Radically Unchurched: Who They are and How to Reach Them.* Grand Rapids: Kregel, 2002.

Rendtorff, R. "The Problem of the Process of Transmission in the Pentateuch." *JSOT*, 1990: 101.

Reyburn, William David, and Euan Mc G. Fry. *A Handbook on Genesis (UBS Handbook Series).* New York: United Bible Societies, 1997.

Richards, E. Randolph. *Paul And First-Century Letter Writing: Secretaries, Composition and Collection.* Downers Grove: InterVarsity Press, 2004.

Richardson, A, W Schweitzer, and ed. *Biblical Authority for Today*. Philadelphia: Westminster Press, 1951.

Roberts, Alexander, James Donaldson, and Cleveland Coxe. *The Ante-Nicene Fathers Vol.I: Translations of the Writings of the Fathers Down to A.D. 325*. Oak Harbor: Logos , 1997.

Robertson, A. T. *An Introduction to the Textual Criticism of the New Testament*. London: Hodder & Stoughton, 1925.

Robertson, A.T. *Word Pictures in the New Testament*. Oak Harbor, MI: Logos Research Systems, 1933, 1997.

Robinson, G. L., and R. K. Harrison. *The International Standard Bible Encyclopedia, vol. 2*. Grand Rapids: Eerdmans, 1982.

Robinson, John A. T. *Can We Trust the New Testament? "The New Testament Dating Game," Time*. Grand Rapids: Eerdmans, 1977.

—. *Redating the New Testament*. Philadelphia: Fortress, 1976.

Rogers, Jack B, and Donald K. McKim. *The Authority and Interpretation of the Bible, An Historical Approach*. New York: Harper & Row, 1979.

Rooker, Mark F. *The New American Commentary, vol. 3A, Leviticus*. Nashville: Broadman & Holman Publishers, 2000.

Ropes, J. H. *The Synoptic Gospels, 2nd Impression with New Preface*. Cambridge: Harvard University, 1960.

Ruether, Rosemary Radford. *Women-Church: Theology and Practice of Feminist Liturgical Communities*. San Francisco: Harper and Row, 1986.

Russell, Letty M, and ed. *Feminist Interpretation of the Bible*. Philadelphia: Westminster Press, 1985.

Ryken, Leland. *Choosing a Bible: Understanding Bible Translation Differences*. Wheaton: Crossway Books, 2005.

—. *The Word of God in English*. Wheaton: Crossway Books, 2002.

—. *Understanding English Bible Translation: The Case for an Essentially Literal Approach*. Wheaton, IL: Crossway Books, 2009.

Sayce, A. H. *The Early History of the Hebrews*. London: Rivingtons, 1897.

Schaeffer, Francis A. *Genesis in Space and Time: The Flow of Biblical History*. Downers Groves: Intervarsity Press, 1972.

Schreiner, Thomas R. *The New American Commentary: 1, 2 Peter, Jude.* Nashville: Broadman & Holman, 2003.

Schweitzer, Albert. *The Quest of the Historical Jesus. Introduction by James M. Robinson. Trans. By W. Montgomery from the first German Edition.* New York: Macmillan, 1906, 1968.

Sisson, Dick. *Evangelism Encounter.* Chicago, IL: Victor Books, 1988.

Smith, Gary. *The New American Commentary: Isaiah 1-39, Vol. 15a.* Nashville, TN: B & H Publishing Group, 2007.

—. *The New American Commentary: Isaiah 40-66, Vol. 15b.* Nashville, TN: B&H Publishing, 2009.

Soulen, Richard N, and R. Kendall Soulen. *Handbook of Biblical Criticism. Edited by Richard N. Soulen.* Atlanta: John Knox, 1981.

Souter, Alexander. *The Text and Canon of the New Testament.* New York: Charles Scribner's Sons, 1913.

Speiser, E. A. *Genesis Anchor Bible 1.* Garden City: Doubleday, 1964.

Spinoza, Baruch. *Theological-Political Treatise, in Complete Works, trans. Samuel Shirley, ed. Michael L. Morgan.* Indianapolis: Hackett Publishing Company, 2002.

Spong, John Shelby. *Living in Sin: A Bishop Rethinks Human Sexuality. .* New York, NY: HaperCollins Publishers, 1990.

Sproul, R.C. *Knowing Scripture. .* Downers Grove, IL: Intervarsity Press, 1978.

Stanton, Elizabeth Cady. *The Woman's Bible .* Seattle, WA: Kindle Edition 2012, 1895.

—. *The Women's Bible.* Boston: Northeastern University Press, 1993.

Stein, Robert H. *A Basic Guide to Interpreting the Bible: Playing by the Rules.* Grand Rapids: Baker Books, 1994.

—. *The New American Commentary: Luke.* Nashville, TN: Broadman & Holman , 2001, c1992.

Stonehouse, , Ned B. *The Origins of the Synoptic Gospels.* Grand Rapids: Eerdmans, 1963.

Strauss, David Friedrich. *A New Life of Jesus. Authorized Translation. Second Edition.* Williams and Norgate: Covent Garden, 1879.

—. *The Life of Jesus Critically Examined. Edited by Peter C. Hodgson. Translated by George Eliot.* Philadelphia: Fortress, 1972.

Streeter, Burnett H. *The Four Gospels, A Study of Origins.* London: Macmillan, 1953.

Streeter, Burnett Hillman. *The Four Gospels, A Study of Origins.* London: Macmillan and Co., 1924.

Stuart, Douglas. *Old Testament Exegesis: A Handbook for Students and Pastors (Fourth Edition).* Louisville: Westminister John Knox Press, 2009.

Tacitus. *The Histories, Books IV-V, Annals Books I-III (Loeb Classical Library No. 249).* Cambridge, MA: Harvard University Press, 1931.

Taylor, Vincent. *The Formation of the Gospel Tradition.* London: Macmillan, 1953.

Tenney, Merrill C. et. al. *Zondervan Pictorial Encyclopedia of the Bible.* Grand Rapids: Zondervan, 1975.

Terry, Milton S. *Biblical Hermeneutics: A Treatise on the Interpretation of the Old and New Testaments.* Grand Rapids: Zondervan, 1883.

Theissen, Gerd. *Psychological aspects of Pauline Theology.* Philadelphia, PA: Fortress Press, 1987.

—. *Sociology of Early Palestinian Christianity.* . Philadelphia, PA : Fortress Press, 1977.

—. *The Social Setting of Pauline Christianity.* . Philadelphia, PA : Fortress Press, 1982.

Theissen, Gerd, and Annette Mertz. *The Historical Jesus: A comprehensive Guide.* Minneapolis, MN: Augsburg Fortress, 1998.

Thiselton, Anthony C. *The Two Horizons: New Testament Hermeneutics and Philosophical Description* . Grand Rapids: Eerdmans, 1980.

Thomas, Robert L. "Current Hermeneutical Trends: Toward Explanation or Obfuscation?" *JETS* , 1996: 241-256.

—. *Evangelical Hermeneutics.* Grand Rapids: Kregel Publications, 2002.

—. *Three Views of the Origins of the Synoptic Gospels.* Grand Rapids, MI: Kregel, 2002.

Thomas, Robert L. ""Current Hermeneutical Trends: Toward Explanation or Obfuscation?" *JETS 39*, June 1996: 241-256.

Thomas, Robert L. "Current Hermeneutical Trends: Toward Explanation or Obfuscation?" *JETS 39* , June 1996: 241-256.

—. *Revelation 1-7: An Exegetical Commentary* . Chicago, IL: Moody Publishers, 1992.

Thomas, Robert L., and F. David Farnell. *THE JESUS CRISIS: The Inroads of Historical Criticism in Evagelical Scholarship.* Grand Rapids, MI: Kregel Publications, 1998.

Torrey, Reuben A., and Edward D. Andrews. *DIFFICULTIES IN THE BIBLE Alleged Errors and Contradictions: Updated and Expanded Edition.* Cambridge: Christian Publishing House, 2012.

Turner, Henry E. W. *Historicity and the Gospel.* London: A. R. Mowbray, 1963.

Vine, W E. *Vine's Expository Dictionary of Old and New Testament Words.* Nashville: Thomas Nelson, 1996.

Virkler, Henry A, and Karelynne Gerber Ayayo. *Hermeneutics: Principles and Processes of Biblical Interpretation.* Grand Rapids, MI: Baker Academic, 1981, 2007.

Wainwright, William J, and ed. *The Oxford Handbook of Philosophy of Religion.* New York: Oxford University, 2005.

Walker, Williston, Richard A Norris, David W Lotz, and Robert T. Handy. *A History of the Christian Church, 4th ed.* New York: Charles Scribner's Sons, 1985.

Wallace, Daniel. *Greek Grammar Beyond the Basics.* Grad Rapids: Zondervan, 1996.

Walls, David, and Max Anders. *Holman New Testament Commentary: I & II Peter, I, II & III John, Jude.* Nashville: Broadman & Holman Publishers, 1996.

Walsh, Jerome T. *Old Testament Narrative: A Guide to Interpretation.* Louisville: Westminster John Knox Press, 2009.

Walton, John H. *Zondervan Illustrated Bible Backgrounds Commentary (Old Testament) Volume 1: Genesis, Exodus, Leviticus, Numbers, Deuteronomy.* Grand Rapids, MI: Zondervan, 2009.

—. *Ancient Near Eastern Thought and the Old Testament.* Grand Rapids: Baker Academic, 2006.

Walton, John H. "Isaiah 7:14: what's in a name?" *Journal of the Evangelical Theological Society 30,* 1987: 289-306.

—. *Zondervan Illustrated Bible Backgrounds Commentary (Old Testament) Volume 5: The Minor Prophets, Job, Psalms, Proverbs, Ecclesiastes, Song of Songs.* Grand Rapids, M: Zondervan, 2009.

Walton, John H. *THE NIV APPLICATION COMMENTARY Genesis.* Grand Rapids: Zondervan, 2001.

Walton, John H., and Sandy. D. Brent. *The Lost World of Scripture, Ancient Literary Culture and Biblical Authority.* Downers Grove: InterVarsity Press, 2013.

Walton, John H., Victor H. Matthews, and Mark W Chavalas. *The IVP Bible Background Commentary: Old Testament.* Downers Grove: IVP Academic, 2000.

Weber, Stuart K. *Holman New Testament Commentary, vol. 1, Matthew.* Nashville, TN: Broadman & Holman Publishers, 2000.

Wegner, Paul D. *A Student's Guide to Textual Criticism of the Bible: Its History Methods & Results.* Downers Grove: InterVarsity Press, 2006.

Wellhausen, Julius. *Prolegomena to the History of Israel .* New York: BiblioBazzar, 1878, 2009.

Westcott, B. F., and Hort F. J. A. *The New Testament in the Original Greek, Vol. 2: Introduction, Appendix.* London: Macmillan and Co., 1882.

Wheelock, Frederic M, and Richard A Lafleur. *Wheelock's Latin, 7th ed.* New York: Harper Collins, 2011.

Whiston, William. *The Works of Josephus.* Peabody, MA: Hendrickson, 1987.

Whitney, Donald S. *Spiritual Disciplines for the Christian Life with Bonus Content (Pilgrimage Growth Guide).* Colorado Springs, CO: Navpress, 1991.

Wolf, Herbert M. "Solution to the Immanuel Prophecy in Isaiah 7:14-8:22." *Journal of Biblical Literature 91 ,* 1972: 449-56.

Wood, D R W. *New Bible Dictionary (Third Edition).* Downers Grove: InterVarsity Press, 1996.

Woodhead, Linda. "Spiritualising the Sacred: A Critique of Feminist Theology." *Modern Theology,* 1997: 197.

Wright, N. T. *Hebrews for Everyone.* London: Westminster John Knox Press, 2003.

Yarbrough, Robert W. "Evangelical Theology in Germany." *Evangelical Quarterly LXV ,* October 1993: 329, 353.

Young, Pamela Dickey. *Feminist Theology/Christian Theology: In Search of Method.* Eugene: Wipf and Stock, 1990.

Zodhiates, Spiros. *The Complete Word Study Dictionary: New Testament.* Chattanooga: AMG Publishers, 2000, c1992, c1993.

Zuck, Roy B. *Basic Bible Interpretation: A Prafctical Guide to Discovering Biblical Truth.* Colorado Springs: David C. Cook, 1991.

www.ingramcontent.com/pod-product-compliance
Lightning Source LLC
Chambersburg PA
CBHW072344090426
42741CB00012B/2922